"History offers Mr. Gordon plenty of interesting material, and he takes full advantage of it."

—*The Wall Street Journal*

"[Gordon is] a natural storyteller with abundant grace and wit."

—*The New York Times*

"A satisfying blend of history and business."

—*Dallas Morning News*

"John Steele Gordon's business is to amuse and instruct at the same time . . . his constant theme is the variety and ingenuity of human action."

—Richard Brookhiser, author of
Alexander Hamilton, American

"Reading John Steele Gordon's excellent stories about American business history . . . is an entertaining and instructive pleasure. Having them collected now in one volume neatly multiplies the pleasure-effect."

—Jean Strouse, author of *Morgan, American Financier*

JOHN STEELE GORDON

THE BUSINESS

OF AMERICA

WALKER & COMPANY   NEW YORK

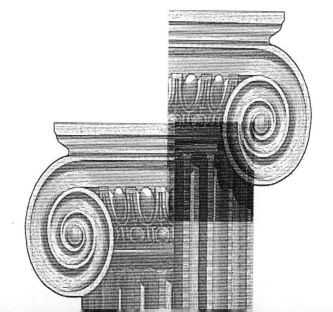

First published in the United States of America in 2001 by
Walker Publishing Company, Inc.; first paperback edition published in 2002

Published simultaneously in Canada by Fitzhenry and Whiteside,
Markham, Ontario L3R 4T8

For information about permission to reproduce selections from this book, write to
Permissions, Walker & Company, 435 Hudson Street, New York, New York 10014

Library of Congress Cataloging-in-Publication Data

Gordon, John Steele.
    The business of America / John Steele Gordon.
       p.   cm.
    ISBN 0-8027-1383-1
    1. United States—Economic conditions.   2. Business enterprises—United
States—History.   3. Businesspeople—United States—History.   I. Title.

HC103.G67   2001
330.*73—dc21   2001017690

ISBN 0-8027-7635-3 (paperback)

Book design by M. Fadden Rosenthal/mspaceny

Visit Walker & Company's Web site at www.walkerbooks.com

Printed in the United States of America

10 9 8 7 6 5 4 3 2 1

TO KEN AND LOIS LIPPMANN,
MAJOR MOGULS IN THE BUSINESS OF FRIENDSHIP

I have always recognized that the object of business is to make money in an honorable manner. I have endeavored to remember that the object of life is to do good.

—Peter Cooper

CONTENTS

Preface   xi

PART I   THE EARLY DAYS OF THE AMERICAN DREAM
Profits in the Wilderness   3
The Corners of Wall and Broad   8
Technology Transfer   13
King Cotton   18

PART II   FARMING AND FOOD
The Tragedy of the Commons   25
Sowing the American Dream   30
The Late, Great Liederkranz Cheese   35
Sawdust Pudding   40

PART III   MANUFACTURING AND MINING
Industrial Revolutionary   47
Sewing and Reaping a Fortune   52
The California Gold Rush   57
Opportunities   62
The Revenge of the Trust   67

PART IV   TRANSPORTATION
The Steamboat Monopoly   75
To the Swiftest   80
The Atlantic Stakes   86
The Towering Boondoggle   91
"The Public Be Damned"   96
Nice Work If You Can Keep It   100
Henry Ford's Horseless Horse   105
The Man Who Saved the Cadillac   110
Through Darkest America   115

PART V BANKING

We Banked on Them   123

The Freedman's Bank   128

The People's Banker   133

Politicians Versus Bankers   139

PART VI THE BUSINESS OF WAR

USS *Pork Barrel*   147

Paying for the War   152

The Armor-Plate Scandal   157

The American Superweapon   162

PART VII BUSINESS AND GOVERNMENT

The Great Crash (of 1792)   169

The Other Great Depression   174

R.I.P., ICC   179

Engine Charlie Wilson   183

PART VIII RETAILING AND REAL ESTATE

The Perils of Success   191

No Respect   196

Where and When   201

Woolworth's Cathedral   206

Unintended Consequences   211

PART IX THE TELEGRAPH, TELEPHONE, AND TELEVISION

Technology of the Future   219

Postalization   224

Technological Turkey   229

The Death of a Monopoly   234

Desi Arnaz   239

PART X AFTER HOURS

The American Game   247

Saint Straus   252

The Philanthropist   257

Bibliography   263

Index   273

PREFACE

I HAVE BEEN WRITING the Business of America column for *American Heritage* magazine since 1989. In doing so, I have confirmed in my own mind the truth of Noel Coward's adage that "work is so much more fun than fun." I have enjoyed every column inch of this job.

Economic history—like economics—is often thought to be deadly dull. But thanks perhaps to a grandfather who was both a successful Wall Street broker and a good storyteller, I have always loved the tales of adventure and daring to be found in economic history and the fascinating men (and now, increasingly, women) who made it.

It should not be surprising that there is so much of interest in economic history. Although it is a cliché that we spend one-third of our lives asleep, curiously it has been far less noticed that we spend another third in the marketplace. Whether we are buying (when it's called shopping) or selling (when it's usually called working—selling our skills, labor, and the products thereof), we are part of the economy. We earn money by creating value and spend those earnings on necessities and, once those are met, the pursuit of happiness. How we spend our money determines how others make theirs.

How we have acted in the marketplace over the years—what goods we brought to sell, what we bought in exchange, what ideas we found there to exploit, what happened in consequence—has been a large part of the history of the modern era. Indeed, in many ways, business in the modern era has been the successor to war and exploration, fields that in earlier times so attracted men of action. As early as the middle of the nineteenth century, the shift was noticeable. "Men no longer attempt to rule by the sword," wrote James Gordon Bennett in 1868, "but they find in money a weapon as sharp and more effective; and having lost none of the old lust for power, they seek to establish over their fellows the despotism of dollars."

Bennett, of course, was sacrificing journalistic accuracy for alliteration in the phrase "despotism of dollars." Bennett himself, after all, was one of the giants of nineteenth-century American business and certainly never thought of himself as a despot. By combining elements developed by others and many of his own ideas, he invented the modern newspaper in the 1830s and made it a major force in Western culture. By doing so, he greatly enriched and enlarged the lives of his fellow citizens, profoundly changed both politics and everyday life, made for himself one of the great American fortunes, and came to possess a power that no journalist had known, or even dreamed of, before.

Bennett's experience in the marketplace has been duplicated many times. To be sure, there have been businessmen aplenty who fit the stereotype found in the works of, for instance, Charles Dickens and Oliver Stone. Russell Sage, a Wall Street trader of genius, would have foreclosed a mortgage on his mother if she fell behind in her payments. Worth perhaps $70 million at the turn of the twentieth century, he was too cheap to hire cabs. When he tried to jump onto a moving trolley, missed his footing, and fell to the pavement (he was eighty-six at the time), he sued the trolley company for his injuries. It was his long-suffering wife who, finally inheriting his fortune (they had no children), established the philanthropic Russell Sage Foundation that has been giving it away ever since.

But even the most rapacious of the so-called robber barons did much more good than harm, especially in the long term. John D. Rockefeller seized control of the burgeoning American oil industry in the late nineteenth century by means that would get you a lengthy jail term today and made himself the richest man in the world in the process. But the price of petroleum products fell relentlessly (and demand, therefore, soared) throughout the Standard Oil era. The automobile that so dominated the twentieth century would not have been possible without a steady and affordable supply of fuel. Andrew Carnegie and Henry Clay Frick had no hesitation in breaking the Homestead strike, but they made the American steel industry the largest and most efficient in the world, setting the stage for the American century. And all three men used their fortunes for philanthropy on a scale never previously imagined.

But business history is not just about people like Bennett, Rockefeller,

Carnegie, and Frick. It is equally about Samuel Slater, who illegally carried the plans for textile machinery out of England in his head and set this country on the road to industrial supremacy. It's about Adolph Tode, who invented one of the world's great cheeses to sell in his New York delicatessen, a cheese now lost forever thanks to an utterly brainless corporate decision. It's about an old New York men's club that expertly exploited the intricacies of the zoning laws to outfox one of the city's largest real estate developers. It's about Desi Arnaz, who persuaded CBS to film *I Love Lucy* instead of having it performed live, thus creating the market for syndication rights that has greatly enriched two generations of actors.

That is why I think William Wordsworth was flat wrong when he wrote that in "getting and spending we lay waste our powers." In fact, in getting and spending we often enlarge those powers and the powers of others in the process. Henry Ford hoped to free the common man from the tyranny of the horse and make a buck in the process. He certainly did that. But he also ended the terrible isolation of nineteenth-century rural America, changed the landscape of the country, and made the suburbs the linchpin of American politics. (It might also be noted that by causing the population of draft animals to plummet, he was instrumental in creating vast agricultural surpluses—as land for fodder crops was turned to growing food for humans—that depressed farm prices in the 1920s and helped set off the Great Depression in the 1930s.)

Business history, like all history, seethes with human passion. And because it is so very human, it is rich in the grandeur and pettiness, triumphs and tragedies of which we as a species have proved ourselves so capable. And that, of course, makes for good stories. I have been very privileged to be able to write these stories, and I hope the reader enjoys reading them as much as I enjoyed researching and writing them.

PART I

THE EARLY DAYS
OF THE
AMERICAN
DREAM

PROFITS IN THE
WILDERNESS

History, like most aspects of human existence, has fashions that come and go. In the nineteenth century, the Great Man theory was very popular. Columbus was certain he could reach the Orient by sailing toward the setting, not rising, sun. He talked Ferdinand and Isabella into footing the bill, and the rest, as they say, is history.

Today the Great Man theory is about as out of fashion as poor Columbus himself, and so-called people's history is in vogue. Rather than Columbus, the fate of the native tribes he accidentally discovered and— equally accidentally—largely destroyed is now seen by many as all-important. The truth, as usual, lies somewhere in between.

Both these schools of history, of course, also routinely ignore the fundamental importance of technology itself. It was only because the full-rigged ship was fortuitously developed during Columbus's lifetime that he was able to do more than theorize about the best way to reach Japan.

Even more ignored than technology as a driving force in history is organization. The full-rigged ship was extraordinarily expensive in the economic universe of Columbus's time. If exploration's full commercial potential was to be exploited, new ways of financing it beyond appealing to princes were needed. Spain did not develop these new ways and soon stagnated. England and Holland, however, developed the joint-stock company and prospered mightily.

Unlike a partnership, where every partner's entire net worth is at risk, in a joint-stock company only the amount invested can be lost. Using this form of organization, many capitalists (not that the word would be invented for another couple of centuries) could join together to seek the potentially huge profits in exploration and distant trade without having to fear being wiped out by the equally huge risks.

In England, the Moscow Company and the East India Company were chartered by the Crown in the late sixteenth century and evolved into vast, and vastly profitable, enterprises. Holland's East India company would make the Netherlands the richest country in Europe in the seventeenth century.

The joint-stock company is the direct ancestor of the modern corporation and thus, together with the nation-state itself, the most important organizational invention of the Renaissance. Without it, the modern world simply could not have come into being.

And without the joint-stock company, the history of the United States would have taken a very different turn indeed. In a fascinating book, *Profits in the Wilderness*, John Frederick Martin makes plain the crucial importance of the joint-stock company and the pursuit of profit to the settlement of New England.

To begin with, both the Massachusetts Bay Colony and the Plymouth Colony were organized as joint-stock companies. Some of the participants in these companies were known as "planters." They were those who came to New England and contributed their labor to the success of the enterprise. Many of these, to be sure, while technically part of a commercial endeavor, looked for their rewards only in heaven. The men who contributed money but stayed in England, however, were known as "adventurers," and they were certainly hoping for a quicker and more earthly return. (The old meaning of the word *adventurer*, by the way, still echoes in the modern term *venture capitalist*.)

Whatever the motives of the original settlers and their financial backers, the toehold the first New Englanders established on the American continent soon proved a refuge from the rapidly deteriorating political situation in old England after Charles I dismissed Parliament and assumed personal rule. In the first great Atlantic migration, about 25,000 people came to New England between 1630 and 1643. How to settle these people in so vast a wilderness in so short a time was no small problem.

The usual image of the settling of America is one of a frontier line slowly, inexorably creeping westward as individual pioneers cut down the next patch of wood, fenced the next field, built the next homestead, and, eventually, established the next town.

It was not quite that simple, and certainly not in the earliest days. To try to push back the frontier on an individual basis in the early seventeenth century would have been nearly impossible, if not suicidal (and, anyway, entirely outside the Puritan mind-set). Just consider all the things that had to be accomplished before people could actually take up residence in a new area of settlement. The colony's government had to give permission. The site had to be chosen. The land had to be purchased from the Indians and surveyed (and the survey accepted by the government). The various lots—home lots, wood lots, planting lots, meadow, and swampland—had to be laid out and allocated fairly among the settlers. River frontage had to be divvied up and roadbeds situated. Bridges had to be built.

All of this took a great deal of organization and cost a great deal of money. The only suitable organizational model the Puritans had at hand was the joint-stock company, and it was immediately pressed into service as a model for town founding. Now, instead of planters and adventurers, there were "goers," who settled permanently in the new community, and "stayers," those who provided money and/or expertise but usually did not take up residence at all or moved on shortly.

The trouble was, there were lots of goers and not enough stayers to go around. As Thomas Hooker, a founder of both Cambridge, Massachusetts, and Hartford, Connecticut (and one of the foremost clergymen of his time), explained, towns all "want men of abilities and parts to manage their affairs, and men of estate, to bear charges."

Because of the shortage, such men as there were were used over and over again; the colony involved them deliberately in the process of town founding and rewarded them with land allocations, which they either sold or rented out. Before long the stayers were often initiating the process of town founding, hoping to prosper in a manner not altogether dissimilar to that of a modern-day real estate developer.

Some of these men, like Daniel Boone 150 years later, stayed with the frontier, moving on as each settlement was firmly established. Cornelius Waldo, born in England in 1624, moved first to Ipswich, Massachusetts. In the 1650s he was one of the founders of Chelmsford and in the 1670s Dunstable. In the following decade he was an investor in the purchase of land on the Merrimack River that would become Lowell. As he moved from town to town, Waldo held on to the land he left behind as well as the small businesses he founded. His descendants, far more prominent than he ever was, would be major land speculators in the next century, thanks to the patrimony he established.

Because the General Court, the legislature, had to grant permission to found a town, members of the court, and especially of the committee that dealt directly with these matters, were often granted lands in towns they never lived in. Joshua Fisher, who had come to Massachusetts as an indentured servant, ended up the owner of more than thirty parcels of land in four different towns, largely because of his membership in the General Court. Today such shenanigans, while hardly unknown, would be regarded as gross corruption. In the seventeenth century, however, it was strictly business as usual.

Men with expertise in dealing with Indians were especially valued. Fur traders, who often spoke the languages of the natives, were often used in negotiations regarding purchasing of Indian lands. They often ended up owning some of the land purchased. Joseph Parsons was one of the first settlers of Springfield and witnessed the deed signed with the Indians in 1636. He soon was active in Windsor and Hartford. In the 1650s he was an active trader with the Indians and a founder of Northampton. He sold some land he had bought from the Indians to the new town of Hadley and negotiated with the Indians for the land on which the town of Northfield was situated.

Altogether Joseph Parsons was active in the settlement of at least five towns in the Connecticut River Valley over a period of nearly fifty years. In the process he turned his expertise with the Indians into a considerable fortune. At his death in 1683, his estate was worth £2,088, one of the largest probated in western Massachusetts in the seventeenth century, and a sizable sum at that time even in England.

To be sure, some of these profit-seeking town founders were less than completely scrupulous. James Fitch, having taken title to more than 1 million acres from the Indians in eastern Connecticut, worked vigorously at enticing settlers. But the settlers often complained that what they were promised and what they received were two different things. In a formal complaint, the settlers alleged that while they had been promised good land, Fitch had kept all the good land for himself, leaving them only "pore rockey hills."

Regardless of such occasional lapses, the town-founding system improvised in the wilderness by the Puritans proved very effective, and southern and coastal New England was settled with astonishing speed. To a large extent this was due to a new breed of men, a type so new there was not even a name for them in the English language until the middle of the nineteenth century: entrepreneurs.

So while no one can doubt that what brought most of these people to New England in the first place was the dream of building a shining city on a hill—a project still under construction after 350 years—many of them also worked hard to make a buck in the meantime.

Welcome to America.

THE CORNERS OF WALL AND BROAD

THE MORE THINGS CHANGE, the French are fond of saying, the more they stay the same. The French have never been exactly renowned for their respect for the free market, but nowhere is their famous proverb more true. The laws of economics that rule the market are immutable, and traders through the ages have employed the same tactics over and over again in pursuing their fortunes. Sometimes they have won, sometimes they have lost, but the market, like the Mississippi, "just keeps rollin' along."

The most spectacular—and potentially the most remunerative—market tactic has always been the corner. A trader with a corner owns all of a commodity—whether it be corporate shares, gold, or pork bellies—that is available for sale, and thus any potential buyer must buy from him or do without. The reason a corner can be so rewarding is that short sellers, often, cannot do without.

A short seller tries to make money by a decline in price. To do this, he sells a commodity he does not own, promising delivery at a certain time in the future. He hopes to buy the commodity later at a lower price, make his delivery, and pocket the difference. In a successful corner, the short sellers discover—too late—that they have sold something they do not own to a trader who already owns all there is of the commodity in question. Thus, in order to make their deliveries, they must first buy from him, and at whatever price he sets because, as the old Wall Street adage has it, "he who sells what isn't his'n/Buys it back or goes to prison." When a true corner is achieved, the short sellers, caught in a financial pincers, are said to be squeezed—an exciting, often noisy, sometimes messy event.

But achieving a true corner is very difficult. Somehow, all the supply has to be bought up or neutralized, without others finding out and fleeing the trap or sending the price through the roof. Pulling off a successful corner, therefore, calls for luck, skill, courage, and financial resources in large amounts. Through the ages, despite the difficulties, there has been no lack of traders willing to try.

The first corner in New York took place in 1666 when the city was only forty years old and Wall Street was not its financial center but its northern defensive boundary. That was the year Frederick Philipse cornered the wampum market. Philipse had been born in Holland in 1626 and moved with his father to New Amsterdam in 1647. Trained as a carpenter, in 1652 Philipse actually helped build the wall that gave Wall Street its name.

Philipse did not remain a carpenter for long. Capable and ambitious, he soon took one of the royal roads to wealth: He married a rich widow. With his wife's money behind him, Philipse began to engage in trade with the Indians as well as with the West Indies and Holland.

The Indians, the source of the furs that were the mainstay of New York's economy in the seventeenth century, did not want gold and silver in payment for them. They wanted what they regarded as real money: wampum. Wampum are tubular beads, usually strung together in intricate patterns, made from clamshells. In 1650 six white beads or three black beads were worth one Dutch stuiver. (Equal to one-twentieth of a gulden, a stuiver was, in effect, the Dutch equivalent of a nickel.)

Unfortunately, wampum inflation set in, and by 1659 it took sixteen white beads to equal a stuiver. This played havoc with the local economy, not only by driving up the cost of furs but because the settlers as well as the Indians used wampum in day-to-day transactions. Governor Peter Stuyvesant tried the usual government remedies, such as price controls, with the usual results, for the price controls were ignored.

Then Frederick Philipse, well supplied with capital thanks to his new wife, began buying wampum and taking it out of circulation, burying it in hogsheads. He soon controlled the market in wampum and succeeded in raising its price dramatically. By 1666 it took only three white beads to equal a stuiver.

The concept of a central bank would not even exist until the eighteenth century. But Frederick Philipse in the middle of the seventeenth century was, in effect, acting as one, regulating the money supply and, doubtless, making a tidy profit in the process. He would go on to become the colony's richest citizen (not so coincidentally marrying a second rich widow along the way), with trading interests as distant as the East Indies and Madagascar.

As Wall Street's financial markets increased in size and scope, so did the number of corners attempted. By the middle of the nineteenth century, it seemed to one ardent speculator of the day that "hardly a week goes by without a recurrence of these singular phenomena." Commodore Cornelius Vanderbilt earned Wall Street immortality by cornering Harlem railroad stock twice and Hudson Railroad stock once, all in twelve months' time. Perhaps the most famous corner in Wall Street history took place in 1869 when Jay Gould and Jim Fisk nearly cornered gold.

But as the size of stock issues increased, the money required to corner one increased as well, and the number of corners began to decline. The last one to take place on the New York Stock Exchange was in 1923. Today, with a host of regulations that firmly discourage corners if they don't actually forbid them, it is highly unlikely there will ever be another.

But if corners are extinct on the Stock Exchange, they are not altogether gone from Wall Street. Indeed, one of the Street's greatest corners occurred when Nelson Bunker Hunt and his younger brother, William Herbert Hunt, tried to corner the silver market in 1980.

Silver, unlike gold, has numerous industrial uses, especially in the electronic and photographic industries, so there is a strong demand for the metal even apart from its monetary uses. But because silver *was* used as money, the U.S. government had long fixed the price at $1.25 an ounce. By the mid-1960s the government found it could no longer maintain this policy because demand for silver was growing swiftly, while world production lagged.

The United States, in effect, was forced off the silver standard. The Treasury recalled the old one-dollar silver certificates and reduced or eliminated the silver content of coins. (Gresham's law—"bad money drives out good"—of course, immediately kicked in, and the old silver coins vanished from circulation almost overnight.)

In the early 1970s Bunker Hunt thought he saw opportunity in silver, just as Frederick Philipse had seen it in wampum. Inflation was rising, which meant that the prices of gold and silver were likely to rise as the dollar sank in value, even apart from the fact that demand continued to outstrip supply.

At that time it was illegal for Americans to own gold in bullion form, and so Hunt set out to acquire silver. Being one of the richest men in the world, he bought silver on a massive scale and almost single-handedly doubled the price in 1974 from $3.27 to $6.70 an ounce. And, unlike nearly all modern commodity traders, he took delivery, removing the silver from the marketplace. Again, he was doing exactly what Frederick Philipse had done with wampum 300 years earlier.

By 1979 the Hunt brothers had accumulated a vast hoard of silver, estimated at as much as 200 million ounces, just about the amount of silver that was thought to be in the floating supply. With the silver available for trading rapidly dwindling, the price ratcheted up all through 1979. Tiffany's was even forced to close its silver department at one point in order to reprice everything sharply upward.

As the year ended, short sellers disappeared from the silver market, adding to the Hunts' already massive buying pressure as they closed out their short positions, buying the needed silver to do so. In early January 1980, the price of silver reached $50.06 an ounce, while the prices of gold and platinum soared as well. The Hunts' silver hoard was worth, on paper, $10 billion. The first great Wall Street corner in nearly sixty years seemed to be at hand.

But the problems that have plagued all would-be cornerers plagued the Hunts as well. They had borrowed hundreds of millions to buy the silver on margin, using the metal they held as collateral. With the prime rate at over 19 percent, the interest expense, even for the Hunts, was awesome.

And as with the gold corner of 100 years earlier, the U.S. Treasury could always break the Hunts' corner at will. The government held massive quantities of silver both in the form of bullion and in unreleased silver dollars.

Finally, with the price of silver more than ten times what it had been only a decade earlier, many mines that had been closed for years (because they could not be worked profitably) could now be worked very profitably indeed and reopened. Equally huge amounts of silver began coming out of attics and basements. The metal content of the old silver coins was now worth more than the face value or even the numismatic value, and people sold them while the selling was good. Meanwhile, tens of thousands of American families decided that this was the perfect opportunity to turn grandmother's ugly old tea service into ready cash. No one knows how many tons of Victorian silverware were melted down and joined the floating supply.

With the amount of silver in the market increasing, and the Hunts by now virtually the only buyers, the price of silver crumbled. They were forced to borrow more and more money to prop it up, straining even their enormous resources to the limit. The nation's leading banks and brokerage houses were strained as well, for they had lent the Hunts more than $800 million, equal to about 10 percent of all the bank lending in the country in the previous two months.

By March 1980, the price of silver was below $40 an ounce and falling fast. Then, on March 27, the corner collapsed when the Hunts were unable to meet a margin call demanding more collateral on their borrowings. Their brokers, in deep jeopardy themselves, began to sell them out, and panic reigned on Wall Street. The Stock Market plunged while the price of silver lost half its value in a single day, closing at $10.82. By the time "Silver Thursday" was over, the Hunt brothers had taken a billion-dollar bath.

Fast action by the major banks and by the Federal Reserve prevented the panic from turning into a disaster for the entire financial system of the country. The next day Wall Street rallied sharply, and the markets quickly returned to normal. But for the Hunt brothers things never returned to normal. The bankers and brokers rescheduled their debts, allowing them to pay them off over ten years. It was all predicated, however, on the price of silver at least remaining stable. And in the 1980s demand for silver stagnated while production soared. The price declined steadily during the decade, and the Hunts' financial situation followed right behind. In 1987 they were forced to file for protection from their creditors.

Frederick Philipse came to Wall Street as a simple carpenter, guessed right, and died the richest man in New York. The Hunt brothers came possessed of the mightiest fortune in Texas, guessed wrong, and were bankrupted.

Meanwhile, Wall Street's free market just keeps rollin' along.

TECHNOLOGY
TRANSFER

ON APRIL 30, 1789, George Washington took the oath of office as the first president of the United States on the balcony of New York's City Hall, then serving as the new nation's temporary capitol. Although it was one of the most important moments in his life, Washington, a man of profound personal modesty, wore a simple brown suit with silver buttons, white stockings, and shoes with silver buckles.

But the hero of the Revolution had chosen this outfit with great care. Even at the very dawn of the Republic, politicians were conscious of symbolism, and Washington had made certain he was wearing a suit made of American cloth, woven in Hartford, Connecticut.

Washington's purpose was to encourage American manufactures, as industrial goods were called in those days. Certainly they needed plenty of encouragement. Most manufactured goods, and nearly all quality cloth, were imported from England. The overwhelming majority of the American population lived on farms and made at home nearly everything they needed, from soap to furniture. They dressed mainly in homespun, a crude, loosely woven cloth made by housewives from yarn that they had, as the name implies, spun themselves. It was little different from the fabric that clothed medieval peasants.

Textile weaving is a technology so ancient that it predates history itself, and remnants of woven cloth have been found in the kitchen middens of neolithic Europe. But over the ensuing thousands of years the technology changed little until the middle of the eighteenth century. Fibers of wool, flax, or cotton were washed and picked clean by hand. Then they were "carded" to align the fibers, combed to straighten them further, drawn out a little at a time, and twisted into yarn using a spindle or, from the fifteenth century on, a spinning wheel. Once the yarn was made, it could be woven on a loom into cloth. It was all an immensely labor-intensive process, and only the rich could afford cloth that was much better, to our eyes, than burlap. There was an active market in secondhand quality clothes, and good clothes were so expensive that people frequently left them to relatives and friends in their wills.

Then the industrial revolution began with the mechanization of the English textile industry. In 1733 John Kay invented the "flying shuttle," which considerably increased the speed with which cloth could be woven. Still the weavers could not work any faster than the spinners could supply the yarn. In 1769 Sir Richard Arkwright invented the water frame, a machine that, using water power, could spin many threads at one time. By 1777 Arkwright had 200 employees in his mill at Cromford, in Derbyshire, and six factories operating elsewhere.

The following year the spinning jenny greatly increased the speed of home spinning. Other mechanical devices to speed up the process of carding and combing came into use. With the great saving in labor costs, the price of quality cloth began to drop sharply and demand soared. An already vast English textile industry grew by leaps and bounds in the last half of the eighteenth century, providing much of the wealth that allowed England to rise to superpower status.

Other countries, naturally, wanted in on the action. But as long as Britain could keep the secrets of the wondrous machines that had started the industrial revolution, it could keep its lucrative monopoly of cheap, quality cloth. The British government was certainly determined to try. It was illegal to export the machinery or plans for it. People with textile expertise were forbidden to emigrate. British customs watched closely to prevent any unauthorized departures.

With Britain determined to keep its secrets, if the nascent United States was to fulfill President Washington's hopes and develop a textile industry of its own, it had only two choices: Either the new technology had to be reinvented by Americans, or it had to be stolen from Britain. The first alternative was not very likely. While the early spinning machines seem extraordinarily crude to us who live deep in the computer age, they were the highest of high tech in the eighteenth century. Furthermore, the United States had few, if any, citizens who were familiar with the intricacies of textile production on a mass scale.

So the technology had to be stolen. Although British newspapers were forbidden to print them, clandestine advertisements circulated through the textile areas promising big rewards to anyone who could set up working textile machinery in the United States. One person who surely was aware of these offers was Samuel Slater of Belper, Derbyshire, in the very heart of the textile area. Born in 1768, Slater was apprenticed at the age of fourteen to Jedidiah Strutts, the owner of a textile mill in Belper and one of the first capitalists to make a great fortune in the new industrial age. Slater from the first showed a marked talent and interest in mechanical work. Rather than visit his family on Sundays, he would often go to the factory, so that he could study the machinery. While still a teenager, Slater invented a means of winding the yarn on the spindles evenly and was rewarded by his employer with one guinea, several weeks' wages for an apprentice.

Slater also showed a talent for directing large enterprises. His job at the Strutts factory was what would now be called "middle management," coming between the owner and the workers, overseeing the mill, and repairing and constructing the machinery. By the time Slater's apprenticeship ended in 1789, when he was twenty-one, he had mastered all aspects of this new, high-tech, burgeoning industry.

Freed of his apprenticeship, Slater wanted to emulate his former master and make a fortune in the textile industry on his own. Having little capital, he decided to pursue his self-interest in America, where he knew his talents and skills were in hot demand. Before he left Strutts's employ, he carefully committed to memory the smallest details of the new spinning equipment, fully intending to use his knowledge of the British textile secrets as a substitute for capital. Knowing the vigilance of the British customs, he kept his intentions so secret that he did not even tell his mother until he mailed her a letter from London only a few hours before he boarded ship on September 13, 1789, listed on the manifest as a farm laborer.

George Washington could not have known it, of course, but the hopes that had been symbolized by his simple brown suit four months earlier were about to be realized.

Slater arrived in New York on November 11 and soon heard that Moses Brown, a Quaker of Providence, Rhode Island, had some spinning equipment that would not work. Slater wrote him offering his services.

Moses Brown, one of the numerous Rhode Island clan for whom

Brown University is named, replied that he would welcome Slater's help and offered him all the profits from the machines over and above interest on the capital and depreciation if Slater could make them work. Slater had been right about the demand for his skills. It was a deal he could never have made in England.

When he arrived in Providence, however, and went to examine the inoperable spinning equipment in nearby Pawtucket, he saw that it was beyond hope.

"These [machines] will not do," he told Brown, "they are good for nothing in their present condition, nor can they be made to answer."

Brown could only have been very disappointed, for he had a large investment in what he had just learned was junk. Nonetheless, he persevered.

"Thee said thee could make the machinery," Brown replied in Quaker fashion, "why not do it?"

Over the next twelve months Slater did exactly that, using the plans he had so carefully smuggled out of England in his head. With carpenters and mechanics unfamiliar with textile equipment, it was a struggle, and at one point Slater almost despaired when the carding machine stubbornly refused to work. Then, on December 20, 1790, the first cotton mill in the United States went into operation in Pawtucket, owned by the firm of Almy, Brown, and Slater. Moses Brown soon wrote proudly to Alexander Hamilton that "mills and machines may be erected in different places, in one year, to make all the cotton yarn that may be wanted in the United States."

Brown was getting rather carried away. England, with its large technological lead and many talented textile machinery designers, would continue to dominate the cotton goods trade for another century. Brown was right, however, that the industrial revolution was now under way in the United States. Soon numerous mills were springing up along New England's many swift-flowing rivers. By the end of Slater's life forty-five years later, cotton spinning was a major New England industry, employing many thousands of people. Samuel Slater was a famous, very wealthy, and greatly respected man.

In 1833, two years before Slater's death on April 20, 1835, President Andrew Jackson toured New England and paid a call on Pawtucket's most famous citizen.

"I understand," Jackson told him, that "you have taught us how to spin, so as to rival Great Britain in her manufactures; you set all these thousands of spindles to work, which I have been delighted in viewing, and have made so many happy by a lucrative employment."

"Yes, sir," replied Slater. "I suppose that I gave out the psalm, and they have been singing to the tune ever since."

At the end of his visit, the seventh president of the United States bestowed on the man who had been instrumental in fulfilling the hopes of the first president the honorary title of "father of American manufactures."

KING COTTON

As any faithful reader of the old gossip columns knows, great wealth too easily acquired can be a very mixed blessing indeed. Many of the very rich whose names appeared endlessly in the columns—the Duke and Duchess of Windsor, for instance—simply frittered life away in an endless round of public pleasure-seeking. If they seldom seemed actually to be having a very good time, perhaps their friend Noel Coward put his finger on the reason when he noted that "Work is so much more fun than fun."[1]

Sudden immense wealth can be debilitating for entire nations as well. The fleetfuls of gold and silver that yearly poured into Spain from the New World, as though from some vast trust fund, were used to purchase commodities (not to mention armies) from abroad rather than to develop the Spanish economy. In effect, the wealth of the Indies went to developing the economies of northern Europe, not Spain, which was left far behind. Only in the late twentieth century did it begin to catch up with the countries that, lacking Spain's wealth, had no choice but to "work for a living."

In the modern era it is usually oil that distorts national economies. In the American South, 200 years ago, however, it was cotton. The consequences of the easy profits to be had from growing cotton in the American South in the first half of the nineteenth century echo even unto today's headlines.

The carefully cultivated *Gone With the Wind* mythology of the antebellum South has colored our image of the colonial South; but in truth the southern colonies before the Revolution were economically precarious, and even the wealthiest citizens were burdened by debts to their agents in London. While sugar in the West Indies was hugely profitable and the foundation of many a great British fortune, the major export crops of the southern colonies—indigo, rice, and tobacco—were much more marginal and the competition from elsewhere fierce.

Indigo, from which a blue dye was extracted, was widely grown in warm climates around the world. With British tariff preferences providing a protected market, indigo utilized about 10 percent of the slave labor in the southern colonies. After the Revolution, with the South now outside the British tariff walls, India blew the American indigo industry right out of the water, and it vanished in the 1790s.

Rice culture, which had employed about 20 percent of the slave labor in colonial days, held its own in terms of exports after the Revolution, but what growth there was came only from the relatively small domestic market.

Tobacco had been the main export crop of the Old South, and 40 percent of the slaves were used in its production. But American tobacco had to compete with the West Indies and the Mediterranean lands, which had begun producing tobacco in quantity within a century of its first importation from the New World. Tobacco could be a profitable crop in good years, as the plantation houses of tidewater Virginia testify, but compared with West Indian sugar—a license to steal in the eighteenth century—it was a tough way to earn a buck.

At the beginning of the eighteenth century, cotton had been a very luxurious fabric, within the reach only of those whose names would have appeared in gossip columns had there been any. The reason for this was simple: Its production was extremely labor-intensive. Spinning a pound of cotton thread by hand, due to the natural twist of its fiber, took far longer than spinning wool, linen, or even silk, between twelve and twenty man-days in all.

The industrial revolution, which began in the English cloth industry, changed matters considerably. Only 500,000 pounds of cotton were spun into thread—all by hand—in 1765. Twenty years later 16 million pounds were spun, by machine, and the price of cotton cloth had dropped from the caviar range to the mere smoked salmon bracket. The reason the price stayed as high as it did was, again, labor costs.

A field hand could pick about fifty pounds of cotton bolls in a day, enough eventually to yield about four pounds of cotton "lint" ready for spinning. But removing the seeds from that much cotton took a single worker fully twenty-five days.

A single bale of American cotton was exported to Liverpool in 1784, the year following the treaty of peace. But British trade regulations required that commodities had to enter the country either in British ships or in ships of the country of origin. The cotton had arrived in an American bottom, but customs officials flatly refused to believe that there was any such thing as American cotton, and the bale rotted on the docks.

The British customs officials were not far wrong. The entire American cotton crop grew on less than 200 acres in the 1780s, virtually all of them located in the Sea Islands of South Carolina and Georgia.

Then in 1792 Eli Whitney, a New Englander and natural-born mechanic living in Savannah, Georgia, decided to do something about removing the seeds, a process called ginning. Savannah at that time was the major port for the American cotton trade, such as it was. Whitney realized that if he could find a way around the ginning bottleneck, it would greatly lower the price of cotton, assist the South in meeting the fast-rising demand of the British cloth industry, and help fill the gap being left by the collapse of indigo. Doubtless his own personal prosperity entered into his calculations.

In a month he had found the answer. Perhaps never before or since has a mechanical device of such simplicity had such vast and immediate consequences. In Whitney's gin a roller studded with nails stripped the lint from the seeds by pulling it through a grid too narrow to let the seeds pass. The seeds fell into one compartment, and a brush swept the lint off the nails and into another. Whitney's machine could be built in an hour or so by any competent carpenter and worked by a single laborer, increasing his productivity fully *fifty* times. In a stroke, Whitney had reduced the labor cost of ginning from the dominant component in the cost of cotton cloth to a near triviality. And the cost of cotton cloth dropped as a result from the smoked salmon range to the fish-and-chips bracket.

Once Whitney had thought of it, lesser minds had no trouble at all discerning the gin's utility. Indeed it was so obvious, Whitney's first gin was stolen. And it was so easily constructed that he was never able to enforce his patents. Altogether Whitney realized only about $100,000 from his invention, no small sum at the turn of the nineteenth century, but nowhere near what he might have earned in a perfect world.

Ironically, Whitney's gin did not work all that well with the sort of cotton that grew on the Georgia coast and flowed through the port of

Savannah. Its long staples tended to clog the machine (and, in fact, it remains more or less a luxury fabric to this day). But it was ideal for the short-staple cotton that could be grown inland. Upland cotton, as it was called, required only a growing season of at least 200 days, about an inch of rainfall a week, and, ideally, a rich soil. While it could be grown profitably, once the gin was invented, in the sandy Piedmont region, it thrived in the black earth belt of central Alabama and especially in the rich alluvial soils of the Mississippi Delta country.

The New South, able to grow cotton very profitably at a much lower price than ever before (or anywhere else), became the natural empire of King Cotton as the demand of the British and New England mills became insatiable. That single bale that rotted on the Liverpool docks in 1784 became 4 million bales by 1860.

While the price of cotton had now dropped low enough to reach a mass market, it remained a labor-intensive crop far more than a land-intensive one. In 1850 cotton took up only 6 percent of the improved land in the cotton states but required about 70 percent more labor per acre than corn to produce a crop. One reason for this is that cotton is very susceptible to weed infestation and needs to be hoed regularly. Chopping cotton, as it was called, was backbreaking toil, but there was a cheap, and involuntary, labor supply available: the slaves.

Slavery was not an uneconomic institution in the eighteenth century, as many (beginning with Benjamin Franklin in the 1750s) have claimed. But it was no more than moderately profitable. In the swiftly rising climate of moral opprobrium, slavery might well have soon withered away in the South as it did in the North, including New York, the only northern colony to have a substantial slave population. But cotton made slavery hugely profitable, and the price of a prime field hand rose twentyfold between 1800 and the Civil War.

The Old South, its climate largely unsuited to growing cotton, swiftly adapted to the new realities and began to export human flesh for profit. Between 1790 and 1860, 835,000 slaves were "sold south," to the new cotton lands.

Southern capital became tied up in slaves rather than in other productive assets. And with vast wealth flowing into the South from the cotton trade, other sectors of the economy were neglected as well. Industry settled in the North. Immigrants likewise gravitated to the North, where opportunities were far greater. Even the cotton trade itself was largely brokered through New York.

Like Spain before it, the South failed to evolve with the swiftly evolving economy of the nineteenth century and fell farther and farther behind, clinging to the profitable but increasingly archaic system that produced so much wealth and so little happiness.

It was a tragedy waiting to happen, and in 1861 the tragedy began.

PART II

FARMING AND FOOD

THE TRAGEDY OF
THE COMMONS

IF THE TWENTIETH CENTURY has taught us anything about economics, it is that free markets work better than any other kind. Virtually every possible substitute has been tried since World War I ended, and they have, without exception, failed to work. Indeed, the more they have departed from the free-market model, the more they have failed to create wealth and improve living standards. North Korea, one of the last thoroughly Marxist regimes left, can produce ballistic missiles but not enough food to feed its own people.

There's a very simple reason why free markets work. They automatically send signals—billions of them every day—to buyers and sellers alike, keeping them informed about supply and demand. The buyers and sellers then adjust their own actions, and these, in turn, affect the supply and demand. This all-pervasive economic feedback mechanism acts something like the governor on a steam engine, making the market run smoothly, while it helps allocate resources with an efficiency no bureaucracy could hope to match.

To illustrate the importance of this web of signals, let me suggest a thought experiment where the web breaks down. Suppose a local supermarket served 1,000 families. One day its management decides to try a new system. Instead of every customer paying for groceries as they are purchased, each family gets a bill of 1/1,000th of the total.

What would happen under these circumstances?

For one thing, many of the signals that prices send would be blunted. In a normal supermarket, if the price of, say, oranges suddenly soars because of a frost in Florida, many buyers will switch to something else. But with the price increase spread among the 1,000 families, there would be little incentive to give up fresh oranges for frozen juice or Texas grapefruit.

And, as individual buying decisions would have only a very limited impact on individual monthly bills, the incentive to be frugal in order to save money for some other, nonfood purpose vanishes. Why buy Hamburger Helper, when you pay just 1/1,000th of the price of the filet mignon?

Of course, everyone comes to exactly the same conclusion, and the inevitable result is a sudden, sharp, and continuing escalation of total food costs for all the families involved. To be sure, the supermarket here is only theoretical, but this was exactly how the United States, in very large measure, paid for routine health care for many years. However, instead of each family paying their share of the communal bill, they sent it to their employers instead. Since buyers cared not at all about medical costs, sellers such as doctors and hospitals were only too happy to increase them, year after year, until the costs threatened to become insupportable.

This is an example of what happens when costs are "socialized," in other words, spread among everyone, rather than being borne by the individual. But what happens when, instead of costs, the ownership of resources is socialized? The result, very often, is what economists call *the tragedy of the commons.* The term derives from the old common land that medieval peasants used collectively to pasture cattle, gather berries and nuts, drive swine, and such. This meaning of the term is echoed today in the famous park in the middle of Boston, Massachusetts, still known as "the Common."

The problem is, if ownership is held by everyone, but each individual is allowed to exploit the asset freely, then no one has an incentive to conserve the resources. Indeed, everyone has a powerful incentive to "get his share" while the getting is good. The result, all too often, is disaster.

The greatest "common" of them all, of course, is the world's oceans, which cover 77 percent of the earth's surface. By ancient international law and treaty, they and their resources are free and open to all. For much of history, that worked very well. The earth's population was small, and the oceans and their resources were unbelievably vast. But twentieth-century technology, increasing population, and the common ownership of the world's oceans are rapidly resulting in a tragedy of the commons of epic proportions. This impending tragedy can best be understood, perhaps, by looking at the history of that singular beast, the Atlantic cod, the most important fish in American history.

The cod is not very prepossessing. Although it can be up to six feet long and weigh over 200 pounds, it is rather sluggish and hopeless as a sport fish. (When hooked, it simply gives up, and the angler need only haul it in.) But as a commercial product, the cod is a wonder. Easily caught, its firm, white, nonfatty flesh is relatively boneless and easily prepared by drying and salting. Dried cod (often known by its Spanish name, bacalao) is about 80 percent pure protein. Equally important for its commercial potential, dried and, especially, salted cod has a very long "shelf life." In a world without refrigeration, that was a quality without peer, and cod quickly became a staple of the western European diet and remained one for centuries.

The cod is a cold-water bottom fish, living generally from 20 to 350 fathoms deep and preferring the relatively shallow waters of offshore banks. Many seagoing European nations, from Norway to Spain, sought to exploit this abundant and versatile food resource, but it was the Basques who found the mother lode. The Basques, who live in northern Spain and the southwest corner of France, had hunted whales for centuries, searching far across the Atlantic for them so they could supply a considerable market for salted whale meat. In the late Middle Ages, they began to bring back cod as well, but nobody knew where their cod was coming from.

The traditional European codding grounds were in the North Sea and as far west as Iceland, but the Basque fishermen were not to be found there. Instead, each spring the Basque fishing fleet would set sail and, in the fall, return laden with cod, already dried and salted and ready for market. Fish can't be dried on a ship's deck, however. So where were the Basques finding and drying their fish? The Basques, needless to say, weren't telling.

But in 1492, Columbus discovered islands far to the west, islands, it was thought at first, that lay off Asia and would be a new means of tapping the spice trade. French and British explorers began searching for a northwest rout to the Spice Islands. Such explorers as Giovanni Caboto (usually known by his anglicized name, John Cabot) and Jacques Cartier failed, needless to say, to find the Northwest Passage. But what they did find was cod, lots of cod, and vast stretches of shoreline on which to dry it. They also found something else: Basque fishermen.

When Jacques Cartier first visited the mouth of the St. Lawrence River, in 1534, and claimed the land for France, he noted the presence in his new "discovery" of more than 1,000 Basque fishing boats, all happily catching cod.

From Newfoundland to Massachusetts there is a series of banks, exactly the shallow water that cod prefer. The warm water of the Gulf Stream flows up from the South, while the Labrador Current flows down from the Arctic. Meeting over the banks, the two currents roil the waters as they mix, stirring up huge amounts of nutrients. The result of this chance congruence of geographic factors is, to put it mildly, cod heaven.

With the Basque secret revealed, a *cod rush* followed. (Mark Kurlansky uses this term in his highly entertaining *Cod: A Biography of the Fish That Changed the World.*) By the mid–sixteenth century, 60 percent of the fish being consumed in Europe was cod, most of it caught off North America. One of those who participated in this cod rush, although he would have much preferred to find gold, was Captain John Smith. Immortal for his part in founding Virginia, in 1614 Smith explored a new part of the North American coastline, to which he gave the name New England. Disappointed in his search for gold, he set his men to fishing for cod while he went exploring in the ship's pinnace, mapping the coastline from Maine to the cape that was already named for the fish that teemed in its waters.

Smith's map and description of New England—and his profits from cod fishing—encouraged the Pilgrims to seek a charter from the Crown to settle there. And, indeed, it was the cod that saved the first European New Englanders. In 1640, only ten years after Massachusetts Bay Colony was founded by the Puritans, it exported 300,000 cod to Europe. Cod was soon also being traded to the West Indies, in exchange for salt, sugar, and molasses. Plowing in the cod waste greatly increased the agricultural productivity of the stony New England soil.

The cod proved the basis of a New England prosperity so considerable that Adam Smith singled it out for praise in his *Wealth of Nations.* And to this day, a wooden sculpture of a cod adorns the walls of the Massachusetts State House in Boston to remind the legislators of the foundation of their state's greatness.

The great cod rush differed from the more familiar gold and oil rushes in that cod is a renewable resource. Like a well-managed trust fund, the North American fishing banks should have paid out dividends in the form of cod forever. And for several hundred years they did exactly that. As late as 1885, the Canadian Ministry of Agriculture was of the opinion that "unless the order of nature is overthrown, for centuries to come our fisheries will continue to be fertile."

But one century was all it took for a tragedy of the commons to unfold in this entirely unmanaged trust fund. The major fishing nations, each trying to get their share, exploited newly available technology—especially high-powered engine-driven ships, drag nets, and onboard freezing—that simply caught cod faster than even that prolific species could reproduce. At first only the average size of individual fish declined, as technology such as sonar helped keep up total tonnage. But then that too began to decline precipitously.

In hopes of finally exerting some control, the United States and Canada extended their jurisdictions out 200 miles. Then, in 1992, Canada, trying to give the cod a chance to reproduce unmolested for a period and thus save a priceless asset, banned ground fishing (fishing for bottom-feeding fish, principally cod) in most of Canada's Atlantic waters.

It is still too soon to know if the ban will work. But it is not too soon to declare that the old system of common ownership does not.

SOWING THE
AMERICAN DREAM

IN THE 1960S A magazine asked J. Paul Getty to write an article to be titled "The Secret of My Success." Getty agreed, and a short time later the manuscript arrived in the mail. It read, in its entirety, "Some people find oil; others don't." Earlier, in a similar vein, political boss George Washington Plunkett is supposed to have explained his electoral successes by noting simply that "I seen my opportunities and I took 'em."

Both Getty and Plunkett, of course, found opportunities that made them rich (in money or votes) almost beyond counting, and, as a result, their stories have been told many times and at much greater length than their own one-sentence forays into autobiography.

But in this respect economic history is much like military history, for it is usually generals and admirals, not PFCs and able seamen, however brave, who are remembered and memorialized. Likewise, for every Getty and Plunkett there have been tens of thousands of others who also saw their opportunities in the American economy and took them.

For these people, the opportunities they seized resulted not in the making of a great fortune but only in a good life well lived and still greater opportunities for their children. And that, not unbounded wealth, is the real essence of the American dream. The stories of these people are often no less stirring, their accomplishments no less real, their legacies no less rich—at least when reckoned on a basis other than monetary—than the stories of multimillionaires.

Consider an area of Orange County, New York, about sixty miles from Times Square by land—and vastly farther in spirit—that is known as the black-dirt country. One hundred years ago Polish and Volga German immigrants first looked upon the perfectly flat land ringed by low hills. It had been considered worthless swampland by the Dutch and English families who had lived in the area for over a century, good only for firewood and trapping muskrats. To the immigrants, however, it looked a lot like the land they had left in eastern Europe to seek their fortunes in the New World.

At the end of the last ice age, 10,000 years ago, a glacier left behind a shallow lake in southern Orange County, drained by the Wallkill River. The Wallkill runs, most unusually for an American river, northward, but it does so only reluctantly, and its sluggish flow often spills out over its banks to this day despite numerous attempts to tame it. The lake, soon choked with reeds, slowly disappeared as the rotting vegetation built up at the average rate of one foot every 500 years. In time the lake was transformed into a seasonal swamp dotted with the limestone uprises that had once been islands in the lake.

The soil created by this lost lake is almost wholly organic matter. Left undisturbed, it would, in the fullness of time, have become a peat bog and eventually a coal seam. At the stage it is in now, it is known, technically, as muck soil. Orange County, with a total of 26,000 acres, has more of it in one spot than any place else in the United States except the Everglades of southern Florida.

The early settlers of the region were upland farmers accustomed to well-drained soil. They turned the short, once wooded hills and small valleys of Orange County into dairy farms and fruit orchards. In dry years they would run cattle in the swamp and cut the white cedar that grew there for firewood. Numerous projects were proposed to drain the so-called drowned lands of the Wallkill, but the river proved intractable.

In the middle of the nineteenth century, some of the farmers drained and cleared a little of the swampland and discovered how extraordinarily rich the deep, black soil was. But, because they were intimidated by the work involved in making it productive, nothing much came of it. Then the Polish and German immigrants who had been living in New York City and working in the area as seasonal help on the farms saw the opportunities presented by the black dirt and took 'em.

Unlike most of western Europe, many areas of eastern Europe are low-lying and poorly drained. Once these areas were made fit for agriculture, however, they became extremely productive. The black dirt of Orange County, the newcomers recognized immediately, was much the same. Because the "drowned lands" were largely regarded as useless, the im-

poverished immigrants were able to buy small parcels, often as small as
three or four acres, very cheaply and, with a vast investment of "sweat
equity," begin the backbreaking task of making them economically fruit-
ful. Families with names like Poloniak, Bogdanski, Gurda, and Wierzbicki
began to set down roots near the tiny town of Pine Island, located on one
of the limestone uprises in the middle of the black dirt. Volga-Germans
founded the town of Little York on its eastern rim.

The first step to reclaiming the land was drainage. Muck soil is like
no other. Behaving like a sponge, it soaks up water and holds it in large
quantities. The exposed soil on top dries quickly, but the crust then holds
in the moisture below. Jumping up and down on it causes it to tremble
for yards around like a gigantic bowl of black Jell-O. Ditches several feet
deep had to be dug by hand in a checkerboard fashion, dividing the land
into fields an acre or so in size.

Next the wild vegetation had to be cleared. The trees could be cut
down, but the stumps could not be burned, as was the usual procedure
elsewhere. Once drained, the soil, being nearly pure organic matter, caught
fire easily and could burn underground for weeks, creating sinkholes into
which people and even horses and wagons could suddenly vanish, sometimes years after the fire was extinguished. In 1964 a disastrous fire destroyed nearly four square miles of fields.

Instead, the stumps each had to be laboriously cut free of their roots
and then pulled by teams of horses wearing special wooden platforms on
their hooves to keep from sinking into the soft earth.

Under these conditions, the new landowners could clear only an acre
or two of land a year at best. But, once cleared, what land it was. Because
the muck soil is rich, stone free, and deep (it averages fifteen to twenty
feet and in spots is as much as seventy-five feet deep), it is ideal for
truck farming and, when flood, wind, and insect don't interfere, immensely
productive.

In the early days a wide variety of vegetables were grown for the
burgeoning New York market so close by. From the beginning, however,
onions were usually the most profitable crop. Today the Orange County
black-dirt country produces on average 30,000 pounds of onion per acre,
and some areas of it average over 60,000. (That, for the mathematically
inclined, is more than one and a third pounds of onions per square foot
per season.)

Onion farming, however, especially in the early days, was extremely labor-intensive. At first there was no machinery designed to deal with onions, and they thus had to be planted, weeded, and harvested entirely by hand, often by people who were down on their knees for most of the day. To relieve the hard labor and increase productivity, the people of the black-dirt country soon began to design their own homemade onion planters and harvesters.

Onions, unlike many vegetables, lend themselves to mechanical agriculture. Today there is even a complicated self-propelled gizmo—called for some mysterious reason a "mule train"—that lifts the onions from the dirt, tops them, and bags them in one continuous operation. The mechanization of onion farming led, in turn, to more and more of the black-dirt country being given over to onions, with all the advantages and disadvantages of monocultural husbandry.

The success of truck farming caused the value of the land to soar. In the 1880s it could be bought for about $10 an acre. Twenty years later it was worth $200 and, by the 1960s, $3,000 an acre. The once desperately poor Polish and Volga-German farmers, who had at first often lived in shacks on their black-dirt acres, began to build substantial houses and barns on the "islands" that rose above the black dirt.

As more and more muck soil was brought under cultivation, the original small farms, worked by individual families, coalesced into larger ones both to take advantage of economies of scale and because the children and grandchildren often moved off the land and into other trades and professions. Today there are several farms of over 1,000 acres and one of more than 2,500 acres that is one of the larger businesses in the county.

The tides of capitalism, however, are seldom still. The proximity to New York City that was once one of the black-dirt country's greatest assets has now turned into a liability. The drop in transportation costs has made produce from more distant areas competitive in the New York market, while the state's swiftly rising property taxes have had a major impact on profitability. "Fifteen or twenty years ago," Walter Chimelowski explained in 1990 to the *New York Times*, "it cost $300 to produce an acre of onions, and we'd get $5 or $6 per 100 pounds. Today, it's $1,400 to produce an acre of onions, and last fall we only got $7 or $8."

To make matters worse, the black-dirt country produces a pungent, richly flavored onion that has now gone out of fashion. For reasons that no one is quite sure of, a Texas-developed hybrid known as granex, when grown in the light sandy soil of southeast Georgia, produces an extraordinarily mild, sweet onion. Sophisticated marketing of these onions, under the appellation Vidalia, has taken away much of the business during parts of the year.

In other areas in the environs of New York City, including Orange County, property taxes have brought about the residential development of much of the farmland. But that is not a solution to the current economic problems of the black-dirt country. The muck soil, so perfect for growing vegetables, is useless for houses. The deep, loose, stone-free soil makes a very poor footing for buildings (that's the origin of the Leaning Tower of Pisa's problem), and unless the ditches are faithfully maintained, the land will soon revert to swamp.

As a consequence, black-dirt farmers are turning back to other crops, lessening their reliance on onions alone. Celery, radishes, lettuce, and endive are all increasingly important. More and more often these are being sold directly at retail to fancy restaurants and at New York City's burgeoning farmers' markets. Another crop recently introduced is sod, and now more than 10 percent of the black-dirt country is devoted to its production. There is little doubt that one of the most agriculturally productive areas in the United States will adapt to changing conditions.

It was luck and black gold that lifted J. Paul Getty to the ranks of the superrich. It was hard work, onions, and black dirt that transformed a group of impoverished eastern European peasants into middle-class Americans. Which is the greater aspect of the American dream?

THE LATE, GREAT LIEDERKRANZ CHEESE

EXASPERATED, as he often was, by the French genius for dividing into multiple and irreconcilable political factions, Charles de Gaulle is reported to have once thrown up his hands and lapsed into apparent non sequitur. "How can anyone," he asked, "govern a nation that makes 365 different kinds of cheese?"

This is not a true non sequitur, however, for the greatest French statesman of the twentieth century seems to have discovered an underlying correlation between cheese and political instability. Consider the United States. It has produced only three uniquely American cheeses: Monterey Jack, Brick, and Liederkranz. But since 1789 the nation has also flourished under a single constitution. Meanwhile France, with 365, has run through three kingdoms, two empires, and five republics.

Even aside from cheese, wholly North American foodstuffs are notably few in number, the cranberry and maple syrup being about the only uniquely North American delicacies we have to offer. This is not to say, however, that the United States has had little effect on the world's eating habits. Far from it. Beginning in the nineteenth century, the United States took what had been always a necessity and sometimes an art, food preparation, and turned it into an industrial process. The world's dinner tables have not been the same since.

Soft drinks were invented in this country by businessmen, not chefs, and Coca-Cola may well be the most famous American product in the world. So were canned soups, nondairy coffee creamers, breakfast cereals, and—I regret to report—TV dinners.

Even many basically foreign foods have been so industrialized as to seem, now, as American as apple pie. Ketchup originated in Southeast Asia and was brought to the West by the sauce-loving British. But it was H. J.

Heinz and Company that put the tomato-based variety on the tables of six continents. McDonald's turned a meat-patty sandwich named for a German city into a multibillion-dollar global capitalist triumph.

The essence of industrialized food, of course, is uniformity and huge production. Pepsi-Cola tastes exactly the same in Boston, Brisbane, and Buenos Aires, and Pepsico goes to a great deal of trouble and expense to see that it does. Ritz Crackers have been turned out in the millions by Nabisco every day since 1934. However, fine cheese is idiosyncratic and, almost always, in very limited production because natural cheese is a living thing.

What makes cheese possible is the happy property of milk protein to coagulate in the presence of acids and certain other chemicals produced by microorganisms. The protein and fat form curds, allowing most of the liquid to be separated out. The curds are then molded and stored while the microorganisms continue to work their magic, slowly producing the flavor, aroma, and consistency of each type of cheese.

It is the infinite variety of these microorganisms that makes for the infinite variety of cheeses. But their existence wasn't even discovered until the seventeenth century, and their role in cheese making wasn't learned until a little over 100 years ago. Only then could cheese making begin to change from an art to a process. The American food industry proceeded to do exactly that (although to be fair, many of the methods were pioneered in Europe).

According to an official publication of the U.S. Department of Agriculture, processed cheeses are "made by grinding fine, and mixing together by heating and stirring, one or more cheeses of the same or two or more varieties, together with an added emulsifying agent, into a homogeneous plastic mass."

The homogeneous plastic mass (the Department of Agriculture certainly has a way with words) is then cut into uniform chunks or squeezed by rollers into thin sheets, cut into squares, and packaged. The result is a nearly sterile, absolutely consistent product whose chief virtue is a notably long shelf life. Of course by this point, processed cheese is to real cheese about what military music is to music.

But if the technology of processed cheese is very new, the history of natural cheese is very ancient. It was known to the Sumerians, and the future King David encountered both Goliath and immortality because he was carrying bread and grain to his brothers serving in the Hebrew army, together with ten cheeses for their commander.

Cheese doubtless was discovered by accident and came to be exploited as a way to extend the period of the year in which dairy products could form a part of the human diet. Originally, milk was available only when the herds were bearing young in the spring. Turned into cheese, however, it remained edible for months, in some cases years.

When Europeans began settling the New World, they brought with them the cheese-making know-how that had developed over many thousands of years and began making cheese. As early as 1676, Virginia militia regulations called for three and a half pounds of cheese per man per week, and the American colonies were soon exporting large quantities to the West Indies.

Each immigrant group also brought a taste for the particular cheeses they had known at home, and cheese makers necessarily catered to these tastes. This is why this country has always produced so many excellent imitations of European cheeses and so few native American ones.

One major immigrant group in the nineteenth century was the Germans, many of whom settled in New York City, especially in an area of Manhattan that was once known as Kleindeutschland—Little Germany—and is now called the East Village. As early as the 1850s German immigrants accounted for over half of the city's bakers, confectioners, tobacconists, and, of course, delicatessen owners.

Many of these middle-class Germans were partial to a cheese they had known in the old country called Bismarck Schlosskaese (literally, castle cheese). Schlosskaese is a soft, ripened cheese that is prepared in brick-shaped molds measuring about four inches by one and a half inches by one inch. It is intensely flavorful and, at least for those who don't like it, intensely smelly.

New York City delicatessens began importing the cheese to meet demand, but, unfortunately, like all soft cheeses, Schlosskaese has a very limited life span. In the late nineteenth century, by the time it arrived in New York by ship from Germany, it was often spoiled and unsalable.

Adolph Tode, the owner of a very popular deli in New York, wanted to do something about that. Tode also owned the Monroe Cheese Com-

pany, in Monroe, New York, about twenty-five miles northwest of the
city. In 1889, he asked his cheese makers to try to duplicate Bismarck
Schlosskaese.

A twenty-two-year-old Swiss immigrant named Emile Frey took on
the challenge, although he had been with the company only a year. He
tried for two years to come up with an acceptable substitute. then in one
of the inspired accidents with which the history of cheese is littered, he
inadvertently invented a whole new cheese. It had the same soft creamy
texture of Schlosskaese and an equally pronounced aroma but quite a
different, indeed, unique, flavor.

Tode thought it was delicious and ordered more, but Frey, to his
horror, found he could not duplicate it. For another two years Frey
searched for the gastronomic equivalent of the lost chord, and at last, in
late 1892, he found it again.

Tode tried the new cheese out on his fellow members of a German
singing club in New York called the Liederkranz Society. A distinguished
group, the society included Theodore Roosevelt and Carl Schurz among
its members. They were enthusiastic, and Tode promptly named Frey's
discovery in their honor.

He started selling the new Liederkranz cheese in his deli, and soon
other deli owners were ordering it from the Monroe Cheese Company as
well. By the 1920s demand around the country had become so great that
Monroe's local milk supply was no longer adequate to meet the demand.
In 1926 the company decided to move to Ohio and set up a brand-new,
state-of-the-art cheese factory in the town of Van Wert in order to produce the cheese that had made it famous and that now had a national
market.

But when the company produced its first batch of Liederkranz at the
new plant, the result was a disaster. Not only did it not taste like Liederkranz, it tasted terrible. Emile Frey realized that the company's new spic-
and-span facilities were a little too spic and span for its own good.

He quickly had the wooden parts of the old factory, deeply embedded
with countless generations of the right microorganisms, dismantled and
shipped to Van Wert, where he installed them in the new factory. Then
he spread Liederkranz cheese all over the gleaming walls in hopes of per-
meating the very fabric of the new factory with the right bugs. The second
batch, doubtless to Frey's immense relief, tasted like Liederkranz.

In 1929 the Borden Company bought out the Monroe Cheese Company. Although Liederkranz could only have amounted to a tiny part of Borden's vast product line, the company continued to produce it with all the care and passion a great cheese needs.

Nor did Borden sell it only at fancy stores. For nearly sixty years, as mom-and-pop grocery stores gave way to supermarkets, and Fannie Farmer to Julia Child, one of the world's great cheeses could always be found, most improbably, at the nation's ordinary dairy counters, nestled right between the waxy, bright-orange processed American cheese slices and the equally bright-orange slabs of Velveeta.

But today, alas, more than 100 years after its invention, Liederkranz is no more. In the corporate restructuring that so marked the 1980s, Borden sold its natural cheese division to General Foods in 1982. In 1988 General Foods was bought by Philip Morris and the following year was merged with Philip Morris's Kraft division into Kraft General Foods. At some point in this process, General Foods stopped making Liederkranz. The decision was apparently taken so casually that there is not even a record of it in the corporate archives. Unless somewhere there is some frozen Liederkranz that could be used to re-create it, it is probably lost forever.

It is ironic that just as the country was beginning to develop a serious gastronomy of its own and a rapidly increasing interest in American, not imitation European, cheeses, one of the quiet—if noisome—glories of the American table vanished in the snap of a corporate decision. Hardly anyone even noticed.

In France, it would have brought down the government.

SAWDUST PUDDING

IN FIRST TIMOTHY, St. Paul advises his young disciple to "drink no longer water, but use a little wine for thy stomach's sake and for thine often [i.e., common] infirmities." It might amuse St. Paul to learn that after nearly 2,000 years, the U.S. government has finally agreed with him. In its 1995 guidelines for nutrition, the federal government acknowledged that a modest intake of alcohol is not harmful and might even have benefits for the heart.

This is an astonishing development. After all, if there has been one consistency in dietary advice through the years, it has been—to use the title of an amusing book on food fads—"If you like it, don't eat it." Virtually everything that people regard as delicious or pleasurable, from cream to gin, has been regularly denounced by diet "experts," beginning at least as far back as Pythagoras—a vegetarian as well as a mathematician—in the sixth century B.C.

And heaven knows there have been few other consistencies. Hardly a single food that is extolled as the very elixir of life itself in one book is not excoriated as the purest poison in another. Even some fruits, usually considered the centerpiece of good nutrition, are occasionally condemned. One recent advertisement for a heavily promoted diet book extolled the virtues of grapes and plums but warned against raisins, prunes, and an assortment of other fruits.

Raisins and prunes, of course, are nothing but dried grapes and plums, but I'm not about to spend my money buying the book to learn why the author thinks a grape is good for you, but a grape with some of its water content evaporated is not.

It has only been in the twentieth century that nutrition became a science at all. The very word *vitamin*, for instance, entered the English

language in 1912 when these substances were first being chemically analyzed and their role in human nutrition determined. There are still vast
gaps in our scientific knowledge, largely because there are severe ethical
constraints on experimenting on human beings. As a result, we know
much more about the real nutritional needs of, say, chickens than we do
of our own species.

This has left plenty of room for the philosophers and cranks, who
dominated the field of nutrition in the nineteenth century, to continue to
be influential, aided and abetted, of course, by a gullible, often ignorant,
and always headline-hunting media.

There appears to be a nearly bottomless market for nutritional nonsense, just as there is for astrological advice. Hundreds of diet books are
published every year in this country. Their authors crisscross the land on
lecture tours to feed this longing for a Rosetta stone to the secret of good
health and longevity and to make very tidy incomes in the process. The
man who first discovered this market, and exploited it profitably, was an
American named Sylvester Graham.

Graham was born in West Suffield, Connecticut, on July 4, 1794. His
father was seventy-two when Graham was born and had sired sixteen
children before him by two wives. He had been the minister at the local
church for fifty years, and as such had been one of the most important
and respected men in the community. But when he died, two years after
his last child's birth, his wife soon found herself unable to cope with
raising seven children alone with little income.

A few years later the local probate court ruled that Graham's mother
was "in a deranged state of mind." Graham himself wrote years later that
"my mother's health sank under her complicated trials, the family was
broken up, and . . . I fell into the hands of strangers." This fall in status
from minister's son to foundling profoundly affected Graham, who began
to exhibit increasing eccentricities, including a profound egocentrism. He
would suffer several nervous breakdowns over the course of his life.

And although the family was restored in later years, when Graham and
his mother went to live with one of his older siblings in Newark, New
Jersey, his education was hit-or-miss at best. Regardless, he decided to
follow in his father's footsteps and become a minister. He enrolled in the
Amherst Academy, a secondary school attached to what would become
Amherst College, in 1823, when he was nearly thirty. His unpopularity

with his fellow students caused him to be expelled on a trumped-up charge after only one quarter. But even in that one quarter, he made himself remembered as "an ardent and eloquent speaker, arrogant and forceful." One faculty member thought him a "stage actor," which was intended as no compliment, but would stand Graham in good stead later in his career. Thereafter he studied privately with a minister and was ordained in 1826, the year he married a woman who had nursed him through one of his breakdowns.

The following year he earned his first income as a minister when he was paid ten dollars to preach a sermon. But Graham soon began widening the field of his endeavors beyond simple soul-saving. In 1830 he became a lecturer for the Pennsylvania Society for Discouraging the Use of Ardent Spirits. Like many early temperance societies, this one aimed only at moderating the then-staggering per-capita consumption of alcohol. But Graham from the first advocated total abstinence.

Soon he was talking about diet and sex as well as alcohol. Graham boasted that he never read books and developed his theories entirely on his own. But he was familiar with several medical writers of the time—when medicine was just beginning its conversion from an art to a science—and, indeed, he plagiarized several of them in his own books and pamphlets.

It was the cholera epidemic of 1832 that put Graham on the map. The disease had been spreading from its base in India since 1826 and had hit Europe by the early 1830s. There was no doubt that the New World would be next. Virtually nothing was then known about the disease except its deadly nature. Its causative microorganism would not be determined until the 1880s, and even the fact that it was spread by contaminated water supplies was not understood till the 1850s. People flocked to hear anyone who could tell them about the disease, and Graham, with his histrionic talents, was soon in great demand. The fact that he ascribed cholera to both chicken pie and "excessive lewdness" did not dissuade them in the least.

With the waning of the epidemic, Graham began to lecture widely on diet and sex and their effect on other aspects of human existence. As with most food faddists, Graham was opposed to virtually anything that might be thought of as pleasurable. Graham's basic premise was that anything "stimulating" was automatically debilitating. Stimulants, of course, included not only alcohol but also meat, warm baths, and sweets.

Graham's most famous dietary advice was that bread should be the mainstay of the diet, should be made from the whole grain, and should be baked at home, by the woman of the house, not the servants. White bread was fashionable because it was more expensive than whole wheat and also had a much lighter texture. But Graham, quite accidentally, was correct that it is nutritionally inferior, as much of the vitamins and minerals in the wheat are lost when the bran is removed.

Graham was soon lecturing up and down the East Coast, often commanding lecture fees of as much as $300 a night. In a time when $1,000 a year was a middle-class income, that was serious money. Graham was delighted with his success. "No man," he was soon boasting, "can travel by stage or steamboat . . . or go into any part of our country . . . and begin to advocate a vegetable diet . . . without being immediately asked . . . What! Are you a Grahamite?" Indeed, Grahamite hotels and boarding-houses sprang up, catering to people who followed his dietary advice. Horace Greeley, ever earnestly in search of the pure and wholesome, often dined at one in New York.

Equally, others made fun of Graham and his bland diet. Ralph Waldo Emerson described him as the "poet of bran bread and pumpkins." Even his own hometown newspaper (he lived in Northampton, Massachusetts, the last fifteen years of his life) called him "the philosopher of sawdust pudding."

Others, however, took less tolerant exception to Graham. Butchers, not surprisingly, objected to lectures on a strictly vegetarian diet, especially when they were accompanied with vivid descriptions of slaughtering practices. Bakers, meanwhile, equally resented calls for baking bread at home and accusations that they adulterated their bread with bean flour and even chalk and plaster of paris.

In Boston, they struck back. The butchers and bakers intimidated the owner of the lecture hall where Graham was scheduled to talk, and he canceled the booking. Graham went to the owners of the not-yet-finished Malborough Hotel, the nation's first temperance hotel. The owners courageously allowed him to use it, even though Boston's mayor said he could not guarantee the peace.

The Grahamites boarded up the windows on the first floor and stationed men on the roof with bags of slaked lime. When the butchers and bakers attacked the hotel, they were showered with the lime. In the words of *Harper's Magazine,* "The eyes had it, and the rabble incontinently adjourned."

Graham's audience eventually turned to other interests (phrenology and "premature burial" were popular in the 1840s), and Graham retreated to Northampton, where he wrote books and became increasingly eccentric and increasingly in poor health (a common characteristic, perhaps not coincidentally, among health reformers). He died in 1851, only fifty-six years old.

Some of his early followers went on to fame and fortune. The Kellogg brothers, influenced by Graham, founded a great American industry. But Graham himself is completely forgotten, despite his own prediction that a granite shaft would be erected on his grave and his house would become a place of pilgrimage. (In fact, it became a tavern.)

But in one respect Graham is not forgotten. Even today, at morning recess in thousands of schools across the country, the kids are served a snack: a glass of milk—and graham crackers.

PART III

MANUFACTURING AND MINING

INDUSTRIAL REVOLUTIONARY

OLIVER EVANS DID NOT live to see railroads. He died in 1819, and the first real American railroad line, the Baltimore and Ohio, was begun only in 1828.

But in another sense he saw railroads very clearly indeed. Just look at what he wrote in 1813: "The time will come when people will travel in stages [i.e., stagecoaches] moved by steam engines, from one city to another, almost as fast as birds fly. . . . A carriage will set out from Washington in the morning, the passenger will breakfast in Baltimore, dine at Philadelphia and sup at New York on the same day. . . . To accomplish this, two sets of railways will be laid . . . to guide the carriage, so that they may pass each other in different directions and travel by night as well as by day."

Oliver Evans not only foresaw railroads but also described precisely how modern refrigerators would one day work. He designed central heating systems, a solar boiler, a machine gun, a gas-lighting system. Most of these inventions, like so many of Leonardo da Vinci's three centuries earlier, were impracticable given the technology of Evans's day. They were just the fancies of an endlessly fertile engineering imagination.

But Oliver Evans also made two singularly practical contributions to the technology of his times. The high-pressure steam engine he invented (his contemporary Richard Trevithick of England also invented one independently) would be the driving force of the nineteenth-century economy. And his automatic flour mill foreshadowed the industrial process by which Henry Ford would transform the world in the twentieth century. Together they give him a claim to the title of "founding father of the American industrial revolution" that few can match.

Born near Newport, Delaware, in 1755, Oliver Evans was the fifth child in what would eventually be a family of twelve. His father was a farmer of modest prosperity, and at seventeen Oliver was apprenticed to a wheelwright and wagon maker in Newport.

While learning the trade, Evans also read widely, especially in mathematics and mechanics. Only a few years before, in 1769, James Watt had produced his first steam engine, four times as fuel efficient as earlier ones, and the young Evans devoured the details of the new energy source. He would be deeply concerned with steam engines for the rest of his life, and, in middle age, his own design rendered Watt's obsolete.

But there was no market for steam engines in late colonial America, and in 1782, the year he married, he joined with two of his brothers in building a flour mill on land they bought from their father.

The technology of flour mills had not changed in any essential aspect since waterpower had first been utilized hundreds of years earlier. To make flour, sacks of grain were carried, one by one, up to the top of the mill, where they were poured into a device that separated the grain from dirt and chaff. Then the wheat dropped through a chute to a lower floor, where it was ground into meal by the millstones.

The meal then dropped into a chest on the ground floor and was shoveled into buckets to be hoisted back up to the third floor. There it was spread out to cool and lose moisture. The meal was then pushed into a chute, where it fell into the bolting cylinder, a device that separated the meal into flour, middlings, and bran. Finally, the flour was packed into barrels and was ready to ship.

The only parts of this complicated process that were powered by the waterwheel were the actual grinding and bolting. Everything else was accomplished by human physical effort. Evans immediately thought he saw a better way. Over the next few years he designed a series of bucket elevators and screw conveyors, powered by the waterwheel, that moved the grain, meal, and flour from one process to another automatically. He also designed a "hopper boy" that spread and cooled the freshly ground meal and slowly pushed it into the bolter. It too was powered by the waterwheel.

Except for the hopper boy, none of Evans's devices were entirely new. The bucket elevator was an adaptation of the chain pump, known since Roman times, and the screw conveyor was merely a horizontal version of

Archimedes' screw, a device so ancient it might even antedate Archimedes himself.

What was stunningly new was the conception of an integrated, automatic, industrial process. Automatic machinery, which worked without human operators, had been around for some time (the clock was one of the first). In the late eighteenth century the number of automatic machines grew swiftly. Textile and nail-making machines were developed, among others. And, of course, there was Watt's steam engine.

But until Oliver Evans, no one had conceived of the factory itself as a machine, yet Evans's flour mill was exactly that: You poured grain in one end, and flour came out the other. Except for adjusting, maintaining, and monitoring, the process needed no human labor whatever.

Having invented a better mousetrap, Evans expected the world to beat a path to his door. He was very disappointed. Flour mills already in operation were profitable as they were, and their owners saw no reason to install expensive machinery. Also, most of them were family enterprises, and the owners feared the new machines might put their own relatives out of work.

For the rest of his life Evans was to rail ill-temperedly against the human tendency to stick with the status quo and to bemoan the fact that fate had made him a genius in a world where geniuses were not appreciated. "He that studies and writes on the improvement of the arts and sciences labours to benefit generations yet unborn," Evans wrote at a particularly gloomy period of his life, "for it is not probable that his contemporaries will pay any attention to him . . . ; therefore improvements progress so slowly."

Evans patented his flour-mill process in several states, and after the new federal Constitution went into effect, he received the third patent the new government issued. (The first Patent Board consisted of three members of the new cabinet, including another prolific American inventor, Secretary of State Thomas Jefferson. Jefferson must have been impressed, for a few years later he would set up an Evans-type flour mill at one of his own plantations and pay Evans a forty-dollar license fee for the privilege. George Washington, also always receptive to new technology, bought a license for his mill at Mount Vernon as well.)

Despite Evans's grumpy attitude about people's reluctance to change, the Evans process relentlessly spread through the industry over the next twenty years while its essential idea spread to other industries as well. Its success was greatly helped by a book Evans wrote, titled *The Young Mill-wright and Miller's Guide*. A how-to book on building and running flour mills, it would have fully fifteen editions, the last printed on the eve of the Civil War, forty years after the author's death.

While his flour-mill inventions were a solid success, the license fees were not yet enough to earn a living. So Evans moved to Philadelphia and became a merchant, specializing in flour-mill equipment. But while he sold bolting cloth and bucket chains to earn his bread, his restless mind was turning back to his adolescent passion: steam.

When he had first learned about Watt's engine, he had dreamed of building a steam carriage. But Watt's engine did not produce anywhere near enough power to move itself, let alone a carriage. The Watt engine operated on low pressure and worked at what today seems an almost surreally slow pace, about twelve cycles per minute. In the Watt engine, steam pushed the piston to the bottom of the cylinder and then was drawn off and condensed, creating a vacuum that sucked the piston back up.

Evans developed an engine using high-pressure steam that not only pushed the piston down but pushed it back up as well. Watt's separate condenser was dispensed with. The result was a steam engine that was far smaller than Watt's and yet produced far more power per unit of weight, because it operated at many times the speed. Evans's first engine, built in 1803, had a cylinder about six inches in diameter and eighteen inches long. It produced about five horsepower. The great Watt-type engines that had been installed the year before to power the Philadelphia waterworks at Central Square, in contrast, each had a cylinder diameter of thirty-two inches and a stroke of six feet. Yet they each produced only twelve horsepower.

Evans set his engine to stationary work, powering a device to grind plaster of paris and another that sawed slabs of marble. But he soon returned to his steam carriage idea. He was commissioned to build a steam dredge for Philadelphia harbor. He did so near his shop, which was about a mile from the Schuylkill River up Market Street. The vessel, improbably named the *Orukter Amphibolos*, was twelve feet wide and thirty feet long. It weighed fully seventeen tons. To get it to the river, he put it on two sets of wheels, attached the engine to one axle with a chain drive, and proceeded up Market Street "with a gentle motion."

When he got to Central Square, he gave a demonstration, circling several times around the waterworks located there. He was, of course, both literally and metaphorically running rings around Watt's low-pressure engines with his high-pressure one. The demonstration over, the first land vehicle in America to move by means other than muscle power tootled off down Market Street to the river, dropped its wheels, and entered both the Schuylkill and the oblivion that is the fate of dredges.

But its engine did not. Evans had redesigned his high-pressure engine for his steam dredge to make it smaller, lighter, and more efficient. Further refined and enlarged, it proved the perfect power source for the steamboats that were soon operating in the shallow and treacherous waters of the Mississippi River system as well as for myriad industrial uses and, later, the early railroads. Together with the licensing fees of his flour mill, it made Oliver Evans's old age a prosperous one.

Oliver Evans, still grumpy and convinced of the stupidity of his fellow man despite his prosperity, pointed the way to the nineteenth century. His fellow man, not so stupid after all, took it from there.

SEWING AND REAPING
A FORTUNE

As the stock market gyrated in 2000, there was much talk about the "old economy" and the "new economy." But the old economy, however temporarily unfashionable it may be on Wall Street, is still very much with us. Buildings are still made of steel and concrete. Oil and the internal combustion engine still dominate transportation. You are probably reading this book with the help of an invention Thomas Edison first demonstrated in 1876.

And there are many parts of planet earth where even the old economy has not yet reached, and the people still live in what we might call the old old economy. This is one of subsistence agriculture and hand labor; grinding poverty for the many and immense wealth for the few. That was the condition of the Western world as well 250 years ago. The only way out of that condition is to do what the West did: industrialize. An industrial economy creates wealth at a much faster rate than does a nonindustrial one, and if history is any guide, however rich those at the top of the economic ladder become, the rest of society becomes much richer as well, and the percentage of the population below the poverty line steadily decreases as the economy expands.

Obviously, the process of building an industrial economy has to begin somewhere. In the Western world it began with cloth, when the manufacture of textiles was industrialized starting in the middle of the eighteenth century in the English midlands. Today, however, the textile industry is a highly mechanized and capital-intensive one, not suitable for third-world conditions. Instead, for the last century and more, it has been the manufacture of clothes that has often served as the beginning to industrialization.

Clothes is one of those curious English words that has no singular. The reason is simple enough: The singular used to be *cloth.* Clothes, after all, are just pieces of cloth sewn together to match the body's contours. Thus it is sewing that turns cloth into clothes, and sewing is about as ancient a technology as still exists. But although cloth making was industrialized very early on, clothes continued to be made by hand for another century and more. Sewing, after all, couldn't become an industrial process until someone invented a practical sewing machine.

Once it was invented, however, clothes making rapidly became industrialized because the technology was inexpensive (one sewing machine per worker, who supplied the power) and easy for uneducated workers to master. Wherever there has been a large supply of cheap labor—New York's vast immigrant population late in the nineteenth century, the third world today—the sewing machine has often proved the first rung up the ladder out of poverty. The development of the sewing machine was thus one of the triumphs of the early industrial revolution, as important in its way as the railroad as an engine of wealth creation.

But it was no easy matter to devise a means to do mechanically what had always required delicate and complex movements by the human hand. Like so many important inventions of the early nineteenth century, the sewing machine was not really the invention of one man. Instead, many contributed parts to the puzzle over many years. But as with George Stephenson and the railroad and Samuel Morse and the telegraph, the historical credit has largely gone to the man who finally put the pieces together: Isaac Merrit Singer.

Singer is a classic example of Adam Smith's "invisible hand" at work. Although an extraordinarily self-centered man who used others, especially women, shamelessly, his own pursuit of fortune greatly increased the standard of living of millions of others, especially women.

Isaac Singer's father, Adam, was born in Germany in 1753. Isaac was his youngest child, born in upstate New York in 1811, when Adam was fifty-eight. The family fell apart, however, when Isaac was ten. In 1821 Adam's wife, after thirty-three years of marriage and numerous children, had apparently had enough of her husband's chronic philandering, divorced him—a rare proceeding in early-nineteenth-century America—and moved to a Quaker community in Albany. She never saw her family again. Adam quickly remarried, and neither the divorce nor his behavior seemingly had any adverse impact on his health: He lived to be 102, dying in 1855.

Isaac was more or less on his own by the time he was twelve, when he moved to burgeoning Rochester, apparently living with an older brother. He managed to get a little schooling but would never write with fluidity or even good spelling. At nineteen he became an apprentice in a machine shop, where he quickly demonstrated a marked talent for mechanics. Isaac Singer was a born tinkerer. Unfortunately for Singer and his family, he wanted to be an actor instead. Acting, then as now, is a profession of notoriously dubious financial rewards, and Singer, while undoubtedly possessed of considerable personal charm, had, at best, only a pedestrian talent.

The pattern of Singer's young life established itself while he was still a teenager. He would act when he could and take jobs as a mechanic when he had to. In between, he pursued women with the same cheerful relentlessness as his father had. He married in 1830, when he was nineteen, and by 1837, he had two children to support. Staying in Baltimore while touring with an acting company, he met an attractive young woman and soon became engaged to her. Needless to say, he did not bother to tell her he was already married. Not long after he returned to New York, his wife returned to her parents. The marriage was over, although he would send her money when he had any.

Singer's fiancée then appeared in New York expecting to marry the young, handsome, and charming man who had won her heart in Baltimore. Singer had no choice but to tell her at least some version of the truth, and he persuaded her to accept the situation. Their first child was born July 27, 1837, and nine more followed, but he never did marry her (indeed he left her for someone else whom he did marry), and he fathered numerous children by other women as well.

Singer continued his acting/mechanical career, inventing a rock drill in 1839, the patent for which he sold for $2,000, no small sum. But despite the rock-drill windfall, the family, or rather families, lived a hand-to-mouth existence until Singer, approaching middle age, finally gave up acting and took up mechanics full-time. He invented a carving machine for making wooden type and interested a businessman named George B. Zieber in marketing it. They took it to Boston and rented space in a machine shop to show it to potential clients. But although several printers looked at it, no one wanted to buy it. Zieber and Singer were just about out of money when destiny called.

The machine shop where they rented space had been making a line of sewing machines, but they seldom worked. "Of a hundred and twenty completed machines," Zieber said, "only eight or nine worked well enough to use." The machine was based on a design by Elias Howe, who had obtained a patent on it in 1846. The machine produced a lock stitch, using a curved needle for one thread and a shuttle that moved in a circular fashion for the other. The curved needle was very fragile, and, when the machine worked at all, the cloth had to be reset after every few stitches. It was, in fact, more trouble than it was worth.

At first Singer was reluctant to pay attention to such a "paltry business," as he called it. Further, he didn't like the possible social effects. "You want to do away with the only thing that keeps women quiet, their sewing!" he told Zieber.

But being broke can be a powerful stimulant to creative endeavor, and Singer was soon at work designing an improved machine, one using a straight needle and a back-and-forth shuttle motion. Most important, it fed the cloth through the machine in a continuous fashion, allowing much quicker operation, seams of any length, and the ability to sew on a curve, obviously a necessity where clothes are concerned.

Late one night, with both Zieber and Singer exhausted, they were finally ready to try it out. While Zieber held a lantern, Singer worked the machine. But the stitches were much too loose to hold the pieces of cloth together properly. Discouraged, the two began walking back to the cheap hotel room they shared.

"Sick at heart," Singer remembered afterward, "we sat down on a pile of boards, and Zieber asked me if I had noticed that the loose loops of thread on the upper side of the cloth came from the needle. It then flashed upon me that I had forgotten to adjust the tension upon the needle thread. Zieber and I went back to the shop. I adjusted the tension, tried the machine, and sewed five stitches perfectly." Isaac Singer had a sewing machine like none before it: It worked.

Singer's sewing machine was an immediate hit. It is not hard to see why. A shirt that took a seamstress fourteen hours and twenty-six minutes to sew by hand could be produced in one hour and sixteen minutes with the new machine. Many clothing workers (there were an estimated 5,000 shirt makers in New York alone in 1853) feared for their livelihoods at first. But, as usual with laborsaving devices, the effect of the sewing machine was to enlarge their business, not destroy it. As the price of ready-made clothes dropped, the increasing market for them made up for it many times over, one of the fundamental reasons capitalism has made the world a richer place.

The only problem for Singer and his partner was the patent situation. Elias Howe had a patent on a sewing machine, even though his model was not a practical device. Isaac Singer had a practical machine, but no patent on the entire device. With big money now at stake, a court fight was inevitable. When the dust settled—and the lawyers had been much enriched—the final result was a patent pool, the first use of that very handy device in a mechanically complex age.

Isaac Singer, ever the showman, began to lead a life of conspicuous consumption even by the standards of the nouveau-riche nineteenth century. He was often seen driving around New York in a vast carriage painted bright yellow and drawn by nine horses. He died in 1875, at age sixty-four, leaving an estate of between $13 million and $15 million, a huge fortune indeed at the time. In his will he tried, as he had in his own way in life, to provide for his children and some of the numerous women who had shared his bed. Not surprisingly, the newspapers had a field day. "Under the terms of the will," the *New York Herald* gleefully reported, "some twenty or more of his offspring by diverse and sundry mothers are entitled to an average of about $200,000 each."

But while the sewing machine made Isaac Singer a great fortune, it also made the lives of countless housewives and factory workers better too. Indeed it is still doing so in many countries that are just beginning to enter the modern world.

THE CALIFORNIA GOLD RUSH

ON JANUARY 24, 1848, a man named James Marshall was inspecting a millrace that he had just constructed on the American River, not far from Sacramento, California. He had turned the water into it the night before to clear the debris, and now something "about half the size and the shape of a pea" glinting in the water caught his eye. "It made my heart thump," he remembered later, "for I was certain it was gold." To his workmen he said, "Boys, by God, I believe I have found a gold mine."

He had indeed.

It is an oddity of the American past that one of the most significant events in the nation's history—the California gold strike—should have taken place in a foreign country. But it was not until February 2, 1848, that negotiations to end the Mexican War resulted in the Treaty of Guadalupe Hidalgo. And it would be May 30 before the treaty was ratified and the stars and stripes rose over the Southwest in exchange for $15 million. Had Marshall made his discovery only a few weeks earlier, the history of both countries might have been very different.

Needless to say, the attempt by James Marshall and his employer, John Sutter, to keep the gold find secret was doomed to nearly instant failure. Indeed, John Sutter, the owner of 50,000 acres in the Colima Valley, was ruined by the onrush of gold miners, and both men would die broke.

The irresistible allure of gold is not hard to grasp. Not only was it worth $20.66 an ounce at that time (a very good week's wage), it is one of the few metals that can often be successfully mined by people without major capital.

Unlike most metals, gold is chemically inert, only very rarely combining with other elements to form molecules. Therefore gold is usually found in nature in its pure form, although often in the form of "dust" or small flakes. But another characteristic of gold, its very high density, makes it relatively easy to separate the small particles from other minerals. Density is measured in grams per cubic centimeter. By definition, one cubic centimeter of water weighs one gram. Quartz has a density of about 2.6 grams per cubic centimeter. Iron's density is a little less than eight. Gold's is over nineteen. In other words, a gold nugget equal in volume to a mere cubic inch weighs well over half a pound; a cubic foot weighs half a ton.

This very high density meant that as gold eroded out of the hills and was carried downstream, it settled out of the moving water before anything else. Thus it was concentrated wherever the water slowed down, such as in an eddy or on the inner side of a bend in the stream. Swirling the gravel found in such places with water in a broad shallow pan was enough to find significant gold in rich deposits.

In the early days of the gold rush, it was not uncommon for a man to pan ten or more ounces a day out of a good stream, with always the hope of finding a large nugget. So while panning for gold was very hard work, it was possible to earn more in a week than the average workman could earn in a year, with the possibility always present that one might find a fortune.

Thus it is hardly surprising that when news of the gold strike spread, the effect was electric. San Francisco, with a population then of less than 1,000, was nearly emptied, and its harbor became choked with shipping as sailors headed for the gold fields, stranding their vessels. An entire platoon of soldiers deserted from a local fort. As one soldier explained, "The struggle between *right* and six dollars a month and *wrong* and seventy-five dollars a day is rather a severe one." Men poured in from Oregon, Hawaii, and South America. But it would be from the East Coast that the main army of gold seekers would come, although it took nearly a year for the news to reach there. That's why San Francisco's football team is not called the Forty-Eighters.

It is hard for us to imagine today just how remote California was 150 years ago. The sea passage around the Horn could take more than six months and was expensive. But it was also the most comfortable and safe (if the weather at the Horn cooperated at least). The shortcut over the Isthmus of Panama reduced the sailing time to only six weeks, but people could wait for months for a ship in the fever-ridden pesthole that was

Panama City. The overland journey across plain, mountains, and desert was the quickest, but often the most perilous.

So it was only in late summer of 1848 that the first rumors reached the East Coast, and it was December 8 of that year, almost eleven months after James Marshall saw that first yellow gleam, that official news was released. That day President James K. Polk—the man most responsible for making California American territory—sent Congress a message declaring the gold strike authentic. He sent along a guaranteed-to-get-your-attention piece of proof: a twenty-pound gold nugget. Only the size of a large fist, it was then worth about $4,800, enough for a large family to live in comfort for two years or more.

The result, quite literally, was mass hysteria. Ninety thousand people set off for California in 1849 and as many again in 1850. By the time the rush petered out a few years later, California had been transformed. Before the rush, except for a few small towns along the coast, it had been a nearly uninhabited wilderness. But only two years and three months after California became American territory, it was admitted to the Union. At the time of statehood, however, California's population was still fully 92 percent male.

That imbalance, needless to say, was quickly arbitraged out of existence. The subsequent history of California, both economic and demographic, is unparalleled. Its mineral wealth is more varied than that of any comparably sized area in the world, and gold has long been supplanted by oil as the most valuable commodity to be pulled from its earth. Today, California has not far from twice the population of any other state, and were it a sovereign country, it would have the world's sixth-largest economy and be a great power in its own right.

But the story of the California gold rush is at least as interesting for its effect on the entire country as on the history of California. The California gold strike moved the country's center of gravity sharply westward in a historical instant. As early as 1851, at the gold rush's height, John L. B. Soule wrote in the *Terre Haute Express*, "Go west, young man, go west!" a phrase quickly picked up by (and forever after attributed to) Horace Greeley.

Immediately the country's connections to the Pacific became a prime political issue. Where and by what means a railroad would be built to California occupied much congressional debate. The state was then more than 1,000 miles from the nearest fellow state, Texas. In terms of communications, it was months away from Washington, D.C. The Panama railway soon made the trip across the Isthmus a quick one and, together with regular steamer service in the Pacific, reduced travel time from months to weeks. In 1860 the storied Pony Express reduced communication time to about ten days. In 1861 a telegraph line linked the West Coast directly to the rest of the country. Finally, in 1869, the Union Pacific Railroad joined California to the Union in geographic as well as political fact.

In economic terms, as well, the California gold strike profoundly affected the country. It would be hard to overstate the centrality of gold to the world financial system in the middle of the nineteenth century. The Bank of England had gone on the gold standard in 1821, declaring itself ready to buy or sell unlimited amounts of pounds sterling for gold at the rate of one ounce of gold for £3/17/10^1/$_2$ (a ratio set more than a century earlier by Sir Isaac Newton, of all people, enjoying the perks of a largely no-show job as master of the king's mint). As the United Kingdom dominated the world's economy in the nineteenth century and the Bank of England was the world's de facto central bank, all major trading nations were soon forced to follow and peg their currencies to gold.

The good thing about a gold standard is that it makes inflation impossible, for if a country begins to create too much money, gold will begin to flow out of its treasury. But that means that under a gold standard, the money supply is limited by the amount of gold available to back the currency.

The United States was not a major gold producer in the early nineteenth century. In 1847, a typical pre-California year, the nation produced 43,000 ounces, mostly as a by-product of base-metal mining. The following year, 1848, however, it turned out 484,000 ounces, thanks to California. In 1849 the output was 1.9 million ounces. By 1853 output was no less than 3.1 million ounces, worth almost $65 million. (To put the latter figure in perspective, in that year the federal government spent a grand total of only $48 million.)

The result of this sudden influx of gold into the American economy was a period of great prosperity and economic growth. Government revenues, a rough measure of economic activity, had been only $29 million in 1844. By 1854 they were over $73 million. Railroads had only 9,021 miles of track in 1850. By 1860 there were 30,626 miles. Telegraph wires spread quickly. Shipping, iron smelting, and textile manufacture increased sharply. Other industries likewise expanded in the early 1850s.

This economic development was by no means evenly distributed, however. It was disproportionately concentrated in the northern states, where population also grew faster than in the South. As a result, when the long-dreaded Civil War began in the next decade, the relative strengths of the two sections had shifted markedly in the direction of the North.

Perhaps equally important, California gold helped to fund the titanic cost of the war, while the South, necessarily trying to finance its war effort with paper, saw its economy collapse under uncontrollable inflation. Thus, although they doubtless never knew it, those hundreds of thousands who pursued their self-interests in the early 1850s by moiling for gold in the foothills of the Sierra Nevada helped mightily to save the Union in the 1860s.

OPPORTUNITIES

IN CAPITALIST ECONOMIES, whenever a new opportunity appears, entrepreneurs quickly find means to profit from it. But because entrepreneurs are free to pursue their self-interests as they see them, they profit as well from a myriad of ancillary opportunities initially undreamed of by most.

Consider the personal computer industry, which did not even exist until Steven Jobs and Stephen Wozniak got the ball rolling in 1976 when they developed the Apple I computer. They have both profited handsomely from their seminal concept, but so have tens of thousands of others, often in ways far removed from the manufacture of computers.

Today, computer word processing is slowly squeezing the life out of the typewriter business. Desktop publishing is profoundly changing the printing and publishing industries. Companies making computer games are thriving. Other companies manufacturing modems, scanners, backup and storage devices, monitors, and other hardware have appeared in the hundreds. Software companies have proliferated. Information retrieval services, electronic bulletin boards, and databases profitably provide their subscribers with information on everything from stock prices to genealogy to astrological forecasts.

Often the greatest fortunes are created not by exploiting the basic technology itself but from these ancillary endeavors. Bill Gates never designed a personal computer; he and Paul Allen designed the basic software that allows most of them to work.

Earlier industries have had similar success stories. Television made such visionaries as David Sarnoff and William S. Paley immensely rich, but nowhere near as rich as Walter Annenberg became. Annenberg was not even in the television industry, but his idea to publish a weekly magazine that listed TV programs soon became the largest-circulation magazine in the world, *TV Guide.* Annenberg recently sold his publishing company for $3.2 billion, mostly thanks to its flagship magazine. Likewise, A. C. Nielsen gave his name to the language—and greatly affected the history of both television and advertising—by developing a way to measure just who was watching what on the tube.

A very early example of an American ancillary fortune is that made by Darius Ogden Mills in the California gold rush. Mills arrived in the first wave of forty-niners, and while very, very few of those who rushed to California to dig for gold died rich, Mills died very rich indeed. He never dug or panned a single ounce of the precious metal, however. Instead he sold shovels so that others could dig, and he opened a bank to store the treasure they found.

D. O. Mills (as he was known to family and friends) was born in 1825 in North Salem, New York, then deep in the countryside but now on the outer edge of New York City's suburbs. The Millses were a locally prominent family (his father was North Salem's town supervisor in 1835), but poor investments reduced the family circumstances considerably. When his father died in 1841, Mills had to seek employment.

He became a clerk in New York City, and five years later his older cousin E. J. Townsend, who was impressed with Mills's energy and competence, invited him to become the cashier of his Merchants' Bank of Erie County in Buffalo, giving him a one-third interest in the enterprise. The bank prospered, and Mills with it. The cousins soon enjoyed excellent credit with both the local Buffalo banks and even with the big New York City banks.

The news of gold in California first reached the East in the late summer of 1848. Almost immediately two of Mills's brothers, James and Edgar, set out for San Francisco with a cargo of merchandise, sailing the 12,000-mile route around the Horn. At first, D. O. was not interested in joining them. He was making very good money in Buffalo and saw no reason to abandon a promising and lucrative banking career in order to pursue the will-of-the-wisp of rumored gold in far-off California.

But when gold fever swept up and down the eastern seaboard, Mills changed his mind about making the trek to California. His cousin readily assented to Mills's journey. In fact he promised to look after their interests in Buffalo, cover any drafts Mills made on the bank, and take a partnership interest in any enterprises Mills might establish in California.

Having decided to go, Mills acted with all the quickness and determination that would characterize him throughout the journey and indeed his life. When the friends who were planning to accompany him were held up by business, he told them that, regardless, "I am going and I shall start in ten days."

Mills booked a passage to San Francisco via Panama on the steamer *Falcon* in the Atlantic and, for the Pacific leg of the journey, the new steamer *California*, which had been sent around the Horn. The virtue of the Panama route was speed. It was thousands of miles shorter than the one around South America. Except for the ghastly trek by dugout and mule back across the rain-soaked and fever-ridden isthmus itself, it was far more comfortable as well. Setting off from New York, Mills expected to be steaming past the Golden Gate in seventy days.

When he reached Panama City, on the Pacific Coast of the isthmus, however, he found no *California* waiting for him and, in fact, no northbound ships at all. Instead he found 3,000 Americans camped out in the muddy streets of the dismal little provincial capital, all desperate to get to San Francisco by any means available.

Mills realized that he might wait forever if he did not take action himself, so he took passage on a ship headed southward. He hoped to find in one of the ports on South America's west coast a ship that he could charter. But both Buenaventura, Colombia, and Quayaquil, Ecuador, had been swept clean of shipping. Finally, in Callao, Peru, a full 1,500 miles south of Panama, he found the bark *Massachusetts*. Her captain agreed to transport 100 people from Panama to San Francisco for $100 apiece.

Mills purchased supplies in Callao that he thought would find a market in California and then, never one to sit idle, went off to see the sights of nearby Lima while the *Massachusetts* made ready.

After fitting out, the *Massachusetts* proceeded to Panama City and picked up her passengers for the passage to San Francisco. The voyage turned out to be a nightmare. Instead of the normal two or three weeks, the trip took fully two months because of contrary or nonexistent winds. For sixteen straight days the ship was entirely becalmed, its sails flapping idly as she rolled heavily and slowly in the long Pacific swells beneath a merciless equatorial sun.

Even when the *Massachusetts* finally arrived off the coast of San Francisco, there was more delay, for the captain at first refused to enter the bay and anchor. Perhaps he was afraid that his crew would immediately desert and rush to the gold fields. Certainly the bay was choked with ships whose crews had done exactly that. Refusing to wait further while in sight of his goal, Mills had a boat lowered and, helped by a flowing tide, was rowed through the Golden Gate and landed, at last, in California on June 9, 1849. The trip that had been scheduled to take seventy days had taken nearly six months. And instead of arriving in the luxury of the spanking new steamer *California,* Mills had stepped ashore in San Francisco from a rowboat. But he was there, and, it turned out, he had beaten his brothers. When they finally arrived after a nine-months passage around the Horn, one of the first people they encountered was the brother they thought they had left behind in Buffalo.

When the *Massachusetts* finally docked a few days later, Mills had already purchased a boat to carry his goods to Stockton, at the southern end of the mining area. It turned out that the merchandise he had bought in Callao was not what the miners needed, and Mills incurred a small loss on the venture after selling the boat. But he had learned what the miners did want and where they wanted it: Sacramento.

Returning to San Francisco, Mills used his last remaining cash to purchase new goods. His new cargo nearly filled a schooner that was heading up the river for Sacramento.

The frenzied atmosphere of the gold rush had driven the price of everything to astronomical heights, including freight charges, and Mills had a $5,000 freight bill to pay for having his goods moved less than 100 miles. He had only $40 in his pocket, but, quite undaunted, Mills ordered the captain to start unloading and to prepare his bill. So great was the demand for merchandise in Sacramento that by the time Mills's cargo was completely unloaded, he had sold enough to pay his freight bill in gold dust. In the next six months the twenty-four-year-old Mills made a profit of about $40,000, a moderate fortune by the standards of the mid–nineteenth century, very roughly equivalent to $500,000 today.

Mills had fallen in love with both California and its opportunities. He closed out his interest in the Buffalo bank and used his trading profits to open the Bank of D. O. Mills in Sacramento, which became the city's leading financial institution. And he was soon instrumental in founding the Bank of California in San Francisco as well, for many years the state's largest bank.

D. O. Mills, a forty-niner to be sure, but never a miner, had seen his opportunities in the California gold rush. Because he was free to take 'em, he became one of the richest and most respected men in California long before he was thirty.

THE REVENGE OF
THE TRUST

Wherever opportunities for great wealth are concentrated, there will also be a concentration of men who make up in ambition, genius, and reckless courage what they sometimes lack in scruples. This is as true of Wall Street and Hollywood as it was of the fallen empire of the Incas and the slave coast of Africa. It was true of Butte, Montana, at the turn of the twentieth century.

Montana has never been embarrassed about the source of its greatness. Its official nickname is the Treasure State, and its motto is the briskly straightforward *Oro y Plata*—gold and silver. But it was the copper that came out of "the richest hill on earth" in Butte that really put the state on the map.

At their height, the copper mines of Butte had 600 miles of tunnels, producing 300 million pounds of copper a year, enough, it was said, to fill a freight train twenty miles long. Some of the ore pulled out of the earth at Butte was 40 percent pure metal, and with the soaring demand for electricity the demand for copper was soaring, too. It was a seller's market in the red metal in those days, and men whose names are still household words in Montana, such as William A. Clark and Marcus Daly, battled the stubborn earth and each other as they moiled for copper.

But none of these copper kings, as they are remembered, could match a boy from Brooklyn named F. Augustus Heinze. Heinze combined the rare talents of a born prospector with a gift for politics and a degree of chutzpah rare even among native Brooklynites. He used these attributes to gain—and almost immediately to lose—one of the great American fortunes.

Heinze was born in 1869. His father was a prosperous German immigrant and his mother a Connecticut Yankee with Irish blood. An able student, Heinze graduated from the Columbia School of Mines in 1889 when he was only twenty. With its copper production growing by leaps and bounds, Heinze decided to try his luck in Butte.

At nearly six feet tall, with broad shoulders and brown hair and eyes, Heinze cut a fine figure. In addition, he possessed a powerful personality, a good speaking voice, and the endearing habit of giving his complete attention to whomever was talking. "When he entered a room," his brother remembered, "you could very near feel it." In Butte he immediately got a job as an engineer with the Boston and Montana Company, one of the major mine owners. Heinze was soon intimately familiar with the Boston and Montana properties and the geology of Butte, for he talked to the old-timers and listened to their stories.

Before long he left the company and began to operate on his own. He leased the Estella Mine from James Murray, who was thought "the shrewdest operator in Butte," but he wasn't quite shrewd enough. Heinze had to pay a royalty only on ore that was above a certain grade, and he was careful to mix in enough poor-grade ore with the better to stay just below the point where royalties would be due. Murray quickly canceled the lease. Heinze "made both friends and money rapidly," one early historian of Montana reported, "and spared neither in the promotion and accomplishment of his purposes."

Heinze departed briefly for Canada, where he operated for a while in Trail, British Columbia, and obtained a land grant from the Canadian government to build a railroad from Trail to Victoria. The Canadian Pacific, thoroughly alarmed at the prospect, bought him out for a reported $1.2 million.

Back in Butte once more, with major money in his pocket, Heinze built a smelter and soon bought the Rarus mine, which proved a bonanza, and the Minnie Healy, which had been unproductive until Heinze found the richest vein of copper in Butte a month after he bought it.

By no means the least of the attractions of the Rarus and the Minnie Healy for Heinze was their proximity to the great mines owned by his former employer, Boston and Montana. Most of the stock of Boston and Montana was owned by the Amalgamated Copper Company, the so-called copper trust. The boards of these two companies were a who's who of the powerful eastern financial interests, including J. P. Morgan, the most influential banker in Wall Street, and Henry H. Rogers and William

Rockefeller of mighty Standard Oil. Not the least intimidated by the copper trust's size or connections, Heinze intended to use his great knowledge of the geology of Butte Hill, the proximity of his own mines, and a quirk in Montana's mining law to take it on.

The "apex law," one of the more misguided pieces of legislation in American history, had been passed with the best of intentions. The law said that the owner of the apex of a vein of ore, where it reached or came closest to the surface, could follow that vein downward even if it ran under someone else's property. The purpose was to stimulate prospecting; the result was to foment the "War of the Copper Kings."

"The theory seemed simple and equitable when simple conditions prevailed," wrote Helen Fitzgerald Sanders in her monumental *A History of Montana*, "but when one little hill was found to hold practically inexhaustible mineral wealth, when hostile and battling interests rubbed elbows and outcroppings could be claimed by both as apexes with equal probability of truth, and when the ownership of such apexes—or the lack of it—meant the gain or loss of inestimable millions, it may readily be seen that complications would follow." They did.

While the apex law was to be a great help to Heinze, he also needed the help of a few friendly judges to overcome the enormous economic power of the Amalgamated Copper Company. He set about electing some with the help of William A. Clark, another independent operator. Heinze bought newspapers to carry his party line. He maintained miners' wages when the Amalgamated cut them. He gave his miners an eight-hour day. He hammered endlessly about the power of the "trust," and how he was on the side of the workingman.

Heinze's tactics worked, and his political influence became very strong, especially in Silver Bow County, of which Butte was the county seat. It was said he had 75 percent of the county vote in his pocket.

His most loyal member of the local judiciary was William F. Clancy, a very large man, with a long white beard, bushy eyebrows, "a deep, crashing, bear-like voice," and slovenly habits. When a reporter noticed some debris in the judge's beard, he said, "I see, Judge, that you had scrambled eggs for breakfast this morning."

"No, you are mistaken, John," responded Clancy, unperturbed, "I had scrambled eggs for breakfast yesterday morning."

Clancy did what Heinze had had him elected to do. One Amalgamated lawyer could recall only two occasions when Clancy ruled in his company's favor. The judge regularly allowed Heinze and his employees to inspect the Amalgamated mines to see if they were encroaching on his rights, but denied the Amalgamated the same privilege in Heinze's mines.

Heinze had noted a small triangle of land on Butte Hill, only seventy-five feet long and ten feet wide at the base, which remained unclaimed, probably because of early surveying errors. Heinze bought it, using a company he impudently called the Copper Trust, and promptly claimed that it contained the apexes of the great veins of ore in the adjoining Anaconda, St. Lawrence, and Neversweat mines belonging to the Amalgamated. Judge Clancy was only too glad to agree.

Soon a blizzard of lawsuits, injunctions, appeals, and reappeals ensnared Heinze and the Amalgamated, which set up a special set of books just to keep track of it all while Heinze had thirty-seven lawyers on his staff. Intimately familiar with the maze of tunnels, Heinze could often ignore whatever injunctions were in force and reach a disputed vein by cutting in from another mine. The Amalgamated, no more scrupulous than Heinze, did the same, and underground warfare roared beneath Butte Hill. Shafts were suddenly closed by dynamite. Miners would break into a disputed tunnel only to be met with steam hoses and lime poured down the hoses that supplied the tunnels with fresh air.

When Judge Clancy ruled in Heinze's favor in one dispute, the Amalgamated, anticipating the inevitable outcome in Clancy's court, had prepared ahead of time. No sooner did the judgment come down than the Amalgamated blew the mine up. If it couldn't have the ore, at least neither could Heinze.

The battles above and below ground went on and on until the trust, at last, decided to get tough. *Very* tough. It closed down all its properties in the state of Montana, and 20,000 men, perhaps four-fifths of all the wage earners in the state, were thrown out of work.

The Amalgamated, fed up with being denied justice time and again in Judge Clancy's court, wanted a "fair trial" law, allowing a party to demand a change of venue if it suspected prejudice on the part of the judge. Heinze, in a brilliant speech from the Butte Courthouse steps, convinced an initially hostile crowd of 10,000 miners that it was all the trust's fault, not his, but the governor, faced with the very real threat of statewide starvation, called a special session and the legislature passed the law. The Amalgamated properties reopened for business.

With his loss of Judge Clancy's services and with the Amalgamated now utterly determined both to get rid of Heinze and to use, unashamedly, its immense power, Heinze could see that the party was over. The Amalgamated had dismissed Heinze's real assets as nothing more than "a number of lawsuits and some district judges," but some of those lawsuits were turning out in Heinze's favor even in courtrooms less openly partisan than Clancy's.

Finally, in 1906, Heinze and Amalgamated made a deal. The latter paid Heinze $10.5 million for his mining properties in Butte, and the former dropped fully 100 lawsuits against Amalgamated. Heinze had beaten the big boys.

Dazzled by his own success, he took his money and set off to conquer Wall Street. In Butte Heinze's talents had allowed him to battle Amalgamated and Standard Oil as an equal, but he was no match for them on Wall Street and they had neither forgotten nor forgiven.

In the rapidly darkening financial climate of 1907, Heinze speculated dangerously in the stock of his own United Copper Company, unaware that Amalgamated and Standard Oil were manipulating both it and the Wall Street rumor mills carefully. Suddenly the banks he had borrowed from called their loans, and he had to bail out of his speculations. Because United Copper had few real assets after his deal with Amalgamated, the price dropped from sixty to ten almost at once. This caused worry about the soundness of other Heinze interests, and a run on a bank he owned began, quickly spreading to other banks. Wall Street was in turmoil. Heinze's bank failed, and his brokerage firm collapsed.

One year after he had taken the most powerful financial interests in the world for $10.5 million, Amalgamated and Standard Oil had ruined him, starting the great panic of 1907 in the process.

PART IV

TRANSPORTATION

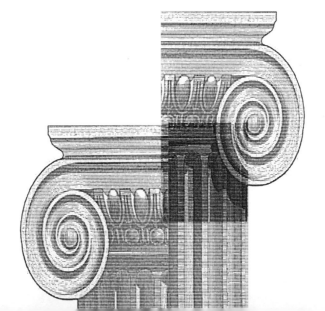

THE STEAMBOAT MONOPOLY

IN THE EARLY 1970S, when Wall Street was going through a particularly bad time, it actually cost half as much money to buy a taxi medallion—a license to operate a taxicab in New York City—as it did to purchase a seat—a license to trade directly—on the New York Stock Exchange.

The reason was simple enough. In the 1930s the city had frozen the number of taxi medallions, to keep otherwise unemployed people who happened to own a car from going into the taxi business and competing with professional cabdrivers. New York City, in other words, created a taxi cartel, and the fortunate medallion holders have been making out like bandits ever since.

There's a lesson here. While we still tend to think of monopolies and cartels as the product of top-hatted, nineteenth-century plutocrats conspiring in private against the public good, the major combinations in restraint of trade in this century have all been government sponsored and just as pernicious.

New York's taxi cartel is pretty trivial in the scale of things (unless, of course, you're in New York, in a hurry, and it's raining). But the federal cartels in the trucking and airline industries, also established in the 1930s, were a different matter altogether. When they were finally broken up in the late 1970s and early 1980s, wrenching economic adjustments were required. Many companies, such as Pan American and Eastern Airlines, failed to make them and have vanished, while unions have had no choice but to give back cushy work rules and featherbedding provisions in their contracts.

The effect for the general public, however, has been almost wholly beneficial. Average airline fares have declined 35 percent in real terms since 1977, while the industry has nearly doubled in size. Many more routes are now served by competing airlines than before deregulation, and the number of direct and nonstop connections between medium-sized cities has increased sharply.

In the trucking industry, meanwhile, the number of "ton-miles" carried has been growing twice as fast as the GNP, while the total number of rigs on the nation's highways has been declining, thanks to greatly enhanced productivity.

All this has had no small effect on the American economy as a whole. Everything we buy, after all, comes from somewhere else, and the "distribution costs" incurred have to be factored into the price. These distribution costs are huge. In 1981 they amounted to almost 15 percent of GNP, or about $650 billion (in current dollars). By 1992, however, distribution costs had fallen to only about 10 percent of the GNP, or about $570 billion. They have continued to fall since.

In other words, the American economy is much larger now than it was twelve years ago, but total distribution costs are much smaller. Even Milton Friedman, the Nobel laureate economist who coined the phrase "There is no such thing as a free lunch," admits that this amounts to, very nearly, a free lunch.

But the cartels established in the 1930s were hardly the first government intrusions into the transportation market in this country. At the very dawn of the industrial age, government-granted monopolies threatened to stifle the new technology of steamboats. Had they succeeded, the history of this country would have been very different indeed.

It is hard to imagine today the difficulties of overland transportation in the eighteenth century. Even in well-developed European countries, roads were often little more than rutted paths, choked with dust in summer and morasses of mud all winter. The Great North Road in England, the main overland route to Scotland, had potholes so large that people and even horses are known to have drowned in them.

As a result, freight moved by water, or it did not move at all. In the young United States, with even fewer and poorer roads than Europe, the broad rivers and estuaries of the East Coast were vital arteries of commerce. As long as most of the population lived within a few miles of tidewater, oceangoing sailing ships served the needs of this commerce adequately.

But as the population began to move across the Appalachian Mountains in large numbers and spread out into the Mississippi River Valley, the problem of moving freight and passengers became critical if this vast, and vastly rich, region was to be developed.

There were, to be sure, plenty of water routes available. The Mississippi and its tributaries total no less than 16,000 miles of navigable water. But there was one big problem: The rivers were, in effect, all one-way roads, with all of them headed toward New Orleans.

As long as freight was headed downriver, flatboats—hardly more than very large rafts, knocked together for perhaps fifty dollars—were able to carry thirty or forty tons of cargo at a clip, swept along by the current. (It was on just such flatboats that the young Abe Lincoln twice traveled to New Orleans.) Once in New Orleans, the cargo would be sold and the flatboat broken up for lumber.

The only way to send freight upriver, however, was by keelboats. These were long, narrow vessels that hugged the shoreline to avoid the current as much as possible and had to be poled upstream solely by human effort, a backbreaking, not to mention extremely expensive, way to transport freight. A trip from the Ohio Valley to New Orleans on a flatboat could be accomplished in as little as a month. The trip back by keelboat was likely to take three.

It is not surprising, therefore, that the technology of the steamboat was immediately hailed as the answer to the problem of inland transportation in the United States. But the developers of the first steamboats, naturally, wanted to be sure that their ventures would be financially successful. Therefore, many early designers applied to the various states for monopolies of steam navigation. There was nothing unusual about this at the time. Governments had been routinely awarding monopolies to the favored for centuries.

John Fitch received such rights in five states, James Rumsey in three. When Fitch was unable to meet the terms imposed by New York State, the grant was revoked and given to Robert R. Livingston, a member of New York's most politically powerful family.

In 1803 the grant was renewed, provided Livingston produced a boat capable of traveling four knots against the current of the Hudson. This requirement was considered impossible, and the measure was passed amid gales of laughter in the legislature. But Livingston was then ambassador to France, where he was negotiating the Louisiana Purchase, and funding the experiments of another American, Robert Fulton, who had a steamboat operating in the Seine that same year. In 1807 the two built the *Clermont* in the Hudson River and made it to Albany from New York City in thirty-two hours, averaging about four and a half knots. The monopoly in New York waters was theirs.

Livingston knew, perhaps better than any other easterner, the potential for steamboats in the Mississippi River Valley, which he had helped so mightily to bring under the American flag. He and Fulton moved to obtain a monopoly there, as well as in New York, writing the various states and territories and asking for exclusive rights.

But although the Livingston name was potent in New York, it was, if anything, a liability in the far more egalitarian West, already resentful of eastern money and commercial power. So the pair got nowhere, except in the territory of Orleans. Livingston's brother Edward had moved to Orleans after being mayor of New York and was soon a political power there. When the territory became a state, in 1812, Fulton and Livingston got their monopoly. Since New Orleans was the break point between ocean- and rivergoing vessels, a monopoly in Louisiana waters was nearly as good as one over the whole Mississippi river system.

In both New York and the West, the Fulton-Livingston monopolies were bitterly resented, both by the public and by other would-be entrepreneurs. "Our road to market must and *will* be free," thundered the *Cincinnati Western Spy;* "this monopolizing disposition of individuals will only arouse the citizens of the West to insist on . . . the privilege of passing and repassing, unmolested, on the *common highway* of the West."

Many defied the monopolies. Henry Shreve, for whom Shreveport is named, ran his steamboat *Enterprise* into New Orleans and often evaded those trying to enforce the monopoly. When finally caught, he won the case, for the court ruled that the territory had no authority to grant a monopoly. By this time Fulton and Livingston were both dead, and their heirs did not pursue the case in a higher court. The Mississippi was free.

The number of steamboats exploded, and their naval architecture quickly evolved into a form more suited to the often shallow and snag-ridden western rivers, the classic steamboats of Currier and Ives lithographs. Freight out of New Orleans increased from 65,000 tons in 1810 to 4.7 million in 1860. As early as 1841, a westerner could write: "Steam navigation colonized the West! . . . Steam is crowding our eastern cities with western flour and western merchants, and lading the western steamboats with eastern emigrants and eastern merchandise. It has advanced the career of national colonization and national production at least a century!" The monopoly still held in New York waters, however. New York courts, under the thumb of the Livingstons and their allies, upheld the grant. Finally, the case made its way to the U.S. Supreme Court in 1824. Senator Daniel Webster and Attorney General William Wirt, acting as private lawyers, argued the case for the plaintiff. Webster's presentation took two and half hours to deliver, and it has been regarded ever since as a masterpiece of both legal histrionics and legal reasoning. No one present—the courtroom was packed—ever forgot it.

Webster argued that the federal government's right to regulate interstate commerce was total and exclusive and that therefore the monopoly was null and void, as were all other such laws. Chief Justice John Marshall and the rest of the court bought Webster's argument whole. Indeed, as Webster described it, with typical lack of reticence, "The opinion of the court . . . was little else than a recital of my argument."

Regardless, the decision in the case of *Gibbons v. Ogden* is considered one of the great chief justice's two or three most important. Its immediate practical effect was considerable. A year after the decision, the number of steamboats operating in New York waters had increased from six to forty-three.

Its philosophical effect, perhaps, was even more so. For 100 years the idea of government monopolies in this country was unthinkable.

TO THE SWIFTEST

IF THE MODERN OLYMPIC Games demonstrate anything, it is that the urge to be the fastest lies deep in the human soul. And from the earliest days of humankind, this urge has had its practical rewards beyond mere glory. The fastest caveman, after all, not only caught the most gazelles but was more likely to be regarded with favor by potential mates.

Today, the need to be the fastest lives on, not just in individuals but in our business enterprises as well. All major automobile companies have invested heavily in racing at one time or another because racing both rigorously tests cars and helps mightily to sell them too. This corporate competition to win business by being the swiftest is not merely an artifact of the automobile age, however. Indeed it goes back to the earliest days of the industrial revolution in this country, when steamboats first appeared on American rivers and waterways.

Beginning in 1807 with the *Clermont*, the first practical—which is to say, moneymaking—steamboat, the forces of technology and economics soon combined to produce an extraordinary craft of extraordinary beauty. By the 1840s the brief glory days of the river steamboats in the United States had arrived, before the railroads could compete with them in either speed or luxury.

Steamboating was always an intensely competitive business, and steamboat owners soon began trying to limit the competition in pricing by forming cartels and carving up markets. These cartels worked splendidly, at least from the owners' point of view; one year the Hudson River Association was able to declare a dividend amounting to fully 70 percent of the owners' invested capital.

The greatest of all the steamboat owners, however, Commodore Cornelius Vanderbilt, had no objection to competing by means of price. Far from it. "Wherever his keen eyes detected a monopoly," the *New York Times* would write at his death in 1877, "he pounced down upon the offenders and literally drove them from the rivers. Nor did he, when he had vanquished them, establish a monopoly of his own. His principle of low rates, founded upon acute reasoning, was never violated, so that in every way the public were the gainers." Of course the commodore was always willing to withdraw from a particular run if he was paid enough by the opposition to do so. Usually, the opposition was only too happy to oblige.

With the cartels often regulating the price of steamboat travel, competition among the owners was carried on by providing the greatest luxury and the fastest speed. This lust for speed manifested itself most often in impromptu races between rival captains, during which the passengers were hostages to the urge to sport, and constant attempts to better the fastest time were undertaken. This often led to such obviously dangerous practices as unloading passengers at intermediate stops onto smaller boats while still under way and even tying down the safety valves in order to extract the greatest possible speed from the boilers.

All too frequently the boilers exploded, often with great loss of innocent life. The *Lexington* caught fire in the middle of Long Island Sound in January 1840, and 123 people died as a result. So frequent did these disasters become that many boats took to towing behind them an auxiliary vessel in which passengers, for twice the usual price, could enjoy all the speed and luxury of steamboat travel without the danger of being blown to kingdom come.

Newspapers routinely reported new steamboat records and often egged on the competition, for the results made good copy no matter what happened. On May 26, 1847, the *New York Herald* ran the following brief article, titled "Splendid Affair": "We learn that George Law, esq., the owner of the famous steamer *Oregon* has challenged the proprietors of the new steamers *Bay State* and *Cornelius Vanderbilt* [the Commodore had named his latest boat after himself, although it was properly called the *C. Vanderbilt*] . . . to make a trial of speed of their splendid steamers; . . . the purse to be $500, $1,000, or $10,000, or nothing; no passengers to be taken. This will be a splendid affair, and no risk run by uninterested individuals; and it will settle the question between these boats as to which moves fastest over the water. This is what the public want; it will prevent racing . . . in the future." (Needless to say, it did no such thing.)

The *Herald* surely knew that Vanderbilt could not resist such a challenge, for if the commodore liked to compete by means of pricing, he liked to compete by means of speed equally well. In truth Vanderbilt just liked to compete whatever the contest, and he was always fiercely, passionately determined to win.

George Law was an opponent entirely worthy of the commodore's attention. Born in upstate New York, he had become a contractor and had built parts of the Croton Aqueduct and its famous High Bridge over the Harlem River. He then moved into shipping, a field in which he was so successful that he, too, enjoyed the honorific "commodore" along with Vanderbilt. Later he would be president of the Dry Dock Savings Bank and builder of the Eighth and Ninth Avenue streetcar lines in New York City.

Vanderbilt rose to the bait planted in the *Herald* like a trout to a fly, and the next day the newspaper printed a letter that Vanderbilt—a master of gamesmanship a century before Stephen Potter invented the word— had sent over by messenger.

"I observed," wrote the commodore in mock wonderment, "in your paper of this day, a paragraph stating that Mr. Geo. Law had challenged the *Bay State* and *C. Vanderbilt* for a race. This is the first I have heard of the challenge, nor do I believe Mr. Law authorized its publication. . . .

"Now, I say I will run the steamer *C. Vanderbilt,* untried as she is, against any boat afloat to any place they name where there is sufficient water to float her, for any sum from $1,000 to $100,000. This challenge is open until Saturday next, when I propose trying my boat."

It was soon agreed that the *Oregon* and the *C. Vanderbilt* would race to Sing Sing (modern Ossining and even then the site of the prison) and back for $1,000.

The weather was not perfect on June 1, the day of the race, being overcast and somewhat hazy as New York often is at that time of year. But this did not stop New Yorkers from turning out in droves for the big race. The *Sun* recommended that viewers use the balconies of Castle Garden, the old fort which was then still offshore from Battery Park and reached by a short causeway, while the *Tribune* reported that "the wharves of the city were a mass of spectators." The *Tribune* also noted, with a characteristic air of disapproval, that the side bets amounted to $100,000, though one can only wonder how the figure was arrived at if it wasn't simply plucked from thin air.

"A few minutes before eleven o'clock," reported the *Herald,* which having started the whole thing was now making the most of it, "the *Vanderbilt* appeared off the Battery, when the *Oregon* left her berth, passed around her larboard side, and at four minutes before eleven o'clock, every thing being ready, the signal was given for the start, and both boats appeared to spring from their positions. The race was contested with so much spirit on both sides, that the boats kept side by side for thirty-three miles, neither one gaining a foot on the other."

At the speed the boats were traveling—about twenty-five miles per hour, a breathtaking pace then—only the spectators who had bought passage on other steamers that accompanied the contestants had much view of the race, but there was plenty of other activity in New York harbor that day to keep the crowd diverted. The Upper Bay at that time was far busier with shipping and small boats than it is today when local traffic has been shifted to bridges and tunnels. "The bay and harbor," reported the *Sun,* with less than perfect rhetoric, "were literally alive with steamboats, yachts, and small craft, some moving rapidly between the city and adjacent shores, others sailing down majestically to the Narrows, while small boats darted across the surface in every direction."

The *Oregon* and the *C. Vanderbilt* were as well matched as their owners, the *Oregon* having slightly finer lines while its rival had a slightly more powerful engine. Having been neck and neck nearly all the way to Sing Sing, Vanderbilt at last began to edge ahead. Law in response poured on the power, increasing the revolutions of his paddlewheels from nineteen and a half to twenty-two per minute. By the turning point he had pulled half a boat length ahead.

The turn was the critical point of any race that involved a round-trip, for Hudson River steamboats, swift and gracile creatures of the water though they were—their length sometimes ten times their beam—were not adept at turning. This was not only because of the extreme ratio but also because their twin paddlewheels could not turn at different speeds and the paddlewheels themselves were quite fragile.

There were two schools of thought on how best to manage the turn. One was to make a wide turn at full power, taking a mile or more to turn the full half-circle. The other was to reduce power and make a much tighter turn, hoping to make up in the shorter distance traveled what was lost in momentum.

The *Oregon* was inshore of the *C. Vanderbilt,* and Law opted for the wide turn. He apparently thought himself far enough ahead to clear Vanderbilt, but the commodore fouled him and caused minor damage to the *Oregon's* wheelhouse. In the confusion that followed, either the engineer below who was answering the signals from the bridge made a mistake, or possibly Vanderbilt himself in his excitement sent contradictory instructions, for the *C. Vanderbilt's* engine stopped, instead of merely slowing for the turn. By the time both boats were settled on the homeward course, the *Oregon* was two full boat lengths ahead, and Vanderbilt could only have been wild with fury—either at himself or at the luckless engineer—and the air thick with his profanity.

Down the magnificent Hudson the two steamboats pounded, their huge paddlewheels churning at twenty-two revolutions per minute, while the sun broke through the clouds and cheers drifted out over the water to the boats from spectators along the shore.

Try as he might, Vanderbilt could not make up the lost time. But Law, in his turn, had also made a serious mistake in calculating how much fuel would be needed. He didn't want to carry any more than was necessary, of course, and off Harlem, then still miles north of the city, his bunkers were empty. The steam pressure began to drop, and Vanderbilt began to gain.

Law had spent $30,000 on the furnishings of the *Oregon*—a moderate fortune in the mid–nineteenth century—and they were the last word in luxury, but he didn't hesitate to consign them to the furnaces. "Berths, settees, chairs, doors, and everything else of a combustible nature they could get their hands on" were thrown into the flames in order to keep up steam. Vanderbilt's last chance went up in smoke.

Half of New York City, it seemed, had turned out to watch the finish of the race. "About two o'clock," the *Sun* reported, "the *Oregon* and *Vanderbilt* hove in sight. Quick as thought or an electric flash, the spectators at the foot of Hammond Street"—now West Eleventh Street—"rent the air with a spontaneous shout, which was caught up by those further off and reverberated along the piers for the distance of six miles, extending round to Whitehall."

The *Oregon*, consuming herself as she came, crossed the finish line a quarter mile ahead of the outraged, sputtering commodore.

Vanderbilt, an honorable man if not a particularly gracious loser, presumably paid off the bet promptly and would encounter Law again and again both in business and in sport. In the 1850s they competed with oceangoing ships on the Panama run until Law and his allies paid the commodore $56,000 a month to take his boats elsewhere. Vanderbilt began operating on the Atlantic run and soon snatched the Blue Riband (i.e., the speed record) for the crossing.

No longer personally commanding their ships, the two old commodores continued to assuage their individual need to cross the finish line first by taking part in the informal trotting races held most afternoons on upper Manhattan roads. To Vanderbilt's irritation, Law was one of the few who could beat him regularly.

By the 1860s railroads—a form of transportation that did not lend itself easily to racing—had become the cutting edge of transportation technology (not to mention potential profits), and both men moved into that business, leaving steamboating behind. It would be the twentieth century before racing as a form of regular commercial competition would appear again with automobiles and airplanes.

THE ATLANTIC STAKES

When I was a child in the 1950s, the most magical day of the year for me was the day—usually a week or two after New Year's—when my grandparents would leave on their annual trip to someplace warm. My brother and I would get a day off from school, and a hired car would take everyone to the piers that then lined the West Side of Manhattan for several miles. There, we would board a passenger ship bound for the Mediterranean, South Africa, Hong Kong, or some other place as distant from New York as it was exotic to my young mind.

Once we were all on board, there would be a small party in their cabin, my grandfather would take us around to inspect the ship, and I would wave to the people on the pier far below, pretending that I was going too. Then, inevitably, the loudspeakers would begin announcing departure, and visitors would be asked to disembark. I would obediently go along and stand on the pier, fascinated as I watched tugs push the great ship out of her dock and she set off down the Hudson River, bound for the ends of the earth.

Sadly, I would never get to sail on a transatlantic passenger ship out of New York harbor. By the time I was grown up, they were all gone (except for a few fair-weather cruise ships), unable to compete with the Boeing 707 that began flying in 1958. One of the most storied and romantic businesses in history simply vanished in less than a decade.

Curiously, the passenger ship business had a precise beginning. Until 1818, passenger carrying had been nothing more than a supplement to cargo hauling, and ships left when they had a full hold. But that year a New York merchant named Isaac Wright and several partners decided to change things. Engaged in transatlantic trade that required frequent crossings, Isaac Wright hated having to wait, so he put up $25,000—as did each of his four partners—to found the Black Ball Line. According to an early advertisement, it would operate a line of vessels "between New York and Liverpool, to sail from each place on a certain day in every month throughout the year." The first, the *James Monroe*, left New York on January 5, 1818, right on schedule.

Equally curious—although the United States was present at both the creation and, as we shall see, demise of the passenger ship business—it was perhaps the only major business of the industrial era that the United States not only did not dominate but, for most of the era, had no role in at all. There was a brief exception to this, in the 1850s, and it involved a now nearly forgotten man, Edward Knight Collins. He would fail utterly in the business and pay a staggering personal price as well, but he would also profoundly affect it.

While the first regularly scheduled passenger service was in sailing ships, steam quickly replaced sail. But, under steam, the passenger ship business was seldom, if ever, really profitable. For most of its existence it depended on the kindness of governments to stay viable. The names of British passenger liners, for instance, were usually preceded by the letters RMS, standing for Royal Mail Ship (translation: big government subsidies hidden in mail contracts).

In 1840 Samuel Cunard, a Canadian, convinced the British government of the need for regular steam passenger service across the North Atlantic, and Parliament agreed to pay him £60,000 a year—no small sum in the 1840s—to do exactly that, provided the ships be available for troop carrying when necessary. Cunard soon dominated the North Atlantic passenger business, but he conceived it to be one of delivering passengers to the other side of the ocean safely and reliably, not comfortably and quickly.

One of his earliest and, by far, most prominent passengers was not amused. When Charles Dickens first visited the United States in 1842, he traveled here on the Cunarder *Britannia.* But he called his stateroom an "utterly impracticable, thoroughly hopeless, and profoundly preposterous box." As for his bunk, Dickens thought that "nothing smaller for sleeping in was ever made, except coffins."

It was in Cunard's spartan accommodations and pedestrian food that Collins thought he saw opportunity. He had been born of seafaring stock (both his father and uncle were ship's captains) in Truro, Massachusetts, on Cape Cod in 1802. When still a very young man he came to New York, then just beginning its extraordinary expansion that would see it become one of the world's largest and busiest ports. He took a job in a commission house on South Street, then the heart of the city's port area, and soon learned the shipping business thoroughly.

When his father retired as a ship captain, he and his son began operating regular service between New York, New Orleans, and Vera Cruz. After his father died, Collins began operating sailing ships on the North Atlantic run.

When members of Congress began calling for American ships to haul American mail to Europe, and the navy wanted ships that could be converted to troop transports when needed, Collins struck a deal with the federal government. He would build five steamships and run them twenty times a year between New York and Liverpool in exchange for an annual subsidy of $385,000.

The first Collins steamship to be ready, the *Atlantic*, was not a beautiful vessel—the early steamships seldom were—but she had features no Cunarder could match. Her cabins were steam heated. She carried forty tons of ice in an ice room, had real bathrooms and even a barbershop. Her saloon and dining rooms were richly decorated in the high, overstuffed Victorian style then at the height of its vogue. Equally important, her engines were far more powerful than anything in a Cunard steamer, and she crossed the Atlantic on the return from her maiden voyage in the record time of ten days and sixteen hours.

The battle was quickly joined between Cunard and Collins, and it appeared at first that Collins might be ahead. The public (egged on by the newspapers) loved the idea of a contest for speed between the two countries, and Collins, flamboyant by nature, accommodated them. Although his ships had a designed speed of 11.75 knots, in 1852 the *Arctic* crossed from New York to Liverpool in only nine days, seventeen hours, and twelve minutes, an average speed of 13.25 knots. Cunard not only couldn't match that speed but wouldn't try, as he was concerned with safety.

The British public was outraged, and *Punch* wrote, to the tune of "Yankee Doodle":

A steamer of the Collins line
A Yankee doodle notion
Has also quickest cut the brine

Across the Atlantic Ocean.
And British agents no way slow
Her merits to discover
Have been and bought her—just to tow
The Cunard Packets over.

In the first eleven months of 1852, according to the *New York Herald*, Collins's ships carried 4,306 passengers across the Atlantic and Cunard's only 2,916. There was just one big problem: Collins was losing money on every voyage. The still-primitive engines, when pushed to their limits, broke down frequently and were expensive to repair. All the amenities took up valuable cargo and passenger space. In 1851 he lost an average of $16,928 per voyage, even allowing for the government's subsidy.

Collins went back to Congress and obtained an increase in his subsidy of $10,984 per voyage. Collins then had a great stroke of luck in 1854 when the British government, having declared war on Russia, exercised its rights and commandeered Cunard's ships to carry troops to the Crimea. Collins had the North Atlantic to himself.

But tragedy soon struck. On September 27, 1854, the *Arctic*, running at high speed through dense fog (the idea, believe it or not, was that the higher the speed, the sooner the ship would be clear of the fog), collided with a small French vessel, the *Vesta.* The *Vesta* was iron-hulled and limped off to safety at St. John's, Newfoundland. The *Arctic*, made of wood, foundered while still twenty miles from land. Only 45 of the 391 passengers and crew on board were rescued. Among the lost were Edward Collins's wife and his two children.

The public, once obsessed with speed and comfort, now saw the virtues of safety, and Cunard noted that between 1840 and 1854 his ships had carried 100,000 passengers on 7,000 voyages across the Atlantic, during which "not a single passenger had been lost nor a pound of baggage damaged."

Less than two years after the *Arctic* disaster, another Collins liner, the *Pacific*, simply vanished in mid-Atlantic and was never heard from again. By this time Cunard was back in business, and Collins began to lose passengers in droves. He built a new ship, the *Adriatic*, larger, more luxurious, and faster than ever. But she was very expensive to operate, and when politics turned against Collins and his subsidy was cut by more than half, it was all over. He suspended operations in February 1858, and his three surviving ships, including the newly built *Adriatic*, were sold at public auction for only $50,000.

Both Collins and the United States turned their backs on the North Atlantic, which would be largely a British pond for the next few decades, and Collins died in 1878 in relative poverty. But his idea that passenger ships should be swift, luxurious, and innovative survived. Cunard's first new ship after the Crimean War was the *Persia*. She was the largest and most powerful ship yet built, designed expressly to recapture the speed record for Britain, which she did.

And every few years thereafter the Blue Riband, as the speed record was called, would change hands as some new steamer would pound her way across the Atlantic in a few hours less time. But no American vessel won the Blue Riband after Collins's *Arctic* took it in 1852 until, precisely 100 years later, the SS *United States* took it from Cunard's *Queen Mary* in 1952.

The *United States* still held it when, on November 15, 1969, it was announced that she would be suspended from service in the face of ever-mounting losses, and regular passenger ship service across the North Atlantic ended. I hope it is some comfort to the shade of Edward Knight Collins to know that, at least, an American vessel will now hold the Blue Riband forever.

THE TOWERING
BOONDOGGLE

BUSINESSPEOPLE, even very savvy ones, make economic mistakes. In 1898, Asa Candler, the founder of Coca-Cola, thought the soft drink's future lay with the soda fountain and sold the bottling rights for one dollar. In the American folk memory, the Ford Motor Company's Edsel has become for corporate disasters what the *Titanic* is for shipwrecks. The reason for these lapses is simple enough. Humans are quirky, and predicting their future behavior, in the marketplace or anywhere else, is hard to do.

But capitalism forces businesspeople to try. And because their own future well-being depends on it, they try very hard. Politicians, however, don't have to worry about market share or profits. They have to worry about getting reelected. That is why politicians have a far worse record in economic decision making than businesspeople. Again the reason is simple: Politicians don't really make economic decisions; they make political ones.

As a consequence, when politicians *do* make the sort of decisions that capitalists should make instead, the results so often make the Edsel seem like a good idea in comparison. Consider New York's World Trade Center. In 2000 the Port Authority of New York and New Jersey—a joint venture of the two state governments that owns the WTC—was paralyzed, unable to make major decisions, economic or otherwise. The governors of the two states were locked in a dispute over how much of the Port Authority's large pool of development money should be spent in each state. One of the decisions hanging fire was whether or not to sell the World Trade Center. In truth, of course, it should never have been built at all.

The Port Authority was established in 1921 so that New York and New Jersey, which share New York Bay, could develop its potential to the fullest. Over the years it built bridges, tunnels, airports, and communication and harbor facilities. But it suddenly found itself in the Manhattan real estate business in the late 1950s because the chairman of the Chase Manhattan Bank wanted to protect the bank's investment in its new downtown headquarters, completed in 1960. The chairman of Chase Manhattan at that time was David Rockefeller, and he wanted to see downtown New York remade. Fortunately for him, his brother Nelson happened to be governor of New York, and Nelson Rockefeller never saw a megadevelopment project he didn't want to build.

After a great deal of political horse-trading between the two states, the Port Authority was authorized to build, in New York, not one but two skyscrapers, each taller and far more spacious than the Empire State Building, on a sixteen-acre site. In exchange, New Jersey's chronically money-losing Hudson tubes, a subway system connecting New Jersey with Manhattan, would be taken over by the Port Authority. In theory, the profits from the World Trade Center were supposed to cover the losses of the Hudson tubes.

The result was, from an engineering standpoint, a marvel. From an aesthetic one, however, it was at best a dubious achievement. The view of Manhattan from the harbor had for decades been one of the world's great vistas. But the huge bulk of the World Trade Center on the western edge made it look as if the entire island were about to capsize into the Hudson.

And from an economic standpoint the World Trade Center has been an utter disaster. The complex was completed just as the deep recession of the mid-1970s hit New York with a vengeance, forcing the city itself to the edge of bankruptcy. The vast new supply of office space in the World Trade Center overwhelmed demand in the downtown area. Had the state of New York not been able to force many of its innumerable agencies to take space there, the twin towers would have been largely empty. It would not be until 1993—ironically the year it was bombed—that the World Trade Center began to show a profit.

The World Trade Center, of course, is hardly New York State's only big business mistake. The state has a rich tradition in this regard. The Erie Railway was New York's World Trade Center of the 1830s. Curiously, it was the result of one of the best economic decisions ever made by the state of New York, the decision to build the Erie Canal. In order to secure the support of legislators from the "Southern Tier," as the counties in

New York bordering on Pennsylvania are called, Governor De Witt Clinton promised them an "avenue" of their own, once the canal was finished, built by or with the substantial aid of New York State.

A canal was impossible across the rugged Catskill and Allegheny Mountains, so at first a toll road was envisioned. With the success of the Liverpool and Manchester Railroad in England in 1828, however, the railroad craze was on, and the Southern Tier made it clear that a railroad was the sort of "avenue" they wanted. But the success of the canal had changed the politics of New York State. The so-called canal ring, the legislators who came from the areas directly served by the canal, now controlled Albany, and they wanted no competition for the canal that was making their constituents so very prosperous.

As a result, the charter, when it finally made its way out of the legislature, on April 24, 1832, virtually guaranteed an economic basket case. The charter established an independent corporation to build a railroad running through the Southern Tier, but specified that the line must lie wholly in New York State. Because New Jersey occupies the western shore of New York harbor, that meant that the eastern terminus of the road would have to be about twenty miles north, at the village of Piermont, New York. And because the canal ring wanted no interference with the canal, the western terminus was set not at burgeoning Buffalo but at the small Lake Erie town of Dunkirk, thirty miles to the south. Only politicians could have designed what would be, upon completion, the longest railroad in the world, running, almost literally, between nowhere and nowhere.

Further, the legislature required that the Erie have a gauge of six feet and that it not connect with any out-of-state railroad without the specific permission of the legislature. In the earliest days of railroading, the tracks were built to whatever gauge suited the engineer in charge. But before long, a gauge of four feet, eight and a half inches became the standard. (The exact origin of that curious width is a mystery.) Other railroads quickly fell in line in order to be able to use off-the-shelf rolling stock, cross ties, and such. But the Erie, long forbidden by its charter to adopt the standard gauge, did not do so until the 1880s, at huge cost.

As for connecting with other railroads, it seems the legislature feared that they might siphon off traffic. That they might equally bring traffic to the Erie was, apparently, beyond the imagination of the Solons at Albany. By 1850 they had, at least, learned that and passed a law requiring all New

York State railroads, including the Erie, to connect with all possible out-of-state lines. As it turned out, geography compelled New York State to allow the Erie to make two small incursions into the state of Pennsylvania. (The state of Pennsylvania, proving that governments are not completely blind to economic possibilities, charged handsomely for the privilege.)

As for the cost of the Erie, with very little experience to fall back on, neither the surveyor of the proposed route, nor the original management of the Erie, nor the politicians who so reluctantly authorized its construction had the faintest idea. This did not stop them from issuing estimates, of course. The surveyor thought that it would cost $4,726,260. The management, in its first annual report, thought that "a sum not exceeding, and probably falling considerably short of $6,000,000," would do the trick (and thought the project would require five years to complete). The Committee on Railroads of the state assembly, haughtily announcing that it was "discarding estimates founded entirely upon conjecture," came up with a figure, based inevitably on conjecture, of $16,435,875, a figure that included double-tracking the entire line.

The committee's estimate proved to be as erroneous as it was precise. In the end, the Erie Railway, with only 60 of its 450 miles double-tracked, cost $23.5 million and took seventeen years to construct. In the context of the time, that was a staggering sum. It was about what the federal government was spending annually in the 1840s and amounted to more than three times what the Erie Canal had cost. To raise it, the Erie Railway had to issue just about every form of security—from stock to preferred stock to debentures to convertible bonds—that existed. And three times it had to be bailed out by the state, lest the entire enterprise collapse into politically conspicuous failure.

As a result, the Erie from its inception was burdened with a capital structure that made it easy to manipulate on Wall Street, where plenty of people were more than willing to do so. It soon became known, in the memorable phrase of Charles Francis Adams, as the Scarlet Woman of Wall Street for the many investors' hearts the railroad broke. Profitable only in the best of times, the Erie passed through bankruptcy and was reorganized no fewer than six times before losing its corporate identity altogether in the early 1970s.

The Erie, at least, became a model of how not to build a trunk-line railroad, just as the World Trade Center, 120 years later, became a model of how not to carry out a major urban development project. But the WTC disaster, at least, had one wonderful consequence. The dirt from the enormous hole dug for the foundations of the World Trade Center had to go somewhere. The answer was the Hudson River, between the rotting piers that were no longer utilized by shipping. For twenty years, this expanse of landfill remained empty. (One year a conceptual artist planted two acres of wheat on it, the first agricultural crop to be harvested in Manhattan in many a year.) But finally, when the real estate market was right, Battery Park City began to rise on this land. A mix of residential, commercial, and public areas designed by many different architects and built by many different real estate concerns under an overall design, it became a masterpiece of urban development.

Further, because it lies to the west of the World Trade Center, those colossal structures no longer stand at the water's edge and the vista of Manhattan from the harbor is once again as aesthetically satisfying as it is awesome.

"THE PUBLIC BE DAMNED"

William Henry Vanderbilt, president of the New York Central and numerous other railroads, was a quiet, honest, modest, and, above all else, moderate man. Although the most important railroader of his time, he would be almost wholly forgotten today were it not for four simple words he so uncharacteristically and incautiously uttered on October 8, 1882: "The public be damned."

Within twenty-four hours of its escaping his lips, the phrase had become one of the great public relations disasters in American business history and appeared on the front page of hundreds of newspapers. It provoked editorials, sermons, cartoons, and political speeches by the thousands. Within two days the *New York Herald* was able confidently to predict that "after he dies posterity will regard it as his epitaph, regardless of what may be carved on his tombstone." The *Herald* was right. William Henry Vanderbilt, who had not the slightest ambition to literary fame, is listed in *Bartlett's Quotations*.

The reason his words resounded around the country like a cannon shot is simple. Vanderbilt, by his own admission, was the richest man in the world. "I am worth $194,000,000," he told a friend not long before his death, and said he would not cross the street to make another million. *Harper's Weekly* noted that Vanderbilt's fortune exceeded the total value of all assessed property in Nebraska, Colorado, Nevada, and Oregon combined. Vanderbilt admitted that England's Duke of Westminster was worth $200 million but pointed out that most of that was tied up in land and didn't pay 2 percent. Vanderbilt's wealth was in government bonds and railroad securities and paid about 6 percent, giving him a take-home income of nearly $1 million a month at a time when $1,000 a year was a decent wage.

It is a measure of how large Vanderbilt loomed on the American landscape in the 1880s that when he suddenly died in December 1885, the *New York Times* carried no other news whatever on its front page the following day, and the story was the lead for several days thereafter.

Although Vanderbilt immediately denied that he had said such a thing at all, there is little doubt that he did. What varies among accounts is the context in which he said it.

Vanderbilt was on his way to a tour of the West and was traveling in his private railroad car from Michigan City, Indiana, to Chicago. Clarence P. Dresser, a young freelance reporter with a reputation as a journalistic agent provocateur, sought an interview. Dresser, according to Melville E. Stone, for many years head of the Associated Press, "was one of the offensively aggressive type—one of those wrens who make prey where eagles dare not tread. Always importunate and usually impudent." In his autobiography Stone wrote that Dresser had barged into Vanderbilt's car and demanded his immediate attention. Vanderbilt said that he was in the middle of eating but if Dresser would wait until he had finished, he would give him a minute.

"But it is late," Dresser said, "and I will not reach the office in time. The public—"

"The public be damned," Vanderbilt burst out; "you get out of here!"

According to Stone, that was all there was to it. Dresser tried to sell the story to the *Chicago Daily News*, where Stone was then working, but the *News* was not interested in the words provoked from a man whose patience and privacy had been assaulted.

Dresser, still according to Stone, then made his way to the *Tribune* and turned in a different story. The crucial part of the interview printed in the *Tribune* and reprinted everywhere went like this:

"Does your limited express [between New York and Chicago] pay?" Dresser asked.

"No, not a bit of it. We only run it because we are forced to do so by the action of the Pennsylvania Road. It doesn't pay expenses. We would abandon it if it was not for our competition keeping its train on."

"But don't you run it for the public benefit?"

"The public be damned. What does the public care for the railroad except to get as much out of them for as small a consideration as possible? I don't take any stock in this silly nonsense about working for anybody's good but our own because we are not. When we make a move we do it because it is our interest to do so, not because we expect to do somebody else good. Of course we like to do everything possible for the benefit of humanity in general but when we do we first see that we are benefiting ourselves. Railroads are not run on sentiment but on business principles and to pay, and I don't mean to be egotistic when I say that the roads which I have had anything to do with have generally paid pretty well."

Still a third version comes from Vanderbilt's favorite nephew, Samuel Barton, who was traveling with his uncle that day. He reported quite a different context a few years later to William A. Croffut, who wrote a biography of Vanderbilt in 1886.

"Why are you going to stop this fast mail-train?" Dresser asked in this version.

"Because it doesn't pay. I can't run a train as far as this permanently at a loss."

"But the public find it very convenient and useful. You ought to accommodate them."

"The public? How do you know they find it useful? How do you know, or how can I know, that they want it? If they want it, why don't they patronize it and make it pay? That's the only test I have of whether a thing is wanted—does it pay? If it doesn't pay I suppose it isn't wanted."

"Mr. Vanderbilt, are you working for the public or for your stockholders?"

"The public be damned! I am working for my stockholders! If the public want the train, why don't they support it?"

None of these versions is likely to be wholly correct. Stone must be suspected of sour grapes, for he let one of the big stories of the year slip through his fingers. Dresser wanted to be sure of selling his story, and Barton wanted to put his uncle's fatal words in the best possible light. (And it can be safely assumed that all these men were perfectly willing that *historians* be damned.)

Both Dresser's and Barton's versions have enough elements in common to indicate a single origin in fact, even though one has Vanderbilt continuing to run a train and the other has him canceling it. One could make a case for either one. Barton's, perhaps, is more provocative, and Vanderbilt would have to have been provoked into saying what he did, for he was not in the least an arrogant or stupid man but had in full measure the family's quick temper. And each is very reminiscent of the attitude toward business of Vanderbilt's father, the commodore, a man William Henry held in the deepest respect, and whose ideas regarding business behavior he followed faithfully.

Dresser's version recalls testimony by the commodore given to a committee of the New York State Assembly twenty years earlier. "I have always served the public to the best of my ability. Why? Because, like every other man, it is my interest to do so, and to put them to as little inconvenience as possible. I don't think that there is a man in the world who would go further to serve the public than I."

Barton's version recalls another occasion when the assembly asked the commodore his system for running a railroad. "My system of railroading is . . . to take care of it just as careful as I would of my own household affairs, handle it just as though it was all mine; . . . and take good care of its income; that is my aim, you know, and give that to the stockholders." The commodore noted that although he was president of three railroads, he took no salary. His compensation, in other words, came only from stock dividends. Both the commodore and his son regarded themselves as fiduciaries for the stockholders, a claim that precious few railroad managers could honestly make in the nineteenth century.

In both versions, William Henry Vanderbilt's purported words, while hard-nosed and certainly impolitic, are embedded in inescapable economic truth that he had learned from his father. Both men thought the key to success was to seek profits by serving the public but knew that companies that seek to serve the public rather than make a profit will not be around very long to do either.

In history, as in so much of life, often "you pay your money and take your choice," and that is certainly the case here. But in either version of the most famous interview in American business history, William Henry Vanderbilt, however infelicitously he phrased it, was only repeating a truth first written by that master of economic felicity, Adam Smith.

NICE WORK IF YOU CAN KEEP IT

THE USUAL IMAGE, as opposed to the reality, of invention is the solitary genius struggling in his garret with an idea only he has faith in. One day he shouts "Eureka!" and the world changes. Sometimes this is actually the case. Thomas Edison, after all, was entitled to shout "Eureka!" more than 1,000 times in his life, although I doubt that he did.

In the modern era, however, most great inventions are under development for long periods of time, sometimes generations, before someone solves the last piece of the puzzle and becomes "the inventor." Dozens of individuals were struggling with heavier-than-air flight at the turn of the twentieth century, but it was the Wright brothers (so close to each other as nearly to be a solitary genius) who solved the last major problem—turning. Their insight was to realize that airplanes turn in three dimensions, not two like land- or sea-bound transportation, and they devised a means to allow the aircraft to do so while maintaining stability, wing-warping. That was enough, however. Orville Wright became the first man to "slip the surly bonds of earth," while Wilbur watched in triumph, and they did indeed invent the airplane, for theirs was the first one that worked.

But many of the most important inventions had no inventor at all. It was known as early as the sixteenth century, for instance, that when a wagon is placed on rails, a draft animal (or, often, a human being) could haul a much heavier load. It is not known who first had the idea of using a steam engine instead of a horse or mule to pull the wagon, and it was only in 1797 that Richard Trevithick developed a steam engine powerful enough to do so. Trevithick's locomotive, however, required a toothed rail to operate, such as cog railways use on steep mountain slopes to this day. Then it was William Hedley who, in 1813, built "Puffing Billy," the first adhesion engine, which relies on friction for traction. Finally, in 1828, George Stephenson built the "Rocket"—much more powerful than previous locomotives, thanks to its multitubular boiler—and solved a myriad of practical engineering problems in designing the Liverpool and Manchester Railway, the first commercially successful railroad.

In our own time, the computer had a thousand fathers, from Charles Babbage in the early nineteenth century to Steven Jobs and Stephen Wozniak in the 1970s and 1980s, before it was ready to sit on half the desks in the country.

The automobile, too, had many contributors, from Roger Bacon in the thirteenth century, who first conceived the idea of a self-propelled vehicle, to Nikolaus Otto, who built the first practical four-cycle engine in 1876, to Wilhelm Maybach, who invented the carburetor in 1893, to Henry Ford, who introduced the assembly line in 1914.

But unlike the other inventions that evolved more than sprang into being from the mind of a single genius, the automobile was patented in its entirety, by someone who never even built one, George B. Selden. Had he been able to make the patent stick, he would have been Forbes-400 rich. And given his actual, minuscule contribution to the development of the automobile, he didn't do badly at all as it was. It was not American patent law's finest hour.

Selden, who lived in Rochester, New York, was an inventor by avocation. But he made his living as a patent attorney and was thoroughly versed in the intricacies of that law, one of the earliest legal specialties.

In 1872 George B. Brayton of Boston had patented a two-cycle internal combustion engine that was exhibited at the Philadelphia Centennial Exposition, where Selden saw it and was inspired. He built his own three-cylinder model, and, around this engine, he designed, but never built, a vehicle. In 1879 he applied for a patent for an "improved road engine" (the word *automobile* would not be coined until 1883) that was powered by "a liquid-hydrocarbon engine of the compression type."

Had that been that, Selden would have received his patent probably in 1881, and thus it would have expired in 1898. But he realized that the automobile was nowhere near a practical (and therefore potentially moneymaking) invention in 1879. Knowing the intricacies of patent law and the foibles of the patent office, Selden filed a series of amended applications, which had the effect of delaying the issuance of the patent while maintaining his priority. Finally, in 1895, fully sixteen years after he first applied and just as the patent office was beginning to tighten up its much-abused procedures regarding amended applications, Selden received U.S. Patent number 549,160. As far as the federal government was concerned, George B. Selden had invented the automobile. And receiving the patent at this point was fine by Selden, for Maybach's carburetor, developed two years earlier, had finally made the automobile practical. There was now money to be made in the aborning automobile industry.

In 1899 Selden cashed in. He sold his patent to a syndicate of Wall Street investors headed by William C. Whitney and Thomas Fortune Ryan for $10,000 (perhaps fifteen times that in today's money) and 20 percent of any royalties they collected from car manufacturers. The following year the syndicate, operating as the Electric Vehicle Company, sued the Winton Motor Carriage Company, then the largest manufacturer of automobiles in the United States. Alexander Winton fought the suit at first but came to realize that the courts were likely to uphold it, and settled. (He was right; the court held the patent valid on March 20, 1903.)

And Alexander Winton and other manufacturers, who had originally seen the Selden patent as a mortal threat to their livelihoods, began to view it instead as a means of limiting competition in the automobile business, which at that time was ferocious, with dozens of companies coming into the business every year (and a more or less equal number leaving it, usually through bankruptcy). Soon thirty-two companies formed the Association of Licensed Automobile Manufacturers and agreed to pay a royalty of 1.25 percent of the retail price of every car they sold. One-fifth of that money was to go to Selden, two-fifths to the Electric Vehicle Company, and two-fifths to the ALAM to finance infringement suits against nonmembers. They would have to apply for membership in the ALAM before being allowed to go into the car business. In other words, the ALAM was a cartel.

But, almost immediately, the brand-new cartel made a serious mistake. A new automobile company, formed that year, wanted to join. But ALAM, which like all cartels was out to limit the number of members of the club, turned down the Ford Motor Company's application, saying it had not demonstrated competence in the manufacture of automobiles. Henry Ford's response, needless to say, was to go right on manufacturing them and, like the majority of American car companies, ignore the Selden patent.

When the ALAM threatened to put him out of business, Ford answered, "Let them try it!" ALAM sued a few weeks later, but not until May 28, 1909, a year after the Model T had been introduced, did the suit finally go to trial.

Henry Ford was perfectly candid under cross-examination. "I invented nothing new," he admitted. "I simply assembled into a car the discoveries of other men behind whom were centuries of work. . . . Had I worked fifty or ten or even five years before, I would have failed. So it is with every new thing. Progress happens when all the factors that make for it are ready, and then it is inevitable. To teach that a comparatively few men are responsible for the greatest forward steps of mankind is the worst sort of nonsense."

By pure coincidence, the first transcontinental automobile race, from New York to Seattle, was getting under way right outside the courthouse in lower Manhattan as the trial was going on. Five cars were in the race, and two of them were Ford Model Ts. One of Ford's lawyers, Frederic Coudert, in the midst of examining a witness, watched the spectacle from the window as William Howard Taft, in the White House, pressed a golden telegraph key, the mayor of New York fired a starting pistol in response, and they were off. Coudert then turned to the judge. "Your Honor," he said, "there is something that puzzles me. I don't see a Selden car. I see a Ford car, two Ford cars, but I see no Selden car!"

Ford was so confident of the outcome of the lawsuit that he left in the middle of it to go to Seattle to watch the finish of the race. To his unconcealed delight it was won by one of the Ford cars. But although Ford triumphed in the race, he did not in court, and the court ruled that any car powered by gasoline that was manufactured without a license from ALAM infringed the Selden patent.

Ford was distraught by the verdict and even thought of selling out to William Durant, the founder of General Motors, but the deal fell through when Durant couldn't raise the cash needed. And meanwhile Ford was appealing the decision.

On January 9, 1911, the appellate court finally handed down its ruling. The gas-powered automobile, it ruled, was a "social invention" and anyone could manufacture the vehicle without payment of royalty.

The following night, the Ford Motor Company held a raucous victory party, featuring guests improvising lyrics to popular songs that made fun of Selden and the ALAM. Ford was there, a broad grin on his face, but his mind was obviously somewhere else, thinking beyond the moment of triumph.

A friend sat down next to him and congratulated him on his victory, but Ford obviously did not hear a word of what he said, for he suddenly turned to him. "Nothing can stop me now," Ford told him. "From here on in the sky's the limit."

Ford was right, of course, and the world changed.

HENRY FORD'S
HORSELESS HORSE

HAVE YOU HEARD THE story of the man who almost made a fortune in the soft-drink industry? He invented 6-Up.

All right, I know it's a very old joke, but it illustrates a point: There are a lot more near misses in capitalism than bull's-eyes. Many of these near misses come about through simple bad timing or bad luck (RCA's Selecta Vision, for instance, blown out of the water by the VCR). Others result from technological overreach (the gigantic *Great Eastern* steamship in the middle of the nineteenth century, or Howard Hughes's equally gigantic airplane, the *Spruce Goose,* 100 years later).

But others happen because an innovator fails to fully conceptualize the new technology he is dealing with and relies on models from the old technology he seeks to replace. The first mechanical pencil sharpener, for example, was not the three helical cutting edges whirling around their own axes as well as a common center. Instead it was a Rube Goldbergian contraption that sought to imitate a human hand wielding a pen knife. Not surprisingly, it didn't work very well.

Or consider Henry Ford's Fordson tractor. While Ford no more invented the tractor than he invented the automobile, his Fordson tractor, like his Model T, revolutionized an industry, brought a powerful new technology within the reach of millions, changed an age-old way of life forever, and had innumerable economic consequences.

But although the Model T made Ford one of the richest men in the world, the Fordson tractor was, finally, a financial failure. The reason it failed, perhaps, was that Henry Ford hated farming and focused too much on simply replacing the horse and not enough on what the horse actually did for the farmer.

American agriculture, from its beginning, had been different from its

European antecedents. In Europe land was expensive and labor cheap; in America it was exactly the reverse. Because of this reality, early American farmers often had a startling lack of interest in husbandry but were very receptive to laborsaving machinery.

At the time of the Revolution, American farmers still had little in the way of equipment unknown to the Romans 2,000 years earlier. It was reckoned that two men and a boy, using two or three horses or twice as many oxen, could plow only an acre or two a day. Yankee ingenuity was about to change that.

As early as 1788 Thomas Jefferson was working on the right mathematical curve for a plow to turn the earth with maximum efficiency. (His equation, elegance itself on paper, was not successful in the field.) Most farmers continued to use simple wooden plows, while the wealthier could afford cast-iron ones.

Then, in 1819, Jethro Wood introduced cast-iron plows with replaceable parts, bringing them within reach of the average farmer. Two decades later, John Deere introduced the steel plow, a great improvement on the cast-iron model and a capitalist bull's-eye of the first order. The John Deere Company used the motto "He gave to the world the steel plow" for well over 100 years. (Of course, as more than one farmer noted, "He may have given it to the world, but I had to buy mine.")

James Oliver promptly improved the tempering process and mounted a plow on wheels and provided the farmer with a seat. Now, using two teams of horses and two linked plows, the farmer could plow twice as fast as previously.

There is much more to farming, to be sure, than plowing, and the industrial revolution also gave the farmer mechanical seed drillers, cultivators, reapers, and threshers. All this had a radical effect on productivity. In 1822 it had taken fifty to sixty man-hours to produce twenty bushels of wheat on an acre; by 1890 the same yield was achieved with just eight to ten man-hours.

The number of "horse-hours," however, had greatly increased, and by 1880 the number of horses and mules on American farms exceeded 12 million and was climbing quickly.

At that time the only alternative to the horse was steam. At first, portable steam engines were employed on very large farms for threshing.

In truth they were portable only in the sense that they were not permanently situated and could be moved, very slowly, by large teams of horses.

Somebody soon had the idea to use a steam engine's own power to move it from farm to farm. It was exactly such a steam engine that Henry Ford encountered one day at the age of twelve when riding in a wagon with his father. It was the first self-propelled device that Ford, already deeply fascinated with anything mechanical, had ever seen, and he was as wild with excitement as only a twelve-year-old boy can be.

"The engine had stopped," Ford wrote half a century later, "to let us pass with our horses and I was off the wagon and talking to the engineer before my father . . . knew what I was up to." The engineer cheerfully explained how everything worked and made a lifelong impression on Ford. Indeed, "from the time I saw that road engine . . . right forward to today, my great interest has been in making a machine that would travel roads."

Steam, however, was not well adapted to farm use. The energy output in steam engines is low per unit of weight, and thus steam engines capable of doing farmwork were very heavy and expensive. Very few farmers could afford to own steam engines, and many could not even afford to rent them.

With all of steam's disadvantages, when the internal combustion engine began to approach practicality, it was soon adapted to farm use. The first gasoline-powered traction engine (a phrase shortened by 1900 to "tractor") was built by John Froelich in 1892, four years before Henry Ford built his first automobile. But Froelich's engine, like most early prototypes, didn't work very well in the real world, and Froelich soon disappeared from history.

However, the major farm-equipment companies such as John Deere and International Harvester, along with a host of smaller companies, were soon experimenting and turning out internal combustion tractors. The early gasoline tractors were largely modeled on the steam-powered ones they were beginning to replace. Thus they were large, heavy, clumsy, and expensive. Few farmers wanted or could afford them. Then World War I changed everything.

American farm prices soared as European grain production plunged and Russia's huge grain exports were cut off. The demand for horses and mules, meanwhile, also increased vastly. The belligerents needed them to haul wagons and guns on the front lines, where they were slaughtered, like the soldiers, by the hundreds of thousands. With the price of horseflesh rising out of sight and money in their pockets from grain sales, more and more American farmers decided to try tractors. Henry Ford decided the time had come to produce one.

In 1915 he announced the Fordson tractor, saying he would sell it for $250. His new tractor was smaller than most then on the market, structurally much simpler, and specifically designed to be mass-produced—a tractor version of the Model T, in other words. It took Ford two years to get into production (and the initial price was $750). Still, from the beginning sales were brisk. By March 1918 he was making 80 a day, and production hit 300 a day by year's end. In 1920 Ford boasted that he had sold 100,000 tractors, twice the total number that had been in use on American farms when the Fordson was introduced.

Although already the largest manufacturer of tractors, Ford then decided to go after market share. In 1921 he slashed prices, selling the Fordson for only $395, less than the price of a good team of horses. The other tractor manufacturers were stunned but had no choice other than to meet his price. Many, Ford included, were losing $300 on every tractor they sold, and many vanished from the marketplace. International Harvester, however, did not.

"Ford was backed," Cyrus H. McCormick, grandson of the founder, explained, "by the most popular commercial name of the time and by the uncounted millions earned for him by his epoch-making car; . . . [but] he was trying to capture a business with which he had no previous contact. International Harvester had on its side many years of training gained from contact with farmers, less capital by far, and utter inexperience with defeat." That contact with farmers and farm equipment was to prove crucial in the contest between Ford and McCormick for dominance in the tractor market.

The old horse-drawn farm equipment had been powered by a "bull wheel." The bull wheel was a large wheel sticking out from the side of the equipment, armed with cleats that dug into the ground. As the horses pulled the equipment, the bull wheel, at least in theory, turned the machinery. When the soil was wet, however, the bull wheel often just slithered along without turning and had to be helped manually, an exhausting and sometimes dangerous job. Farmers hated bull wheels.

But the bull wheel, for all its inadequacy, was the best way there was for powering horse-drawn equipment. As one engineer of the time explained, "Horses are obliged to transmit their power through the ground to the machinery they operate because of their inherent and unchangeable construction."

The construction of tractors is not unchangeable, however, and in the cutthroat market of the early 1920s International Harvester soon offered a vast improvement on the bull wheel, the power takeoff. The PTO is a rotating shaft powered by the tractor's engine that can be connected to the equipment being pulled by the tractor. It has been a feature of every successful tractor model since.

Being a farm equipment manufacturer, International Harvester soon had a line of equipment designed to work with the new, much more efficient, and far more reliable power source offered by its tractors. Farmers loved the PTO, and International Harvester quickly pulled ahead of Ford in tractor sales. By 1928 Ford was forced to withdraw from the tractor market he had largely created in the first place.

When Ford produced his Model T, he produced a practical, affordable horseless carriage, all that the traveler needed to travel and just what the marketplace was looking for. It was one of the great capitalist bull's-eyes of history. His Fordson tractor, however, was no more than a practical, affordable horseless horse. That, in the end, was not quite enough.

Even geniuses don't hit the bull's-eye every time.

THE MAN WHO SAVED
THE CADILLAC

ALTHOUGH THIS WILL COME as a stunning surprise to most academic economists, economics is one of the biological sciences.

Free markets operate according to the rules that govern life itself, rules that are not always fair. And just as in a biological ecosystem, the fit (and the lucky) survive the test of the market, the rest do not. Nowhere is this clearer, in both biology and economics, than when a new technology punctuates the equilibrium and changes what is possible. In both cases there is a flurry of creation as new creatures and products come into being and a rapid evolution as they compete. By the time the dust settles, most will have died out, leaving only the best-designed and most efficient models surviving.

The most famous example of this in the history of biology is known as the Cambrian explosion. It happened between 535 and 530 million years ago when the first multicellular organisms evolved. In only 5 million years, virtually all the basic multicellular body plans that still exist (along with many more that no longer do) came into being. As the paleontologist Stephen Jay Gould has noted, the whole history of life since has really been nothing but endless variations on Cambrian themes.

In the economic ecosystem, the development of the microprocessor—really a tiny, dirt-cheap computer—in the early 1970s likewise made possible many new things under the sun. In no time the handheld calculator drove the slide rule extinct, and the word processor sent the typewriter into irreversible decline.

The new technologies, of course, also competed among themselves, and many have already vanished. The word processor is now only a niche technology, supplanted by the personal computer, and Wang Laboratories, one of the great success stories of the 1970s, is now in bankruptcy. Visicalc, the first all-purpose spreadsheet, is long gone. WordPerfect and Ashton-Tate, software giants of the 1980s, are no longer independent companies.

But the computing power that twenty years ago would have cost, literally, $1 million is now to be found on the desktops of half the teenagers in the country. What they will do with it over the next few years is anyone's guess, but I would strongly advise everyone to step back smartly.

At the turn of the twentieth century, the automobile appeared and also underwent a rapid evolution, proliferation, and partial extinction. In 1903 alone, fifty-seven automobile companies came into existence and twenty-seven went bankrupt. Today, there are fewer than two dozen major car companies in the entire world. The rest, from the Stanley Steamer to the Henry J, have all gone extinct.

One brand of car that survives from 1903 is the Cadillac. But if the Cadillac survived, it certainly had a near-death experience in the early 1930s. It was rescued at the last second by Nicholas Dreystadt, a man who found, in the midst of the Great Depression, a whole new market for luxury cars and developed a whole new way of making them.

The Cadillac came into existence, ironically enough, because Henry Ford walked out of a deal. Several rich men had set up a company, called the Henry Ford Company, in hopes of turning his already undoubted mechanical gifts into automotive gold. But Ford refused to do things their way and quit. In hopes of salvaging something from their investment, they brought in Henry M. Leland, a machine maker who had developed a new type of engine, one built to unusually fine tolerances. Leland quickly designed a new car, built around his engine, and called it the Cadillac, after the French explorer who first came ashore at what is now Detroit.

The Cadillac would long have a reputation for being mechanically innovative. In 1911, two years after the company was acquired by General Motors, it introduced the first electric starter, which quickly caused the difficult and dangerous starting-crank technology to go extinct. In 1915 the Cadillac Model 51 sported the first commercially available V-8 engine.

But this innovation came at a price. By 1921 the top-of-the-line Cadillac was the most expensive car General Motors produced, at a snappy $5,690 (around $40,000 in today's money, perhaps twice that if measured as a percentage of average per capita income).

Although Henry Ford and his next company revolutionized the way in which mass-market cars were produced, luxury cars such as Cadillacs were still made the old-fashioned way, more or less one at a time. The 1920s, of course, were the golden age of luxury automobiles, vehicles of such beauty and style that they still move the hearts of even the most nonmechanical. But the onset of the Great Depression caused the automobile market as a whole to shrink drastically, while the luxury segment of it virtually collapsed.

In 1928 General Motors manufactured 1,709,763 vehicles in the United States, of which 41,172 were Cadillacs. By 1933 GM production was down to a dismal 779,029 vehicles, a decline of more than 54 percent. But that year Cadillac sold only 6,736 cars, a decline of fully 83 percent.

General Motors showed a profit every year of the Great Depression, but it did so only by ruthless cost cutting. Buick, Pontiac, and Oldsmobile were collapsed into one division, for instance, to save managerial overhead.

As for Cadillac, it was losing so much money (with its high costs per unit, it had never been really profitable, not even in the 1920s) that the only question was whether to kill it outright to keep its name alive and wait for better times. The executive committee of the board of directors was meeting to decide its fate when Nicholas Dreystadt knocked on the door of the boardroom and asked to be heard for ten minutes.

Dreystadt was an unlikely GM executive. He had come to this country from Germany in 1911 at the age of thirteen, as an apprentice on a Mercedes racing team, and he always spoke English with the broad accents of his native Swabia. He favored tweed sport coats—spotted with burn holes from his ever-present pipe—over business suits. His secretary kept a pair of men's dress shoes handy for the days when Dreystadt showed up at the office in shoes that did not match. A gifted mechanic, however, by the early 1930s he was in charge of Cadillac service nationwide, a middle management position of responsibility but no real importance in the politics of General Motors.

So for someone like Dreystadt to crash a meeting of the GM executive committee might roughly be compared to a monsignor knocking on the door of the Sistine Chapel to make a suggestion to the College of Cardinals while it was busy electing a pope.

But Dreystadt said he had a plan to make Cadillac profitable in eighteen months, depression or no depression. The first part of his plan resulted from an observation Dreystadt had made traveling around the country to the service departments of Cadillac dealerships.

Cadillac was after the "prestige market," and part of its strategy to capture that market was refusing to sell to blacks. Despite this official discrimination, however, Dreystadt had noted that an astonishing number of customers at the service departments consisted of members of the nation's tiny black elite, the boxers, singers, doctors, and lawyers, who earned large incomes despite the flourishing Jim Crow atmosphere of the 1930s.

Most status symbols were not available to these people. They couldn't live in upscale neighborhoods or patronize fancy nightclubs. But getting around Cadillac's policy of refusing to sell was easy: They just paid a white man to front for them.

Dreystadt urged the executive committee to go after this market. Why should a bunch of white front men get several hundred dollars each, when that profit could flow to General Motors? The board bought Dreystadt's reasoning, and in 1934 Cadillac sales increased by 70 percent and the division actually broke even. (By way of comparison, GM total sales were up by less than 40 percent.) In June of 1934 Nick Dreystadt was made head of the Cadillac Division.

He proceeded to revolutionize the way luxury cars were made. "Quality is design and tooling," he said, "inspection and service; it is not inefficiency." He was willing to spend money on superior design and on better machine tools. He was willing to spend even more on quality control and top-notch service departments. He was not willing to spend money on production itself.

"Nick made us look closely at everything," one Cadillac executive remembered. "If someone else made a part for two dollars—why did ours have to cost three or four?" In less than three years of this attitude at the top, Cadillac's production costs were no higher, per unit, than were General Motors's low-end Chevrolet's.

And because Cadillac still sold for luxury prices despite its drastically reduced production costs, it had become General Motors's most profitable car per unit. In still depressed 1937, more Cadillacs were sold than in roaring 1928. It is ironic that twenty years later, Dreystadt's first employer, Mercedes-Benz, would use his technique of applying mass production to luxury automobile manufacture to transform itself from a marginally

profitable boutique operation into the very model of the modern luxury
car maker.

But Nicholas Dreystadt would never know that irony. His astonishing
turnaround of Cadillac put him on track for big things at General Motors,
and in 1946 he was made head of Chevrolet, far and away GM's biggest
division. He would undoubtedly have been a major contender for GM's
presidency in a few years. But six months after moving to Chevrolet, he
succumbed to throat cancer at the age of only forty-eight.

But for that cruel fate, the whole evolution of the American automobile industry over the last fifty years might have been utterly different.

THROUGH DARKEST AMERICA

As EVERY HISTORIAN KNOWS, great events are often determined by trivial ones. Benjamin Franklin, in *Poor Richard's Almanack*, noted that for want of a single horseshoe nail an entire war could be lost. Franklin was being theoretical, of course, but real examples abound. It was only at the last minute, for instance, that Lincoln changed his mind and decided to go to Ford's Theater, instead of the National Theater, to find an evening's entertainment and thus, alas, an assassin's bullet. Had any one of a thousand things happened (or not happened), the *Titanic* would have missed the iceberg.

Much of the man-made physical world, too, owes its existence to trivialities. In the 1840s New York banned the noisy, dirty, spark-throwing locomotives of the day from the built-up areas of the city. They were ordered to stay north of Forty-second Street, then no more than a country lane. As a result, New York is the only city in the world with two completely separate main business districts, one downtown, centered on Wall Street, and another, miles to the north, centered on the train station that was, necessarily, built at Forty-second Street.

Railroads were the great infrastructure project of the nineteenth century. Infrastructure, because, by definition, it facilitates economic transactions, always has a profound effect on how, where, and why a country as a whole develops.

Being the world's richest nation, the United States has more infrastructure than any other country. Almost all of it, however, came into existence with little or no overarching vision. Rather, it developed from myriad local pressures and entrepreneurial activity, a fact for which the country seems little, if any, the worse. (Washington, D.C., please note.)

There is one glaring exception, however, to this general rule, the greatest American infrastructure project of them all, the Interstate Highway System. It was conceived, planned, and financed as a single entity, and it remains the largest public works project in the history of the world.

But even this immense, and notably successful, undertaking owes its existence in large measure to a strikingly trivial event. In 1919 a U.S. Army captain was bored with peacetime duty. So that summer he volunteered for a trip that promised adventure by taking him, in his words, "Through Darkest America."

In the first decades of this century, American roads did not come close to achieving what might even charitably be called a "system." Although many relatively long-distance roads had been built or planned early in the nineteenth century, the railroads had superseded them as carriers of passengers and freight, and by the end of that century, while the country had about 2 million miles of roads outside urban areas, they were, quite literally, all local roads.

They often terminated abruptly at a state or even county line. As late as 1912 when Henry B. Joy, president of Packard Automobile Company, was in Omaha, he asked the local Packard dealer how to go westward from that city. He was told, in effect, "You can't get there from here." The dealer offered to show him and took him westward out of the city until they encountered a wire fence. "Take down this fence," the dealer told him, "and drive on and when you come to the next fence, take that down and go on again."

"A little further," Joy added, "and there were no fences, no fields, nothing but two ruts across the prairie."

And of those 2 million miles of local roads, only about 100 were paved. The other 1,999,900 miles were often quagmires of mud in the spring and fall and choked with dust all summer. (They were also notoriously lacking in signs. After all, as all roads were local, only locals used them, and the locals, presumably, already knew where they were going.)

But that year, at least, the first national highway since the famous Cumberland Road, suggested by George Washington and built in the first decades of the nineteenth century, was proposed. The Lincoln Highway, as it was called, was a privately funded demonstration project, mapped to reach from New York to San Francisco. By 1919, however, it was still more a cartographic than physical reality.

After the First World War had shown how vulnerable horses were to modern firepower, the U.S. Army decided to test the military capabilities of the internal combustion engine for moving men and matériel. It also wanted to bring attention to the wretched condition of U.S. highways for both military and civilian purposes and to "demonstrate the necessity for the judicious expenditure of federal government appropriations in providing for the necessary highways." So it mounted what it dubbed the First Transcontinental Motor Convoy of 1919, to cross the country on the Lincoln Highway.

This convoy was no small undertaking, for it was to operate under "wartime conditions," and assumed that "railroad facilities, bridges, tunnels, etc., had been damaged or destroyed by agents of an Asiatic enemy." The expedition was to be entirely self-sustaining and to assume it was marching through enemy-held country.

There were sixty trucks—which the army in its inimitable style insisted on calling "Class B vehicles"—together with half a dozen staff cars and the same number of motorcycles with sidecars. Two of the trucks were converted into ambulances, two others were fitted out to act as machine shops, and many towed trailers. But most were standard army vehicles for carrying water and gasoline, troops, weapons, aerial searchlights, and the other paraphernalia of modern warfare.

Altogether there were around 280 officers and enlisted men—drivers, mechanics, medics, engineers, cooks, and telegraphers as well as regular soldiers—under the command of Lieutenant Colonel Charles W. McClure.

The expedition got under way in Washington, D.C., on July 7, with great ceremony (a milestone marking the event is, in fact, still there, just south of the White House grounds). The secretary of war, the army chief of staff, and assorted senators and representatives were there to see the convoy depart. Once the politicians had run out of oratorical steam, the convoy set off at 11:15 A.M. Seven and a quarter hours later, it camped for the night at the Frederick (Maryland) Fair Grounds, having made a less-than-brisk forty-six miles. One trailer had broken its coupling, a staff car had lost a fan belt, and one Class B had to be towed into camp with a broken magneto (alternator, in today's parlance).

And so it went, day after day. The convoy could make a top speed of ten to fifteen miles an hour but averaged only sixty miles a day thanks to frequent stops for repairs and to inspect bridges. In the East the roads were fair and usually paved, but the bridges were often a problem. Some had to be circumvented because they were too narrow (or were covered and couldn't take the big army trucks). Others had to be reinforced. In all, sixty-five bridges were remodeled or rebuilt by army engineers as the convoy made its way west.

Although the convoy was operating as though it were passing through enemy-held territory, the inhabitants of that territory were, if anything, determined to kill the troops with kindness. Virtually every town greeted them with cheers, flags, and, of course, speeches. Brass bands and concerts were frequent, and at least one town, Bedford, Pennsylvania, even had that ultimate in welcoming festivities, dancing in the streets.

When the convoy reached Columbiana, Ohio, the richest man in town—who happened to be the not-entirely-disinterested Harvey Firestone—treated the entire convoy to a picnic on his lawn.

As the convoy moved steadily westward, the population thinned out, and the roads deteriorated into the wagon tracks that they once, not so long before, had all been. In North Platte, Nebraska, one day was lost when torrential rains turned what passed for a road into a sea of mud, and twenty-five vehicles had to be hauled out of ditches.

A second day was lost when, in the midst of the Nevada desert, the convoy found itself facing a sand dune 300 feet high and 3 miles long with no way around. Every vehicle had to be pushed or pulled through it by the caterpillar tractors they had had the foresight to include. In eleven hours they made only twelve miles.

At one point there was no road at all, and they "rolled, tumbled, rocked and tossed over an abandoned railroad . . . [bed] with holes of varying depths." In the Sierra Nevada of eastern California, they faced grades of over 17 percent. (Today the Interstate Highway System has no grades of over 4 percent.)

Despite all the hazards, the convoy lost only two vehicles to accidents, and one that rolled down a mountain beyond reach, in the 3,200-mile trek. It arrived in San Francisco only two days behind schedule, on September 6. There is no doubt that this accomplishment was due far more to the can-do spirit of the officers and men than to the vehicular infrastructure with which they had to cope.

Being an army operation, a full report was filed on the expedition. "The necessity for a comprehensive system of national highways," it noted, "including transcontinental or through routes east and west, north and south, is real and urgent as a commercial asset to further colonize and develop the sparsely settled sections of the country, and finally as a defensive military necessity."

Like countless other army reports before and since, it went into a file draw, for all practical purposes never to be seen again. The federal government began contributing funds to state road-building projects in 1923 for highways that met certain specifications and were given U.S. route numbers. This hardly constituted a comprehensive system, however, being under the political control of forty-eight separate states.

But the army captain who had joined the convoy for no better reason than he thought it would be a pleasant way to spend the summer did not forget his experience.

Thirty-five years later he continued to think that a comprehensive system of national superhighways was in the interests of the country. And because by then he happened to be president of the United States, he was in a position to do something about it.

It was Dwight Eisenhower who determinedly pushed the Interstate Highway System through an initially reluctant Congress.

PART V

BANKING

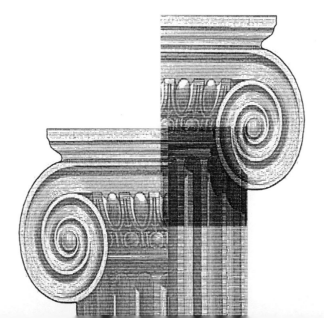

WE BANKED ON THEM

It is not often that even the most ardent believer in capitalism mourns the passing of an economic institution, unless, of course, he or she has personally lost money as a result.

After all, the people involved are still around even if the institution is gone. So, too, are the capital assets, if now in other hands. What is actually lost is just such stuff as lawyers make, the corporate or partnership agreement that governed the way the parts made up the whole. To be sure, one of the miracles at the core of capitalism is how the whole always exceeds the sum of those parts.

But the Baring Bank is different. Old capitalist institutions, like old generals, tend to just fade away when they fail to change with the ever-changing economy. But Barings suffered no such protracted disappearance. It had been adapting successfully to changing times since 1762, seven years before James Watt perfected the steam engine that was instrumental in setting off the industrial revolution. By the time the revolution was far enough advanced to be noticed and the term entered the English language, the Baring Bank was eighty-six years old and flourishing as never before.

It continued to flourish—with one serious illness in 1890—until it suffered something akin to murder at the age of 233 in 1995.

Historians, of course, are likely to have a weakness for the venerable for no better reason than that they *are* venerable. But there is another reason all Americans might mourn Baring Brothers. The firm was a friend of the United States from its earliest days, when most members of the British establishment treated this country as something between a nest of traitors and a banana republic.

How big a friend was it? Consider this: Technically we didn't buy the

Louisiana Purchase from Napoleon Bonaparte. We bought it from Baring Brothers.

The Baring family had its origins in Germany. Their involvement in the wool trade brought them to Exeter, in the west of England, in the early eighteenth century. There they prospered mightily; the family soon evolved into gentry, while the family firm evolved into a new kind of business, one that the British now call merchant banking and Americans call investment banking.

Investment banks, very roughly, are wholesale banks. They do not deal with individuals (unless, of course, the individual is very, very rich). Rather, in the beginning, they facilitated trade by handling cargoes for foreign merchants on consignment as well as trading on their own account. Soon they were financing this trade by making loans to trading firms to cover the period between when a cargo sold and the payment was received.

As their loan business expanded, merchant banks slowly left the actual buying, selling, and handling of commodities behind and concentrated on the finances. Governments and businesses also began using merchant banks to facilitate borrowing money long term, using them as agents to sell bonds in the money markets that were springing up in London, Amsterdam, Frankfurt, and elsewhere.

Barings was active in the American market even before the Revolution, when the firm was only a few years old. The thirteen colonies had become one of the principal markets for British cloth, and Barings helped to finance this trade as well as to participate in it.

After the Revolution, Robert Morris and state senator William Bingham, two financially prominent Philadelphians, and others quickly moved to reestablish relations with Barings, which welcomed their overtures, unlike many other British merchants and financial houses. Alexander Baring, the son of the firm's leading partner, Sir Francis Baring, would marry Bingham's daughter.

But the possibilities for doing profitable business were limited as long as the new United States was mired in the depression and financial chaos that followed the Revolution. Only after the Constitution was adopted and Alexander Hamilton put the federal government on a firm footing did Atlantic trade take off in the 1790s.

It was in dealing with the Barbary pirates that Barings did the U.S. government its first real service. The Barbary pirates ran one of history's largest protection rackets. Their ships regularly attacked commerce in the Mediterranean, unless, of course, they were suitably paid off not to attack.

England, deeply engaged in a war with revolutionary France by the mid-1790s, simply found it cheaper to pay the pirates off than divert the naval force needed to attack the well-fortified ports of Tunis, Algiers, and Tripoli. In 1795 the U.S. government came to the same conclusion. The problem was *how* to pay them off.

Pirates, needless to say, don't accept IOUs, and that was all the United States had to offer right then. To turn paper into something the pirates would accept, the U.S. Treasury needed a banker. It turned to Barings, sending it $800,000 in U.S. bonds. Typical of treasury officials the world over, they instructed Barings both to sell these bonds in London without depressing the market for U.S. securities and to do it with the utmost haste. The proceeds, in silver bullion, were then to be forwarded to David Humphreys, the American minister in Lisbon, who was in charge of bribing the pirates.

Barings had to overcome numerous difficulties to fulfill the contradictory instructions and often risked loss by acting on its own rather than waiting for further instructions from Washington. But when the job was done, Rufus King, the American minister in London, wrote to Francis Baring, to congratulate him "on the liberal and skilful manner in which you have assisted Col. Humphreys in a very critical operation. I have written to the Secretary of the Treasury . . . of my conviction that the United States will entertain a proper sense of your Services in this Business."

At the same time, Barings was also securing muskets and cannon for the United States, to help in the developing "quasi war" with France. In all it sent nearly 10,000 muskets and 330 cannon, advancing £45,000—no small sum at the end of the eighteenth century—for the purpose.

But it was in securing Louisiana for the United States that Barings was nearly indispensable to American interests. At heart, Louisiana was a geopolitical as well as a domestic political problem for Thomas Jefferson's administration, which came to power in 1801. The transappalachian West was growing by leaps and bounds by the turn of the nineteenth century, and much of Jefferson's political support came from the area. But the settlers, blocked by the mountains, were dependent on the Mississippi River and its tributaries to reach eastern and world markets.

While the Mississippi then formed the country's western border, New Orleans and the river's mouth were in the hands of the Spanish. Fortunately, Spain was now a great power in name only, quite unable to seriously threaten American interests. It allowed the United States to maintain a depot in New Orleans, where cargoes could be transshipped without paying Spanish customs duties.

The ever-more-ambitious Napoleon Bonaparte, however, forced Spain to cede Louisiana to France in the secret treaty of San Ildefonso in 1800. News of this cession soon leaked out, of course, and Jefferson was appalled at the idea of a French army on his back doorstep. The British lion, purring smoothly, offered to conquer Louisiana for the United States and turn it over when peace with France was achieved. But Jefferson, needless to say, didn't want a British army any more than he wanted a French one. He moved to buy the east bank of the Mississippi all the way to the Gulf of Mexico, sending James Monroe to help the American minister to France, Robert Livingston, negotiate.

Napoleon quickly realized that Louisiana couldn't be defended against a British attack, and, desperate for money as always, he offered to sell the whole territory. No one knew the precise boundaries at the time. Still, at an asking price of $15 million, no one doubted that it was a fantastic bargain. But as former New York mayor David Dinkins once said, "Two elephants for a quarter is a bargain—if you need elephants and you have a quarter."

The Federalists thought that the answer to both conditions was no. "We are to give money of which we have too little for land of which we already have too much," the *Columbian Centinel* of Boston complained. And certainly the money, while trivial on a per-acre basis, was huge on an absolute one. Today, the U.S. government spends $15 million every five minutes, around the clock. But in 1803 the total expenditures for the year were only slightly more than half that, $7.85 million.

Again, the United States needed a banker, one with vast resources. And it had one. Alexander Baring was with Monroe and Livingston throughout the negotiations with the French government and, at least according to his father, was largely responsible for getting the price as low as it was. Even for Baring it was a very large commitment of capital. "We *all* tremble about the magnitude of the American account," Francis Baring confessed, and he limited the Baring Bank's part in the deal to 60 percent.

Henry Hope and company, another major merchant bank, took the other 40 percent.

In the final deal, Napoleon trusted Barings's paper over that of the United States. He sold Louisiana to Barings and Hope for Fr 52 million, FR 6 million payable in the first month and Fr 2 million a month thereafter. Barings then turned title over to the United States in exchange for $11.25 million 6 percent bonds. (The other $3.750 million was covered by private American claims against France.)

No wonder that a few years later the French foreign minister ruefully acknowledged that "there are six great powers in Europe: England, France, Prussia, Austria, Russia and Baring Brothers."

Then, suddenly, Barings was gone. To be sure, a successor corporation took over, but the history of capitalism lost a living example and the United States lost an old friend.

THE FREEDMAN'S BANK

IT WAS A BANKING system. The act that made it possible slipped through Congress with hardly any debate and little attention to economic reality. Many of its highest-ranking officials knew little or nothing about the peculiar nature of the banking business. More than a few were incompetent, and some were plain crooks. When it failed to flourish, Congress expanded the sort of investments it was permitted to make without regard to the risk involved. It collapsed at great cost.

No, it was not the savings and loan industry in the 1980s. It was the Freedman's Savings and Trust Company in the 1860s and 1870s. But to read Carl R. Osthaus's worthy book on its sad history, *Freedmen, Philanthropy, and Fraud,* is to know déjà vu on a historical time scale.

When the Civil War ended, the Union was preserved, but social and economic chaos reigned throughout the devastated South. No one felt the effects of this chaos more than the freed blacks. They were now free, but in many cases this freedom was "just another word for nothing left to lose." How were they to make a living? The former slaves had no property and, hardly surprisingly, were very reluctant to work under the old system of gang labor, regardless of the wages they might be paid. And the landowners, their liquid assets wiped out by the war, usually lacked the cash to pay wages in any event. Over the next decade, the sharecropper system would evolve to accommodate the new realities, allowing the barter of land use for labor.

But ironically, many of the blacks, who had hardly ever seen cash money in the days of slavery, now had some cash in their pockets. Hundreds of thousands of the men had joined the Union army and received both bonuses for joining up and regular pay. (To be sure, they were paid at rates substantially below those paid to white soldiers.) Many people, educated blacks and whites alike, feared that these soldiers would quickly be fleeced out of their hard-earned army pay by the camp followers and other lowlifes who inevitably surrounded Civil War armies unless a safe place was quickly devised where they could store it.

On January 27, 1865, the Reverend John W. Alvord, a Congregational minister and dedicated abolitionist, but no banker, invited twenty-two prominent New Yorkers to a meeting to discuss the creation of a permanent banking institution to serve the needs of the freedmen. This group, which included such nationally prominent men as Peter Cooper and William Cullen Bryant, decided to act at once and sent Alvord to Washington to ask Congress for a banking charter.

Congress was in the throes of adjournment by the time the bill reached the floor of the Senate on March 2, 1865, moved by the abolitionist Charles Sumner of Massachusetts. Sumner's bill would have allowed, in the words of one objecting senator, "a kind of roving commission for these persons to establish a savings bank in any part of the United States." Sumner quickly agreed to limit the bank's charter to the District of Columbia, and it passed the Senate.

In the House that evening, an amendment was passed adding the chief justice, Salmon P. Chase, to the list of incorporators, which would have ensured high-level government attention to the project. But in the confusion of the last days of the session, both the Senate and the House amendments were lost in the shuffle, and the bill became law as Sumner had originally introduced it. John Alvord, with no credentials beyond good intentions, became president of the bank.

Because the amendment limiting the bank's charter to Washington, D.C., was accidentally dropped from the enrolled bill, and because the intended depositors were scattered widely over the South and border states, the Freedman's Bank quickly became the first since the old Second Bank of the United States—killed by Andrew Jackson in 1836—to have branches in more than one state. (It would also be the last until late in the twentieth century.) By the 1870s the bank had thirty-eight branches in no fewer than sixteen states as well as the District of Columbia.

But although the bank became far-flung, it did not become profitable. In form, the new Freedman's Savings and Trust Company was a simple mutual savings bank. It was owned by its depositors, and their deposits were to be invested in securities issued by the U.S. Treasury. But there was no initial capital subscribed, so the bank would have to be entirely financed out of deposits. This greatly increased the difficulty of earning enough on deposits to pay a good rate of interest.

And the branches, while many, were small, some too small ever to be profitable. Also, because the bank was intended for the use of the poorest stratum of American society, the individual accounts were invariably small as well. But it is an unfortunate reality of the banking business that each account, regardless of size, tends to cost much the same amount to service. As a result, the expenses of the Freedman's Bank were extraordinarily high.

At that time, the rule of thumb was that expenses should be no more than 0.5 percent of deposits. The Freedman's Bank, however, with many branches and no large accounts, had expenses upward of 5 percent of deposits. Since Treasuries, the only investment the Freedman's charter permitted, were paying 6 percent interest at that time, there was little if any profit with which to pay dividends. The pressure to find more lucrative investments never ceased.

The Freedman's Bank had two other grave weaknesses. The first was that, because its expenses were so high relative to deposits, it simply could not afford to pay the going rate for competent bank help. As a result it hired many people whose hearts were in the right place but whose book-keeping skills were lacking and sometimes nonexistent.

The other weakness was at the very top of the bank. In theory, the Freedman's Bank was governed by a board of fifty trustees. The original list was a who's who of the American business establishment of the day. But seven of the most prominent members of the board resigned almost immediately. Apparently their names had merely been used as window dressing to impress Congress, and their consent to serve was never obtained.

The bank's board of trustees, in fact, never kept close tabs on what the bank and its officers were up to. William Cullen Bryant, among others, never attended a single board meeting. Those who occasionally did attend rubber-stamped what the bank officers put before them. By 1870 power at the Freedman's Bank was effectively in the hands of these officers and the three-man finance committee, with no one monitoring their performance. If there is anything that is clear from the history of American banking, it is that whenever a few people, with interests of their own and little supervision, find themselves in charge of large sums of other people's money, disaster is on the way.

The officers of the bank began lobbying Congress for changes in the charter. Soon, a bill allowing the bank to invest in real estate—the most illiquid, and thus potentially the most troublesome, form of investment—passed the House without debate.

In the Senate only two senators raised objections to allowing the Freedman's Bank to risk its depositors' meager assets in such a way. Significantly, one of them was Simon Cameron, the boss of the Pennsylvania Republican Party, who had made his own very considerable fortune in the banking business. "Depend upon it," he warned, "the moment you allow them to put their money . . . in real estate that moment you weaken the credit of the institution and its stability."

But the Senate did not listen to Cameron. It preferred to listen to Charles Sumner, who never knew a good cause he wasn't willing to suspend reality for the sake of. The bank was allowed to make loans on real estate provided that the collateral was at least twice the value of the loan. Of course, the value of real estate, then as now, is a highly subjective matter and highly volatile to boot.

With the new amendment to the charter, the Freedman's Bank, with astonishing swiftness, became highly speculative. It began lending its "available fund," money supposed to be at hand to meet any demand for withdrawal, on such dubious security as railroad bonds, often the junk securities of the day. The trustee who proposed this, in fact, was the director of a railroad that promptly borrowed $175,000 from the Freedman's Bank.

The individual branches began making loans without getting authorization from the head office in Washington. Many of these loans were ill-advised, and many others flatly illegal. One cashier, a minister not a banker despite his job at the Freedman's Bank, loaned his own son-in-law $6,000 to conceal the son-in-law's misfeasance as county tax collector.

And incompetence vied with speculation and fraud to hasten the bank's end. Anson Sperry had been with the bank since its earliest days and had a genuine interest in helping the freedmen. But as the bank's inspector, charged with checking each branch's books, he was hopeless. "I should have known more and had less enthusiasm," he admitted after the bank's failure. Indeed. He certified many of the bank's book balances, labeling them as "correct, E & O E." Asked what that meant by mystified congressional investigators after the collapse, he admitted "E & O E" stood for "errors and omissions excepted." That's rather like certifying a ship as seaworthy except for whatever holes may be found in the hull.

The panic of 1873 dealt a death blow to the bank as depositors rushed to withdraw their money. It weathered the immediate storm by liquidating most of its government bond portfolio and, far too late, tried to reform its ways. The well-meaning but incompetent John Alvord was replaced as president by Frederick Douglass, in the hopes that the great man could reassure the black depositors.

But the comptroller of the currency quickly reported a deficit of $217,886.15. With total assets, many of them questionable, of only $3 million, this was no small sum, and panic withdrawals resumed. Douglass, who had been misled prior to accepting the presidency, quickly realized that the situation was hopeless, and on July 2, 1874, the bank closed. Few depositors ever saw a dime of their hard-earned savings as many of the loans proved uncollectible. The bitterness in the black community over the debacle lingered for decades.

To quote Santayana correctly for once: "Progress, far from consisting in change, depends on retentiveness. . . . Those who cannot remember the past are condemned to fulfill it." The Freedman's Bank and the savings and loan disaster are perhaps the best example of that truth I know.

THE PEOPLE'S BANKER

JOHN KENNETH GALBRAITH AND many other distinguished economists of the mid–twentieth century predicted a future American economy that would be dominated by a relative handful of giant companies, soon nicknamed on Wall Street the "nifty fifty." These, Galbraith thought happily, would necessarily be under close government supervision to prevent them from abusing their quasi-monopoly positions. And certainly the wave of mergers that has swept over the American economy in the last generation has concentrated economic power in fewer and fewer corporate hands, right?

Well, no, actually, it has not. Professor Galbraith's crystal ball—as is usually the case among economists—proved to be a bit cloudy. In 1967 the top 200 nonfinancial companies held 41 percent of the country's business assets, such as buildings, machinery, and land. By 1988 they held only 32 percent, and that number has continued to drop in the years since.

The reason, of course, is that the economy has grown even faster than its largest companies have merged. And new companies, which tend to grow fastest of all, have been appearing like mushrooms after a rain. In 1967, after all, neither Intel nor Microsoft even existed, and now they are being sued by the federal government as monopolies.

An exception to this has been the banking industry. The number of American banks reached its peak in 1921, when we had no fewer than 29,788 of them. The number fell by 20 percent in the 1920s as the automobile and agricultural depression began to transform rural America, and by 1930 the number of banks in the country had fallen to 24,273.

Then came the Armageddon of the Great Depression. Perhaps nothing illustrates so starkly that sickening slide to the edge of the economic abyss as the number of banks in the United States with their doors still open.

In 1931 it was 22,242; the next year, 19,317. In 1933 a mere 14,771 still operated. Banking assets in these terrible years fell by one-third.

But then the number stabilized. There were 14,771 banks in 1933 and 14,435 nearly half a century later in 1980. (Banking assets in those years, of course, increased enormously, from $51 billion to $1.9 trillion.) Then the slide started again, and there were only 12,343 banks in 1990. By 1998 there were only 8,774. Meanwhile banking assets soared to $5.4 trillion.

That, to be sure, still gives the United States more banks than the rest of the world combined. But that is an artifact not of economics but of history and the deep fear of banks held by Thomas Jefferson and his political heirs. Unlike industrial companies, banks were, from the country's earliest days, greatly restricted in their ability to grow and merge by state regulations. Many states limited branch banking, and some, such as Illinois, forbade it altogether. When national banks were chartered, beginning in 1863, they were soon subject to the same restrictions on branching as were banks chartered by their home states, and interstate branching was made illegal.

Slowly, under the pressure of sheer economic necessity, these restrictions have been easing. Banks now find themselves in competition with mutual funds and brokerage houses for banking services such as checking accounts and as repositories for the savings of average families. Meanwhile, the computer and ever-increasing travel have made restrictions on branch and interstate banking hopeless anachronisms.

In the last few years even giant banks, such as Chase Manhattan and Chemical, have been allowed to merge. In 1998 this trend accelerated even more. Most notable was the merger of Nationsbank, based in Charlotte, North Carolina, and the Bank of America, based in San Francisco, to form what was at the time the largest American banking corporation.

The Bank of America has an only-in-America history. American bankers traditionally have had WASPy names like Peabody, Morgan, and Stillman. But the Bank of America was founded by a man named Giannini.

Amadeo Peter Giannini was born in San Jose, California, in 1870. His father, Luigi, had come to California from Italy, drawn by the siren call of gold, but the gold was largely gone by the time he got there in 1860. He went into the hotel business and then bought a forty-acre truck farm. But tragedy struck when a disgruntled farmworker murdered Luigi Giannini in a dispute over two dollars in wages.

Giannini's mother heroically carried on the family farm alone for a couple of years and then married Lorenzo Scatena, a self-employed teamster who made his living hauling produce for local farmers and for a wholesale firm on the San Francisco waterfront. Scatena proved to have no talents as a farmer, and his wife suggested he try his hand at being a commission clerk, working for a wholesale firm.

This turned out to be a *very* good idea, for Scatena had the gifts that make for a good broker: an unerring sense of how the market is moving and an ability to make quick decisions. He was soon earning $250 a month, a comfortable middle-class income at that time. Again his wife pushed him to ask for more, and when the firm refused, Scatena quit and went into business for himself. By the end of his first month, he had made a profit of $1,500, big money in the 1880s.

Giannini decided to leave school after the eighth grade and go to work for his stepfather. "The old waterfront commission business was a pretty stiff school for men," he remembered long afterward. "I used to study them down there and I suppose I picked up the knack of sizing up men."

It quickly turned out that he, too, had what it took to make a great broker. In the summer of 1887, when he was only seventeen, Giannini felt sure that there would be a shortage of pears that autumn. How he knew this is not recorded, but he persuaded his stepfather to trust him on a buying trip to the Sacramento Valley, where he promptly bought up all the pears he could get his hands on for future delivery. It was a huge gamble, but he was right and the price of pears climbed and climbed as the autumn advanced, until the firm cleared a profit of $50,000 on pears alone that year.

Not surprisingly, Giannini was soon in charge of all buying trips into the Sacramento Valley. And he quickly demonstrated that other requirement for economic success, the capacity for hard work. "I used to take a loaf of bread and a big Italian cheese along with me for my lunch and supper," he said. "I never aimed to arrive at a place when they were having meals. It would have meant a serious loss of time."

Giannini soon proved himself indispensable. In 1889 his stepfather gave him a one-third interest in the business and two years later raised it to one-half. In 1892 he married Clorinda Cuneo, the daughter of an Italian immigrant who had made a fortune in real estate. By the turn of the century Giannini was a rich man by the standards of the day. He had income from investments of about $250 a month, plus his half-interest in his stepfather's firm. That, Giannini decided, was enough. "I don't want to be rich," he said. "No man actually owns a fortune; it owns him." He sold his interest in the family firm to a group of employees for $100,000, and at the ripe old age of thirty-one, retired.

But the following year his father-in-law died intestate, and the family asked Giannini to handle the estate, which amounted to about $500,000. Giannini took over his father-in-law's seat on the board of the Columbus Savings and Loan Society, a small bank located in North Beach, San Francisco's Little Italy. Giannini quickly noticed that a competitor, the Italian-American Bank, was growing rapidly by catering to small borrowers.

When the board of directors refused to go after this business—which very few banks at that time regarded as worth pursuing at all—he, along with five other directors, resigned. They and others, including Giannini's stepfather, founded the Bank of Italy in 1904, which opened in a converted saloon, capitalized at $300,000.

From the first, the Bank of Italy was what today is called a full-service bank, providing both savings and commercial checking accounts, while encouraging small loans, some as small as $25. Giannini realized that if he was to enlarge his loan business, he would have to enlarge his deposits. To do so, he used the same tactics he had employed so successfully buying fruits and vegetables. He walked the streets of North Beach, schmoozed with recent immigrants in his fluent Italian, and persuaded them to move their small savings from the mattress to his bank. It worked. In December 1904, loans amounted to $178,400 and deposits $134,413. One year later the figures were $883,522 and $703,024.

The rapid increases in deposits and loans continued until the morning of April 18, 1906, when Giannini, asleep in his suburban San Mateo house, was thrown out of bed by the force of the San Francisco earthquake. After making sure his family was safe (his wife was expecting their eighth child), Giannini set out for San Francisco, traveling the seventeen miles by the only means available, on foot. He found a city in ruins and the raging fires that would consume much that survived the quake. He had small hopes for his bank but was delighted to find it largely undamaged.

However, the fire was quickly headed toward the bank. "I figured," Giannini said, that "we had about two hours to get out of there." He managed to commandeer two wagons and loaded them up with the bank's furniture, records, and, most important, money. Knowing that looters would have a field day if they ever sensed what the wagons were carrying, he piled crates of oranges on top and made it safely back to San Mateo, although the money smelled of orange juice for weeks afterward.

The next day, Giannini returned to find his bank a charred ruin, as, indeed, was most of North Beach, where fewer than 300 of the 4,000 buildings survived. Also in ruins was San Francisco's banking industry. The governor had declared a bank holiday, and many bankers expected it to last weeks. But the Bank of Italy opened almost immediately, offering loans to help rebuild. Giannini, who instinctively understood the immense power of symbolism, put a notice in the *San Francisco Chronicle*, set a desk out on the sidewalk at the Washington Street wharf with a bag of gold prominently displayed, and hung a banner announcing this to be the Bank of Italy's temporary quarters.

But while Giannini could only react brilliantly to an earthquake, the following year, when the financial earthquake called the panic of 1907 swept the country, he was prepared. Anticipating it, Giannini had been quietly hoarding gold, and when the crisis came he let it be known that he was ready and able to pay gold to all who wanted to withdraw their money. He stacked bags of it behind the tellers' windows for everyone to see, and as a result, of course, few demanded their money. "Mr. Giannini and his Bank of Italy," reported the *San Francisco News*, "were once again the talk of San Francisco."

In 1909 California adopted a law, pushed by Woodrow Wilson, among others, that allowed banks to branch throughout the state as long as the state superintendent of banks agreed that it was in the public interest. With a reputation no money could buy, earned in the earthquake and the panic, there was no one better placed to take advantage of this opportunity to create a banking empire than he. And he seized it. In less than ten years, the Bank of Italy had twenty-four branches throughout California and was the fourth-largest bank in terms of assets in the state. By the end of the 1920s, with the name changed to the Bank of America, it was one of the largest banks in the country.

Giannini withdrew from day-to-day management in the 1920s, but when the new management tried to sell off some branches in response to the onset of the Great Depression, he waged a proxy fight to regain control in 1932 and did so. Once more running the show, he got his beloved bank through the banking crisis of March 1933 unscathed and undiminished. Indeed, it was once more poised for expansion, doubling in assets in the next six years.

When Giannini died in 1947, true to his beliefs, expressed when he had "retired" at age thirty-one, he left no great fortune, only about $500,000. What he did leave behind was what was then, and for many years afterward, the largest bank in the world, a bank that had grown to greatness on the once-radical notion of providing banking services to ordinary citizens.

POLITICIANS VERSUS BANKERS

Democracy is usually a slow and almost always messy business. Not infrequently, good politics trumps good policy in the process.

On Friday, November 12, for instance, President Clinton signed the Banking Act of 1999 into law. It allows banks, insurance companies, and brokerage houses to compete with great freedom across state lines and merge with each other to form financial conglomerates. In ten years, the bank at the corner will be as likely to be owned by Merrill Lynch or Aetna as by Chase Manhattan. It will be possible for a family to get only one monthly statement that covers its cash deposits, investments, life insurance, and other monetary assets. And that statement is likely to arrive via the Internet rather than the post office.

The law that makes this new American financial world possible took decades to achieve, and there was much blood on the floor in Washington before it passed. Indeed, the bill is no less than the *twelfth* serious attempt to overhaul banking law since the last major change in the depths of the Great Depression, but the only one to make it all the way through to the president's desk.

When you think about it, that is a monument to the power of the status quo in a democracy. The large city banks and brokerage houses long pushed for change, but the small country banks and S&Ls naturally preferred things as they were in their protected local markets. Insurance companies, often as powerful and far-reaching as the major banks and brokers but largely (and cozily) regulated at the state level, also feared change. Meanwhile, Thomas Jefferson's hatred of banks and commerce still reverberated in the halls of Capitol Hill, despite two hundred years of industrial revolution.

The banking law that was finally replaced, usually known as the Glass–

Steagall Act after its principal congressional architects, was equally the product of a messy process, but not, for once, a slow one. Indeed, it was only the last of many bills enacted during the so-called Hundred Days at the start of the New Deal.

And while only time will tell whether politics trumped policy in the new banking act, there is no doubt that it did in the last one. It greatly weakened the country's strongest banks while protecting the weakest ones from market forces by maintaining restrictions on competition.

Few alive today are old enough to remember the American banking system before Glass–Steagall. While there were many large and powerful banks in the United States, including J. P. Morgan & Co., arguably the most powerful bank that has ever existed, most American banks were small one-branch affairs located in small towns. In 1921 there were no fewer than 29,788 of them, more banks than in the rest of the world put together.

But small one-branch banks are, ipso facto, weak banks. During the 1920s, when the apparent prosperity was confined largely to the cities, these small banks failed at a rate that averaged 550 a year. When the Great Depression struck, the failure rate rose sickeningly. There were 1,300 failures in 1930, 2,000 in 1931, and a terrifying 5,700—more than twenty percent of all the banks in the country—in 1932. With each bank failure the hopes and security of hundreds or thousands of families failed too, and the psychology of depression deepened its grip on the land.

Meanwhile, the great Wall Street banks, who had ridden so high in the 1920s and were still financially sound despite the depression, had seen their reputations sullied by revelations of wrongdoing during the boom years. This moved popular opinion sharply against them. Their power to affect legislation was thus greatly weakened. With the advent of the New Deal, the Senate Banking Committee began holding hearings to investigate, in Roosevelt's words, "all the ramifications of bad banking."[1] The committee's counsel, Ferdinand Pecora, set about the task with relish, at least with regards to the large banks.

What he found made headlines over and over. To give just one example out of dozens, he uncovered the actions of Albert Wiggin, who was president of Chase National Bank (a forerunner of today's Chase Manhattan) in the 1920s and who sat on no fewer than fifty-nine corporate boards.[2] In the summer of 1929 Wiggin, sensing the coming crash, shorted

Chase stock to the extent of 42,000 shares. This was perfectly legal at the time, but of course, it put his own interests 180 degrees around from those of the stockholders, who paid him a colossal $275,000 a year to look after *their* interests. To add insult to injury, Wiggin, in order to finance the short sale, had taken out a large loan from . . . Chase National Bank.

With many of the small country banks still deep in financial disarray and the great money-center banks deeply politically wounded by the Pecora hearings, Congress set about to write a new banking law. It was largely three men who determined the lay of the American financial landscape for decades.

President Roosevelt, an eastern aristocrat with exquisitely sensitive political instincts but few ideological or economic convictions, had little use for the small-town bankers, most of whom were politically well-connected with Congress and, outside the South, Republican. The President favored a national banking system that would effectively put these bankers and their financially weak but politically strong banks out of business.

Senator Carter Glass of Virginia was an advocate of limited government (he opposed most of the New Deal), and actually a firm friend of Wall Street. When Roosevelt, before his inauguration, approached Glass about becoming Secretary of the Treasury again (he had served in that office under President Wilson), Glass said he wanted to take two Morgan partners, Russell Leffingwell and Parker Gilbert, with him. Roosevelt couldn't buy that. "We simply can't tie up with 23," he said, referring to the Morgan Bank's Wall Street address.[3]

Glass, too, favored developing a national banking system, with institutions strong enough to survive bad times. When he had first been elected to the House, in 1902, and assigned to the House Banking Committee. He had been ignorant of both economics (to his later embarrassment he had supported William Jennings Bryan in 1896) and banking. However, he was a very quick study and was soon a leading authority in Congress on both economic and banking issues. He would become the most important congressional influence on banking law in the first half of the twentieth century. In 1913, by then Chairman of the House Banking Committee, Glass was responsible for the legislation creating the Federal Reserve. For the rest of his life he took pride in being called "the father of the Federal Reserve System."[4]

Appointed to a vacant seat in the Senate in 1920, he would remain there for the rest of his life. But while friendly with Wall Street, even Glass recognized the reality of Wall Street's reputation in 1933. Antiblack even by the standards of the Jim Crow South, he wisecracked that, "One banker in my state attempted to marry a white woman and they lynched him."[5]

The third major force was Henry B. Steagall, the son of a prosperous doctor, who practiced law in Ozark, Alabama, before moving into politics. Elected to Congress in 1914, at the age of forty-one, he would remain in the House of Representatives until his death in 1943. Steagall was much more a legislative technician than an economic thinker. And he was deeply concerned with protecting the interests of people, and bankers, from areas such as his own native, and deeply rural, Dale County, Alabama. His main interest was in ending the runs that had devastated so many small banks and the small towns they served.

His proposed means for doing so was deposit insurance. The idea was that, by assuring depositors that their money was not at risk should the bank fail, they would not rush to withdraw their funds at the first rumor of trouble, giving weak banks time to get their affairs in order and sparing sound banks the devastating effects of a run.

Deposit insurance was opposed by many, including the American Bankers' Association, Carter Glass, and President Roosevelt himself. The bankers opposed the idea because they would have to pay insurance premiums, but Roosevelt opposed it because of the "moral hazard" such insurance created. Roosevelt thought that insuring deposits "puts a premium on sloppy banking and penalizes good banking."[6]

But if Roosevelt personally opposed deposit insurance, his political antenna, picking up every whisper of public opinion, persuaded him to go along with it. Steagall, with the help of a flood of supporting letters and Republican senator Arthur Vandenberg of Michigan, was thus able to make the creation of the FDIC one of the major provisions of the Glass–Steagall bill. He was certainly right that it would cure the problem of bank runs; there has not been a serious one since. But Roosevelt was also right about the moral hazard. Much enlarged and extended, deposit insurance would be a major cause of the S&L debacle of the late 1980s.

The concept of deposit insurance created another problem besides moral hazard, however. The major banks were usually both depository banks and investment banks. In other words they were in the securities business as well as the banking business. And while deposit insurance was very popular, no one wanted to insure the securities affiliates of these banks.

The only solution was to command the separation of deposit and investment banking. The big banks fought this tooth and nail. The Morgan Bank pointed out that the already passed Securities Act of 1933 had corrected most of the poor practices that investment banks used in the 1920s, such as concealing loans to companies and countries whose bonds they underwrote. It was also argued that, divorced from commercial banking, investment banks would be capital poor, and thus vulnerable in bad times. This turned out often to be the case.

But no one was listening to bankers, especially big bankers, back then. As Morgan partner Russell Leffingwell explained, "There is so much hunger and distress that it is only natural for the people to blame the bankers and to visit their wrath on the greatest name in American banking."[7]

That great name in American banking, J. P. Morgan and Company, had to spin-off Morgan, Stanley under the new law. It was never quite the same again. Meanwhile, the countless small institutions that dotted the landscape in the thousands survived, ensuring that the American banking system would remain the most trouble-prone in the world, even as the American economy reached new heights.

PART VI

THE BUSINESS
OF WAR

USS *PORK BARREL*

MANY HISTORIANS HAVE ARGUED that, whatever their function in the state religion, the pyramids of Egypt were also politically useful make-work projects. By employing peasants during the season when the Nile flooded the fields, pyramid building provided an income to the poor and thus helped secure political tranquillity for those in power. If this is the case (and Egyptology is hardly my field), the pyramids are not only one of the seven wonders of the ancient world but the earliest surviving government pork-barrel projects as well.

Despite the ancient history of the concept, however, the term itself is at least 4,500 years younger than the pyramids. *Pork barrel* first entered the American language only in 1904, when the Republicans were in the ascendant. Given the phrase's southern origin (it refers to the custom of regularly handing out joints of salted pork, stored in barrels, to each slave family on a plantation), it is highly likely that it is a Democratic coinage. Thirty years later, during the New Deal, *boondoggle* came into English, doubtless courtesy of disgruntled—and now out-of-office—Republicans.

By their nature, of course, these terms are employed by politicians only when their own constituents are not beneficiaries. Some such phrase as "vital national project" is preferred by the rest. And here's the rub. At least since the end of the age of the god-kings, a real, or apparent, utility has been a sine qua non of every well-designed vital national/pork-barrel project. That's why the true motivation behind so many has been impossible to ascertain, at least until the dust of history settles.

Complicating matters still further, many projects that start out clearly justified by circumstances turn into pure pork barrel when circumstances change but the projects roll on relentlessly anyway. For one very early

example, consider the navy's ship-of-the-line program that followed the
War of 1812.

Ships of the line were so called because they were large enough and
powerful enough to stand in the line of battle and slug it out with any ship
afloat. For 200 years they were the ultimate instrument of naval power.

By the mid–eighteenth century the standard ship of the line carried 74
guns and required a crew of about 700 men to sail and fight them. A few
behemoths carried as many as 100 guns on four decks. HMS *Victory*, the
most famous ship of the line ever built, is one of these so-called first
raters. Being the largest and most powerful ships, ships of the line were,
of course, also the most expensive to build and to operate, especially given
the fact that they were intended to function only as a part of a fleet of
similar vessels.

When the American navy came into existence during the Revolution,
it was, naturally, almost entirely an improvised affair of privateers and
converted merchant ships. One ship of the line, however, was built. Called
the *America*, she was launched at Portsmouth, New Hampshire, in 1782,
one year after the war had effectively ended at the siege of Yorktown. Far
too expensive for the nearly bankrupt Confederation government to operate, she was immediately given to the French navy to replace a ship that
had been lost in Boston harbor, thanks to an incompetent local pilot.

Indeed, from 1785 until 1797 the new United States had no navy at all.
But in 1794, with war raging in Europe and our relations with both France
and Great Britain deteriorating, Congress authorized the construction of
six frigates, and the navy was born again, this time permanently. Frigates
were smaller than ships of the line and far better sailors than the lubberly
battleships. They were intended primarily for showing the flag, commerce
raiding, and reconnaissance.

Although money was appropriated for six ships of the line in 1799,
and material for their construction gathered—a lengthy process because
trees of exactly the right size and shape had to be located—they were
never built. It was frigates that would give the U.S. Navy its first taste of
glory.

But although the victories of the American frigates early in the War
of 1812 were a cause of national rejoicing, they didn't affect the vastly
larger Royal Navy's control of the seas one bit. British fleets sealed off

American ports and brought American foreign trade to a standstill. The U.S. Navy was powerless to do anything about this, for it lacked the one thing capable of attacking ships of the line: ships of the line.

Six months after war was declared, with the British noose tightening inexorably around American commerce, Congress authorized the building of four ships of the line, utilizing the materials already gathered for such a purpose. None of these could be completed before the war ended, and one, built for use on Lake Ontario, was never completed at all.

With the return of peace, Congress determined that the navy needed a fleet of ships of the line to defend the country in any future war with Great Britain. It could not hope to match the Royal Navy ship for ship, of course, but any reasonable fleet in being would vastly complicate British strategic planning in the event of war. Moreover, skillfully handled and with the home-ground advantage, such a fleet might well have at least temporarily broken any British blockade.

So Congress, on April 29, 1816, "authorized to cause to be built, nine ships to rate not less than 74 guns each." All nine were eventually laid down, in shipyards ranging from Portsmouth, New Hampshire, to Norfolk, Virginia, and four of them were completed in a timely manner by the end of 1820. None of these ships ever saw action, of course, but the world had entered into an extended era of peace.

As the risk of a naval war diminished nearly to the vanishing point in the years after the War of 1812, and as the industrial revolution ended the age of sail, the five remaining ships in the program lost all military justification but not, of course, their pork-barrel potential to provide construction jobs. Indeed, their history is so laden with pork, it positively oinks.

Although work on them slowed to a crawl (it was usually heavily concentrated in the few weeks preceding elections), only one was ever actually canceled. The USS *Virginia*, laid down in Boston in 1822, was finally broken up uncompleted in 1839, having cost the taxpayers $197,400. (To put that figure in perspective, the navy's budget in 1839 was only slightly over $6 million.)

The USS *Alabama* was the only ship of the five not to be started in an election year, work beginning in 1817 in Portsmouth. She lay on the stocks for a world-record forty-seven years, however, before finally being launched in 1864, two years after the battle between the *Monitor* and the

Merrimac had demonstrated beyond a doubt that the days of fighting sail were over. (The *Alabama,* understandably enough under the circumstances, was launched as the USS *New Hampshire.*)

The *New York,* started in Norfolk in 1818, was burned, still un-launched, by retreating federal forces in 1861. And the *Vermont,* laid down in Boston in 1822, was launched only in 1853. No sooner did she have water under her keel at last than she was mothballed for eight years. At least she was the only one of the five to see action after a fashion, serving in the blockading squadron off Port Royal, South Carolina, during the Civil War.

But the fattest, juiciest, most nourishing ham in this whole barrel was the USS *Pennsylvania.* When Congress specified only that these ships be "not less than 74 guns," the Board of Naval Commissioners, the policy-setting arm of the navy, saw a political opening of irresistible potential. They ordered up a leviathan.

The *Pennsylvania* had gun ports for no fewer than 136 guns, 36 more than *Victory* herself had carried into the Battle of Trafalgar. At 3,366 tons, she was the largest wooden warship ever built in the United States, by far, and by some measures the largest ever built anywhere. Laid down in 1822, she monopolized the resources of the Philadelphia Naval Yard for the next fifteen years, like a cuckoo hatchling in a wren's nest. Fully armed, the *Pennsylvania* would have needed a crew of at least 1,100 men to fight her. Yet in the year she was begun, the personnel of the entire navy was only 3,774.

But she never fought. In fact, she hardly ever sailed. Finally completed in 1837, she proceeded down the Delaware River, stopped briefly in New-castle, Delaware, to pick up gun carriages, and then sailed on to the Nor-folk Naval Yard in Virginia. Her skeleton crew was immediately trans-ferred to other vessels, and she never again spread an inch of the 33,000 square yards of canvas she was designed to carry. She was burned to the waterline in 1861 during the ignominious federal retreat from Norfolk.

Even in her one week's sail down the Atlantic seaboard, her officers found her "cumbersome, leewardly, and crank." This is hardly surprising given her size and the fact that she was, in a very real sense, a sea-going pyramid, not a warship at all.

But if the first *Pennsylvania* was, at best, an embarrassment to demo-cratic government, her twentieth-century namesake redeemed the honor of the name. Commissioned in 1916, the second USS *Pennsylvania* saw no action for twenty-five years until she survived the disaster at Pearl Harbor. In the next three and a half years, however, her great guns hurled fully 5,500 tons of shells at the enemy, more than any other battleship in the history of naval warfare.

PAYING FOR THE WAR

WARS ARE FOUGHT WITH silver bullets. While individual battles are decided by tactics, firepower, courage, and—of course—luck, victory in the long haul of war has almost always gone to the side better able to turn the national wealth to military purposes.

As it happened, the American Civil War was the first great conflict of the industrial era. Indeed it was the greatest military event of the nineteenth century, fought on a scale previously unimagined, and foreshadowed the desperate global struggles of the early twentieth century. As a result, both sides confronted wholly new fiscal demands and had to invent new ways to finance them without wrecking their domestic economies in the process. The fact that the North succeeded in coping with expenses of this magnitude, and the South did not, played no small part in the eventual outcome.

At first, both sides confronted desperate financial problems. The government in Washington had been operating in the red for nearly four years, borrowing mostly short-term to make up the deficit. In December 1860, as the Deep South voted for secession, there was not enough money in the federal Treasury even to pay the salaries of congressmen, let alone fund a great war.

To our jaded ears, the actual sums involved sound trivial. But in mid-nineteenth-century America, $1,000 was a skilled worker's annual wage, and the entire GNP was well under $10 billion. The cost of the Civil War, to those who lived through it, was staggering. At the outbreak of the war, federal spending in all departments was running at only $172,000 a day, raised almost entirely from tariffs. Three months later, war expenses alone were eating up $1 million a day. By the end of 1861, War Department daily spending was up to $1.5 million. Confederate spending was less, but equally unprecedented.

How could these expenses be met? In both peace and war a government generally has only three ways to raise money. It can print, tax, and borrow.

Both sides quickly resorted to the printing press. In December 1861, northern banks had to stop paying their debts in gold, and the federal government was forced to follow suit a few days later. The country had gone off the gold standard, and Wall Street panicked. "The bottom is out of the tub," Lincoln lamented. "What shall I do?" Soon the Treasury was authorized to issue greenbacks, as the new paper money was called, and by 1865 there would be a total of $450 million in circulation.

The consequences of issuing large quantities of fiat money—money that is money only because the government says it is money—are inevitable, and they were as well known then as they are now. First, Gresham's law ("Bad money drives out good") comes into play, and gold and silver disappear into mattresses. Second, inflation takes off.

Four hundred and fifty million dollars amounted to about 13 percent of total government expenses during the war, and greenbacks contributed substantially to the steep wartime inflation in the North. But that inflation was nothing compared to what the South suffered as a result of paying *more than half* of its bills with paper money. As early as May 1861, the Confederacy was issuing Treasury notes that would only be redeemable in gold and silver two years after independence was achieved. During the war, the Confederate government issued over $1.5 billion of these notes, and the effect of this flood of printing-press money on the southern economy was catastrophic. In the first two years alone prices rose more than 700 percent in the South. To make matters worse, the government in Richmond was not the only one printing "money," and state and city governments also issued notes. Because the South lacked good paper mills and elaborate printing facilities, counterfeiting was both easy and widespread. By the end of 1863 the southern economy had spun out of control. Hoarding, shortages, and black markets spread relentlessly, while support for the war eroded as living standards fell.

The South issued so much paper money because its ability both to tax the population and to sell bonds was severely limited. The North had an established Treasury and a revenue-gathering system, with bureaucracy and procedures already in place. The South had to start from scratch. That was no easy task amid the screaming demands of war. Worse, the South suffered from an economy notoriously lacking in liquidity. Wealth, in other words, could not be easily translated into money and spent on military power. While the South had 30 percent of the country's total assets at the outbreak of the war, it had only 12 percent of the circulating currency and 21 percent of the banking assets. The word *land-poor* would not be invented until Reconstruction days, but it perfectly described the southern economy in 1861. In the four years of the war, the Confederate government was able to meet only 5 to 6 percent of its expenses with tax revenues.

The federal government, in contrast, raised fully 21 percent of its total revenues by taxation. The first federal income tax was enacted as early as August 1861, and the Internal Revenue Act, which taxed nearly everything, from professional licenses to newspaper advertisements to yachts, followed in 1862. The Bureau of Internal Revenue was the ancestor of today's IRS, by no means the least of the country's enduring legacies from the Civil War.

The third means of raising revenues, loans, also worked to the advantage of the North, thanks to its large banks and to one banker in particular, Jay Cooke of Philadelphia.

Jay Cooke was born in what would later be called Sandusky, Ohio, in 1821, the son of a lawyer and congressman. He went to work as a clerk when he was fourteen and soon ended up in the Philadelphia banking house of Enoch W. Clark. In 1861, just as the war began, Cooke opened his own bank in Philadelphia, Jay Cooke and Company.

Cooke's younger brother, Henry, had close political connections with Salmon P. Chase, Ohio senator and governor and Lincoln's first secretary of the Treasury. The younger Cooke saw to it that his brother got to handle a $2-million bond issue for Chase.

After the disastrous First Battle of Bull Run in the summer of 1861, Cooke "put on his hat, left his office and, visiting the bankers of Philadelphia, in a few hours collected over $2,000,000 on the security of three-year treasury notes."

A few days later Cooke accompanied Secretary Chase to New York and helped the embattled secretary raise an additional $50 million from bankers there, pending the issuance of government bonds paying 7.3 percent interest. (The interest rate of these bonds, the so-called seven-thirties, was chosen, apparently by Chase, for no better reason than that they would pay two cents a day in interest for every $100 face value.)

Fifty million dollars was a huge underwriting for the banks of those days, but a drop in the bucket compared with what Chase realized would be needed. The national debt had stood at $64 million on July 1, 1860, and a year later had risen to nearly $91 million. Chase estimated that by July 1, 1862, the national debt would be $517 million.

Government debt had been handled until then by quietly placing bonds with the major bankers and brokers, who either held them in their reserves or sold them to their largest customers. Clearly a new system was needed, and Jay Cooke devised it.

Cooke was made the agent of the federal government to sell five-twenty bonds (so called because they could be redeemed in not less than five years nor more than twenty; meanwhile they paid 6 percent interest, in gold). He advertised the bonds widely in newspapers and handbills. He had the Treasury offer the bonds in denominations as low as fifty dollars and accepted payment on the installment plan. He deliberately tried to involve the little guy and make him feel that buying government bonds was not only his patriotic duty but a good investment for his own future as well. Jay Cooke invented the bond drive, a major feature of every great war since.

Before the Civil War far less than 1 percent of the population had owned any securities whatever. Cooke sold government bonds to about 5 percent of the northern population. According to John Sherman, an influential senator from Ohio (and General William T. Sherman's younger brother), Cooke made the virtues of these bonds stare "in the face of the people in every household from Maine to California."

Not content with advertising, Cooke planted stories in newspapers. "Here is a letter from a lady in Camden who orders $300," ran one story called "A Day at the Agency for the Five-Twenty Loan." "There is one from St. Paul, Minn, for $12,500. . . . Near one of the desks is a nursery maid who wants a bond for $50 and just behind her placidly waiting his turn is a portly gentleman, one of the 'solid men' of Philadelphia, at whom you can scarcely look without having visions of plethoric pocketbooks and heavy balances in bank. He wants $25,000."

In May 1864 Cooke was selling war bonds so successfully that he was actually raising money as fast as the War Department could spend it, about $2 million a day at this point. Altogether the North raised fully two-thirds of its revenues by selling bonds. The South, with few large banks and little financial expertise, could raise less than 40 percent of its revenues by this means.

Cooke's successful bond drive caused a breathtaking rise in the U.S. national debt. In 1857, before the onset of the depression, the debt had stood at a minuscule ninety-three cents per person. Eight years later it had grown by a factor of eighty and stood at seventy-five dollars per person, a height it would not reach again until World War I. But because the North could throw so much of the cost of the war onto the future, which the South could not, its economy remained intact, able to churn out the war matériel that finally overwhelmed the rebellion.

Confederate paper money and bonds, of course, died with the Confederacy, but the greenbacks and the national debt went on and on. Whether and when to return to the gold standard was, second only to Reconstruction, the leading issue in national politics after the war. Debtors wanted more, not less, paper money for its inflationary effects, whereas creditors, naturally, wanted "sound money." The latter eventually prevailed, and greenbacks became redeemable in gold in 1879. But they wouldn't be fully legal tender until 1933, and there was a Greenback Party candidate for president as late as 1944.

THE ARMOR-PLATE
SCANDAL

ECONOMISTS FROM ADAM SMITH on have written about the evils and dislocations that monopolies bring to an economy. For more than 100 years, since the passage of the Sherman Antitrust Act, the Smithian ideal has been written into American law with mostly very beneficial results. It is only too bad that the Sherman Act doesn't apply to government monopolies, which are only now beginning to come under sustained political attack.

What has been much less written about over the years, however, are the evils of monopsony.

In the interest of saving wear and tear on the nation's dictionaries, let me hasten to offer a definition. A monopoly is any entity that effectively controls the supply of a commodity, such as petroleum in the case of Standard Oil or driver's licenses in the case of state motor vehicle departments. A monopsony, on the other hand, controls the total *demand* for a commodity.

Obviously monopsonies are much rarer than monopolies. The only one I ever enjoyed happened many years ago when I was traveling in Greece. A photographer, quite unasked, snapped pictures of the members of a tour I was on amid the ruins of Delphi. The next morning he went from table to table in the hotel dining room, offering 8×10 glossies at outrageous prices and doing a brisk business.

When he came to me, however, I told him I'd give him one-tenth his asking price for the photos he had taken of me. He indignantly refused, so I suggested he call up the newspapers and see what *they* would pay for pictures of an utterly unfamous college student walking around Delphi with a guidebook in his hand. He took the money I offered him, turned over the pictures, and said something in Greek that would probably lose nothing in translation.

Monopsonies can have large-scale pernicious effects for much the same reasons as monopolies: They prevent the determination of real prices while their possessors invariably come to abuse their power. And like most monopolies nowadays, monopsonies tend strongly to be government ones. State textbook boards are one example. The African government food cooperatives that farmers must sell to, and that have devastated the agriculture of much of the continent as a result, are another.

But the greatest monopsonies are military in nature. After all, how many customers are there for, say, nuclear missile submarines? Mercifully, perhaps, there is only one, and Electric Boat sells to the navy or it doesn't sell at all.

These military monopsonies are nothing new. One hundred years ago, when battleships, not nuclear submarines, were the measure of naval power, the government had a thirty-year dispute with the country's steel makers over armor plate. It's an instructive tale.

The battle between the *Monitor* and the *Merrimac* in 1862 had spelled the doom of wooden navies. By the 1880s the monitor form had evolved into the battleship, armed with the biggest guns afloat and protected by belts of armor plate. The U.S. Navy, however, had quickly shriveled to insignificance after the Civil War and bought what little armor plate it required from abroad. Then Chester Arthur's administration decided to expand the navy, and it wanted domestic sources to ensure a supply in case of war.

The steel manufacturers, already expanding rapidly to meet exploding demand for steel railroad rails and structural elements, were not interested in building the highly specialized plants that could only manufacture armor. Why should they have been? Demand was subject to the vagaries of politics, the navy would be virtually the only customer, and the technology was very difficult to handle, even by the demanding standards of steel manufacture. Because of inevitable variations in the distribution of impurities and in cooling, each batch of armor plate varied considerably in tensile strength and resistance to penetration.

Nevertheless, both Andrew Carnegie and Bethlehem Iron Company, under government prodding, began to construct armor plants. Carnegie, however, suspended construction when navy bureaucrats insisted that government inspectors be present during every phase of manufacturing and that rigid specifications for the very factors that were inherently difficult or impossible to control be adhered to. Carnegie thought, quite correctly, that the only thing that really mattered was the armor's resistance to gunfire and therefore that a ballistics test should be the sole criterion by which the navy should judge his armor plates.

Bethlehem continued to construct its armor plant but, with far smaller resources than Carnegie, soon ran into financial trouble and had to delay completion. So President Benjamin Harrison personally appealed to Carnegie to resume construction of his armor-plate mill at the Homestead Works, and he did so.

By 1892 it was in operation, producing armor for the cruiser USS *Monterrey* and the battleship USS *New York*. But the great Homestead strike of that year ended production for a time, and when it resumed after the strike failed, disaffection among the workers was, understandably, intense.

The following year, an attorney representing four of the workers went to Carnegie's partner, Henry Clay Frick, whose actions had been mainly responsible for the strike, and offered to sell him "evidence" of fraud on the part of the company in fulfilling its armor contracts. Frick—the very opposite and then some of a wuss—sent the lawyer for what he called the "vermillion-hued" workers packing. But the lawyer then went to the government, which agreed to give the men 25 percent of any fines levied on the basis of their evidence.

The government proceeded to name a three-man board of inquiry, which investigated the matter using only the information supplied by the informants. Not surprisingly, the board submitted a report finding the company guilty. But the first that the Carnegie Steel Company knew of the inquiry was when Frick was summoned to Washington to be told that the navy intended to levy a fine equal to 15 percent of the value of the contract.

It was, of course, a classic star-chamber proceeding, and both Frick and Carnegie were outraged. They appealed to President Grover Cleveland. Cleveland, a Democrat, did not want to seem to be supporting the company responsible for the Homestead strike against his own secretary of the navy. But as a lawyer himself, he realized that the company had gotten nothing resembling justice. He reduced the fine to only 10 percent. But that still amounted to $140,484.94, no small sum in the 1890s.

The nub of the navy's case was that while just three of the plates thus far delivered had been below specifications and therefore rejected, most of the rest had been only 5 percent better than specified, and a few were 20 percent above grade. In the navy's logic, if that is the word, since some of the plates were 20 percent above what the contract called for, all of the plates should have been that good.

Only a bureaucrat profoundly ignorant of the practical difficulties of making uniform armor plate could have decided this was fraud. And much that might appear to have been genuine fraud was, in fact, only an attempt—an extremely ill-advised one, to be sure—to protect the navy from itself.

For instance, the contract called for armor plate with no blow holes, holes caused by uneven cooling. In congressional hearings, Charles Schwab, then the superintendent of the Homestead Works, testified that they were inevitable in first-class armor plate and that while they could be easily prevented by adding silicon to the metal, that would have weakened the whole plate. What did the navy want, he asked in effect, strong armor with blow holes or weak armor with none? He pointed out that the German firm Krupp, the leading armor manufacturer in the world, had exhibited its very best armor plates at the Chicago World's Fair of 1892 and that they had been full of blow holes.

Charles Schwab was a man much given to getting the job done now and worrying about nitpicking rules later. To give the navy the best armor plate, but without blow holes, he had simply patched them when the government inspectors had not been around to object.

The Carnegie company could have gone to court and might have won. But Carnegie and Frick, all too aware of the government's monopsony power, knew that any delay in paying the fine might be grounds for the navy's canceling the contract, leaving them with masses of armor plate and no one to sell it to. They also feared that the navy might well never give them another contract, and they would be stuck with an armor plant with no customer. As practical businessmen, they swallowed their pride and paid the fine.

Matters returned to normal, and the Carnegie Steel Company, part of U.S. Steel beginning in 1901, got its share of armor contracts from the government as the country built itself into a world-class naval power after the turn of the twentieth century.

But when Woodrow Wilson's administration came to office in 1913, it was perturbed by the fact that the bids for contracts by the handful of companies that could produce armor plate were often nearly identical. The reason was simple enough. The navy was afraid that if it awarded an entire contract to the lowest bidder, less efficient companies might drop out of the armor-plate business and the country would not have an adequate supply in wartime. So it made a practice of giving all the companies an equal share of any large contract, provided they met the lowest price. With no incentive to bid low, no company did so.

Josephus Daniels, Wilson's secretary of the navy, thought the solution was a government armor plant. Congress appropriated the money after a navy report estimated that a plant with a yearly 10,000-ton capacity could be built for $8.4 million and could produce armor for only $314 a ton, while the steel manufacturers were then being paid $454 a ton.

The steel companies, hardly happy about the idea of the government, already a monopsony for armor plate, becoming a competitor as well, fought the project tooth and nail. But they needn't have worried. When the plant was finally finished, three years after World War I ended, it was millions over budget and could not produce armor for less than nearly double what the steel companies charged. The plant was shut down after one batch of armor plates was produced, and never reopened.

For the last 100 years leftist historians have been regularly dredging up the "armor-plate scandal" as an example of capitalist greed at its worse. What it really is, of course, is one more example of government incompetence both as a customer and as a manufacturer.

THE AMERICAN
SUPERWEAPON

IN A FIRESIDE CHAT on December 29, 1940, Franklin Roosevelt called upon the country to become the "arsenal of democracy," a phrase that would prove enduring.

The president, coaxing a still deeply antiwar country toward what he thought its real self-interests to be, wanted American industry to gear up for war production in order to help those countries fighting the Nazis and the Japanese. He presented the idea as the best way for the United States to remain neutral. Within a year, of course, Japan made the case for neutrality moot, and the United States needed weapons for itself as well as for those who were now its allies.

When Roosevelt made the speech, the arsenal was largely empty. The navy, to be sure, was the equal of any in terms of ships, but it lacked the munitions to fight for any extended time and much of its equipment was old or unreliable. The army had only 300,000 men, and what equipment it had was so antiquated that George C. Marshall wrote that its status had been reduced to "that of a third-rate power." Many of the recruits who entered the army as a result of the Selective Service Act passed in September 1940 had to drill with broomsticks instead of rifles.

But the arsenal did not stay empty for long. Just four and a half years after the phrase was coined, the United States had 12 million men under arms. Its navy was larger than all other navies in the world combined; its air force ruled the skies of the entire globe. In those years American industry turned out 6,500 naval vessels; 296,400 airplanes; 86,330 tanks; 64,546 landing craft; 3.5 million jeeps, trucks, and personnel carriers; 53 million deadweight tons of cargo vessels; 12 million rifles, carbines, and machine guns; and 47 million tons of artillery shells.

The United States accomplished this astonishing industrial feat by turning the world's greatest free-market economy, virtually overnight, into a centrally planned one. Centrally planned economies have always proved dismally inefficient at producing goods and services wanted by consumers, but they have done far better producing the instruments of war. The Soviet Union couldn't manufacture adequate examples of some of the simplest consumer items (locally produced condoms, for instance, were known in the Russian vernacular as "galoshes"). Their nuclear-powered missile submarines, however, were highly respected examples of the most complex machines ever developed. When total war had to be fought, total control of the economy was essential.

When Roosevelt had first moved to put the economy on a wartime footing, he relied on the alphabet soup that had been so much a part of the New Deal. It didn't work. The NDAC (National Defense Advisory Commission), the OPM (Office of Production Management), and the SPAB (Supplies, Priorities, and Allocations Board) all came into existence during 1941 but coordinated poorly with each other. In addition, the separate supply administrations of the army and navy continued to operate, often at cross-purposes, while they both furiously resisted any outside interference from nonmilitary parts of the government.

Further, American industry, finally booming again after eleven years of depression, was not interested in dancing to Washington's tune.

After Pearl Harbor, Roosevelt quickly decided that a different approach was needed. Although William S. Knudsen and Sidney Hillman were coheads of the OPM, the office theoretically in charge of the effort, in early January 1942, the president called in Donald Nelson, the OPM's director of priorities.

Nelson had been executive vice president of Sears, Roebuck, at a salary of $70,000 a year, before going to work for the government at $15,000. Fifty-three years old, he was a large-boned man, a little overweight (at a time, of course, when men his age were virtually expected to be overweight). His quiet demeanor, spectacles, and thin hair gave him the air, in the words of a contemporary, "of a Middle Western Buddha." There was nothing Buddha-like about his private life, however. Twice divorced and twice widowed, he was married a total of five times.

"I'm tired of the way this production thing has been muddled," the president told Nelson. "How would you like to take over the job?"

"I will if I can boss it," Nelson replied.

"You can write your own ticket," Roosevelt told him, "and I'll sign it."

Nelson, Vice President Henry Wallace, and the president discussed the new government agency to be created that would take over the functions of the earlier ones. Nelson suggested calling it the War Production Administration, but Roosevelt suddenly realized that its initials would then be WPA, and knew that that would never do, so he settled on War Production Board instead.

Nelson went back to his office and proceeded to write the ticket Roosevelt had promised him. He gave the War Production Board the powers it needed to turn the U.S. economy into a war machine. He gave himself as chairman the powers he thought he needed to make it all work. Taking the plan back to Roosevelt, the president signed it as executive order number 9024. With that, Donald Nelson became, in effect, the CEO of the American economy. He was fitted for the job.

Nelson had been born in Hannibal, Missouri, in 1888. He graduated from the University of Missouri with a degree in chemical engineering and planned to go on to get his Ph.D. But first he went to work for Sears, Roebuck as a chemist, where he stayed for the next thirty years. He soon left the laboratory behind, moving into management and rising steadily through the corporate ranks.

During the 1930s Sears stocked in its stores and sold through its catalog more than 100,000 items, ranging from hat pins to prefabricated houses. For years it was Nelson's primary job at Sears to learn what items were needed by the retail and catalog operations, find out who could make them or where they could be purchased, and see to it that the merchandise appeared where and when it was needed. It was, of course, the perfect training for heading the War Production Board, for Nelson developed a familiarity with the width and depth of American industry that was quite unmatched by anyone else in the country.

Once he went to work at the WPB, Nelson had three overriding priorities. First, he had to establish what the services and the allies needed in order to win the war. Second, he had to inventory the raw materials the country had on hand together with the country's industrial resources. Third, he had to find ways to fill any gaps.

One immediate critical shortage was rubber. Natural rubber mostly came from plantations in Southeast Asia, then largely in Japanese hands. The collection of wild rubber in Brazil—an industry that had collapsed early in the twentieth century when it could no longer compete with plantation rubber—was revived. In addition, several latex-producing plants that could grow in the United States, such as guayule, were cultivated. But it was synthetic rubber that saved the day. Nonexistent in 1939, in 1945 the American synthetic rubber industry turned out 820,000 tons. Although this supply was sufficient to meet war needs, civilians had to make do as best they could, and the war years would long be remembered as the great age of flat tires.

The most difficult job facing Nelson was deciding what was to be produced first and what could wait. The Army Air Force wanted bombers; the navy needed pursuit planes. Both wanted them *now*. But there was not enough aluminum in the early days to produce all the aircraft that were needed. The WPB had to decide which came first and take any resulting heat from the armed services.

The WPB was divided into several "industrial branches," each responsible for a particular industry and charged with knowing exactly what every plant in that industry could produce, what it was producing at the moment, what it was already committed to produce in the future, and what inventory it possessed. This data was sent up the line to WPB divisions in charge of overall materials, allocations, production, and procurement decisions. It was at this level that the individual orders for equipment and matériel were weighed against one another, approved, given a priority, and sent to the plant that was to produce them, together with an authorization—given an equal priority—to draw on supplies of scarce raw materials.

In view of the task at hand, it is not surprising that the WPB was soon the largest of the wartime bureaucracies in Washington, with more than 25,000 employees by the end of 1942. It used as much paper every day as a good-sized newspaper. What *is* surprising, perhaps, is that the system worked at all, but work it did as the American economy expanded by 125 percent between 1940 and 1944, from $88.6 billion to $198.7 billion.

What is astounding is how little the civilian economy was disrupted by the immense demands of war production and by the fact that about 20 percent of the male population of the country was in the armed forces.

The places of the soldiers and sailors in the workforce, of course, were taken over by legions of Rosie-the-riveters (with results that are still playing themselves out in American society). And although certain products

were impossible to find (such as new automobiles) and others were severely rationed (such as tires, gasoline, and red meat), the civilian economy
continued to supply the needs of the civilian population at a far higher
level than the economy of any other belligerent was able to do. In the
midst of total war, the U.S. economy produced both guns and butter (or
at least margarine). Indeed, at the end of the war the civilian portion of
the American economy was about the same size it had been in 1939.

Donald Nelson's name today is known only to specialists of the period. But in large measure he was responsible for the American superweapon that won the war. That weapon was not the atomic bomb but the
American economy. Thanks to Donald Nelson and many others at the
WPB who did an immensely complex, largely thankless job, the United
States was able to win the Second World War using the same simple
strategy Ulysses S. Grant had used eighty years earlier: Assemble overwhelming men and matériel and pound the enemy into the ground with
them.

PART VII

BUSINESS AND GOVERNMENT

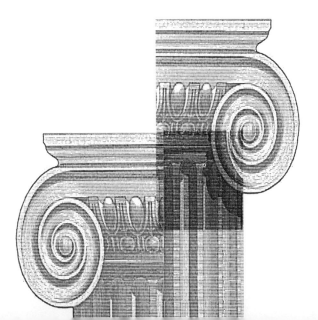

THE GREAT CRASH
(OF 1792)

NINETEEN TWENTY-NINE, like 1066, 1492, and 1776, is one of those dates that summon up an instant picture in the country's collective imagination. For not only did that year see a stock-market crash, it was *the Crash.* The self-defenestrated bodies of ruined investors and brokers are popularly supposed to have rained down on lower Manhattan like hailstones that terrible day (they didn't); the Great Depression is widely believed to have been caused by it (it wasn't); and, for all I know, some people think it was the crash that forced the Joads to move to California (it was a drought—not to mention John Steinbeck's imagination).

And certainly ever since, the crash of 1929 has been perfect for scaring people. Let the slightest hint of "irrational exuberance"—to use Federal Reserve Chairman Alan Greenspan's candidate for *Bartlett's*—appear on Wall Street, and the self-appointed sages on TV talk shows, liberal op-ed pages, and elsewhere start talking ominously about 1929.

But 1929 was only one of a long series of stock-market crashes in American economic history. There were others in 1837, 1857, 1873, 1893, and 1907 that were just as terrible, and each also marked the beginning of a protracted period of economic depression. Therefore it is instructive to take a look at Wall Street's very first crash, in 1792, a crash so early that many of the buildings on Wall Street were still private houses. What makes this crash really interesting, however, is how the federal government handled the crisis.

In one of those neat coincidences of history that help keep people like me off the unemployment rolls, one of its chief victims was a man named Walter Livingston. In 1998 his great-great-great-great-grandson was briefly scheduled to be Speaker of the House.

The cause of Walter Livingston's distress was a man named William

Duer. Born in England in 1747, Duer was the son of a very successful West Indian planter. Educated at Eton, he joined the British army, serving in India with General Robert Clive. He spent some time managing his father's estates in the West Indies and then settled in upstate New York, where he secured a lucrative contract with the Royal Navy to supply masts and spars.

When the Revolution began, however, he sided with the rebels and was elected to the Continental Congress. After he left Congress, he made a fortune supplying the Continental army and married Catherine Alexander, often known as "Lady Kitty," the daughter of the immensely rich American general William Alexander, who claimed (most probably without foundation) the dormant Scottish earldom of Stirling.

After the Revolution, Duer and his wife lived in almost royal style in their New York mansion, with liveried servants and serving as many as fifteen different wines at a single dinner. He was able to afford this lifestyle owing to a number of financial coups during the 1780s, involving land and the Revolutionary debt. In 1785 he was appointed secretary of the Treasury Board of the national government under the Articles of Confederation, a position tailor-made for obtaining insider information. In 1789 Alexander Hamilton (whose wife was a cousin of Duer's wife) appointed him assistant secretary of the Treasury under the new federal government.

Hamilton was personally honest and never tried to profit from his position in the government or to help his friends with inside information. Duer was not so fastidious. When Virginia's Henry Lee asked his friend Hamilton for information on the Treasury's refunding plans, Hamilton refused to tell him anything. But William Bingham, a rich Philadelphian and intimate of Duer, was so sure of the future that he borrowed £60,000—a very considerable fortune at that time—in Amsterdam in order to more profitably speculate in the federal debt.

Federal law forbade Treasury officials from speculating in federal securities, and Duer resigned rather than obey it. But he had always been more interested in Treasury connections, and especially a reputation for having them, than in the job itself.

At the end of 1791 Duer entered into a partnership with Alexander Macomb, one of New York's richest and most prominent citizens. They were to operate together for one year, speculating in stocks and bonds. In effect, the agreement called for combining Macomb's money and Duer's speculative talents and insider connections with the Treasury Department. At the end of the year they were to divide the profits equally.

Duer began buying Bank of New York stock when rumors were about that it was to be bought by the Bank of the United States and converted into a branch. If that were true, the stock was certain to rise, and Duer and Macomb would make a handsome profit. But Duer, it seems, was playing a deeper game. While long in the market with Macomb, he was short Bank of New York in his own account, having sold stock he didn't own, expecting a fall in price. Thus Duer was betting in public that the Bank of New York would be taken over and in private that it would not be. If the merger failed, Duer and Macomb would lose, while Duer, on his own, would make a fortune. But since his agreement with Macomb called for using Macomb's money, not his own, all Duer had to lose by double-crossing his partner was honor, a sacrifice he seemed perfectly willing to make.

Hamilton, unaware of Duer's duplicity, was appalled nonetheless at his speculative activities. " 'Tis time," he wrote on March 2, 1792, "there should be a line of separation between honest Men & knaves, between respectable Stockholders and dealers in the funds, and mere unprincipled Gamblers." Finding that line of separation, of course, has occupied the finest minds of Wall Street and the government ever since, with very mixed results at best.

In the increasing frenzy of speculation, Duer was the center of all attention, and, it seemed, he could do no wrong. Many were only too anxious to loan him money in hopes of getting on the bandwagon. It was at this point that Walter Livingston loaned him $203,000. To get some idea of how much money that was in 1792, consider this: In 1828, fully thirty-six years later, a list of New York's richest citizens was drawn up, perhaps the first "Forbes-400" list. Although the city's population had nearly tripled by that point, there were only fifty-six New Yorkers thought to be worth at least $100,000.

Duer began to buy other bank stocks for future delivery, betting that rising prices would enable him to pay for them when the time came. But among the people Duer had bought bank stock from were several other members of the Livingston clan, who were operating quite independently of their kinsman Walter. They had an interest in seeing that prices fell.

To ensure this, they began to withdraw gold and silver from their bank deposits, contracting the local money supply, and forcing banks to call in loans. In other words, they instituted a credit squeeze. Interest rates soared to as much as 1 percent a day.

This was ruinous to Duer and others who had borrowed in order to speculate. Duer desperately tried to borrow more to cover his obligations, but the man who had been having money thrown at him just a few weeks earlier now found that there was none to be had. Despite his troubles, he maintained a bold front, as the desperate on Wall Street usually do. On March 22 he wrote Walter Livingston that "I am now secure from my enemies, and feeling the purity of my heart I defy the world." A day after this brave statement, however, he was in debtors' prison.

With Duer's fall, panic ensued and prices plunged. The next day twenty-five failures were reported in New York's still-tiny financial community. Walter Livingston, who had gone from door to door assuring anyone who would listen that he was still solvent, announced that he was not. Alexander Macomb failed in early April and was also incarcerated for debt.

Thomas Jefferson, hardly able to contain his glee at the discomfiture of the speculators he hated so passionately, calculated their total losses at $5 million. He also calculated that that was the total value of New York real estate at the time and equated the losses caused by the panic to the losses that would have occurred had the city been leveled by some natural catastrophe.

For some of those caught in the debacle, it must have seemed that they had indeed been hit by an earthquake. Many of the ruined speculators never returned to Wall Street. William Duer would never get out of debtors' prison alive, while Walter Livingston retired to his family's vast upstate property to lick his wounds.

But for the country as a whole, it was not nearly that bad, thanks to fast action on the part of the federal government. Hamilton moved to make sure that the panic did not bring down basically sound institutions. He ordered the Treasury to purchase several hundred thousand dollars' worth of federal securities to support the market and urged banks not to call in loans. Further, to ease the money shortage, he allowed merchants to pay import duties—usually payable only in gold or Bank of the United States banknotes—at the customs house with notes payable in forty-five days. Speaking of the Treasury and the banks, Hamilton wrote that "no calamity truly *public* can happen, while these institutions remain sound."

And it didn't. Calm quickly returned to the Street, the precursor to the New York Stock Exchange came into being a few months later, and the American economy continued to expand rapidly in the prosperous 1790s. The reason is simple enough: Hamilton acted exactly as public monetary and fiscal authorities should act in the midst of a financial panic. He prevented the contagion of fear from getting out of hand and ensured that the panic would not have long-term adverse consequences to the American economy as a whole.

Alas, the lesson went unlearned amid the developing tide of Jeffersonian politics, which held Wall Street and all its works to be, at best, a necessary evil. It would be 195 years—until the great crash of 1987—before the federal government once again moved decisively to prevent a financial panic on Wall Street from turning into a financial disaster.

That is why the panic of 1987 is nearly as forgotten as the first one in 1792. If the federal government has truly learned its lesson, perhaps 1987, not 1929, should be the new image for the nation's collective imagination.

THE OTHER GREAT DEPRESSION

In 1937 THE AMERICAN economy, which had been slowly rising from the depths it had reached in 1933, suddenly reversed course and sank once more. GNP retreated; unemployment increased from its already high levels; tax revenues fell. While this new economic trend enlarged the misery of the American people, it also gave the economists a new problem: what to call it.

Since the start of the nineteenth century, an economic downturn had been called a depression, but in 1937 the country was already *in* a depression. So the economists, probably delighted to have a problem they could actually do something about, pressed the word *recession* into service. Because of the iron law of euphemism ("weak terms drive out strong ones"), *recession* took hold, and we have not had a depression since. Today the latter word effectively belongs to the 1930s and, indeed, is often capitalized to indicate its now unique meaning.

But the Great Depression was hardly the first major downturn in the American economy. In fact, a severe economic contraction followed hard on the heels of the Revolution itself. In 1837, after several years of economic expansion that was reflected in Wall Street's first big sustained bull market, Wall Street was hit with its first really big crash.

The depression that followed lasted well into the 1840s. However, although it deeply affected Wall Street bankers and merchants, it did not greatly alter the daily lives of a majority of Americans. Most citizens lived on farms, grew their own food, and manufactured for themselves most of what they needed. Americans in the 1830s still lived largely outside of what economists call the "cash economy."

By the end of the century, however, the situation was entirely different, and millions of Americans had become dependent on a weekly wage. In

1860, for every worker toiling in a factory, there had been nearly four working on farms. By 1890 the ratio had dropped to two-to-one. In 1860 not a single industrial concern had been listed on the New York Stock Exchange. By the mid-1890s there were twenty, each employing workers by the tens of thousands.

Therefore the depression that struck the country in 1893 has a very good claim to being called the Other Great Depression, for it directly affected the livelihoods not just of the bankers and merchants but of millions. GNP fell almost 12 percent. Unemployment, which had stood at only 3 percent of the workforce in 1892, soared to 18.4 percent two years later. Hunger stalked the streets of the now-vast slum districts in American cities, but only private charity was available to alleviate the misery.

The causes of the depression were partly the usual ones of overexpansion, especially by railroads. In early 1893 the Philadelphia and Reading Railroad and the National Cordage Company, the so-called rope trust, collapsed and touched off panic on Wall Street. By the end of the year another 15,000 companies (and 491 banks) had failed. Before the Great Depression of the 1890s was over, nearly one-third of the railroad mileage of the United States would pass through receivership.

But an equally important cause of the depression was that the government had been ignoring another iron law, this one economic not linguistic.

It is hard to imagine today, but in the last two decades of the nineteenth century, the gold standard was the subject of numerous cracker-barrel colloquies, street-corner harangues, and barroom brawls, reflecting a deep divide in American politics.

Being on a gold standard simply means that a country fixes the value of its currency in gold and stands ready to exchange any amount of it for gold at that value. The gold standard was extremely popular with the "monied classes," the bankers, brokers, and established businessmen epitomized by Wall Street and J. P. Morgan. The Northeast, the most densely populated and wealthy part of the country, strongly supported a gold standard.

The rest of the country, however, was still largely agrarian, not industrial, and farmers are chronic debtors. Many people in the South and West thought that the gold standard was nothing more than a Wall Street plot to drive them into bankruptcy. A gold standard, you see, makes inflation nearly impossible. And inflation is always popular with people who owe money because it allows them to pay back their debts in cheaper dollars. The political career of William Jennings Bryan would reach nearly to the doors of the White House thanks to the overtly inflationary schemes he advocated.

Faced with a strong demand for a gold standard by one politically powerful group, and an inflationary monetary policy by another, the U.S. government, as so often happens in a democracy, tried to have it both ways.

In February 1873 the government began to move slowly back to the gold standard it had abandoned during the Civil War and stopped minting silver coins. The West, where vast new silver deposits were discovered in the mid-1870s, promptly labeled this the "crime of '73." In 1878, however, Congress, while still moving toward a return to the gold standard, also passed the Bland-Allison Act, which required the Treasury to purchase between $2 million and $4 million in silver every month at the market rate and turn it into coins at the ratio of sixteen-to-one. (In other words, sixteen ounces of silver were declared by congressional fiat to be equal in value to one ounce of gold.) This had the effect of arbitrarily increasing the country's money supply, the classic means of generating inflation.

At first sixteen-to-one was approximately the market price of silver, but as the great strikes in the West began to come in, the price of silver dropped steadily, reaching a ratio of about twenty-to-one by 1890. That year Congress passed the Sherman Silver Act requiring the government to buy 4.5 million ounces of silver a month, just about all the silver the country was mining. With the government price for silver well above the market price, this was a sure recipe for inflation.

But the year after Bland-Allison, the country had fully returned to the gold standard, with Congress mandating that the Treasury keep $100 million in gold on hand at all times to meet any demand for the precious metal. With its silver policy greatly increasing the money supply, and the gold standard keeping the value of the dollar steady, the government managed, in effect, both to guarantee and to forbid inflation.

So what happened? Well, as anyone who has studied economics anywhere other than on Capitol Hill could predict, Gresham's law kicked in. This law, an economic truth recognized more than 200 years before Adam Smith was even born, holds that "bad money drives out good." Silver, worth one-twentieth the price of gold in the market, was declared to be worth one-sixteenth the price of gold when coined as money. So, naturally, people spent the silver and kept the gold. Gold began to trickle out of the Treasury.

Because the government ran a persistent surplus throughout the 1880s, the effects of the country's schizophrenic monetary policy were masked. But when the crash of 1893 hit, the trickle rose to a flood. With government revenues plunging, Congress repealed the Sherman Silver Act, but the people had lost faith in the dollar and hoarded gold. The government issued bonds to buy more gold and maintain the reserve, but the metal continued to flow out of the Treasury.

Before long the situation was critical. The Treasury gold reserve dipped below the $100 million required by law in 1894 and reached just $64 million the following January. Congress refused to allow President Cleveland, a staunch supporter of the gold standard, to sell another public bond issue to replenish the vanishing gold reserve.

With a free-coinage-of-silver Congress and a gold-standard president, the government was paralyzed. Soon it was literally possible to watch gold flee the country as every week millions in bullion were loaded on ships in New York harbor headed for Europe. Bets were being made on exactly when the U.S. government would be forced off the gold standard. Badly alarmed, J. P. Morgan took the train to Washington to see that something was done. President Cleveland, all too aware of how "Wall Street" was hated in much of the country, at first refused to see him.

"I have come down to see the president," responded Morgan in his most imperial manner, "and I am going to stay here until I see him." With the situation deteriorating by the minute, Cleveland relented the next morning.

The president, the attorney general, and the secretary of the Treasury all clung to the hope of persuading Congress to permit a new public bond issue, thus sparing them the political embarrassment of having the U.S. Treasury bailed out by the country's ultimate plutocrat. Then a clerk informed them that the New York Subtreasury had only $9 million in gold remaining in its vaults. Morgan said that he knew of a $10-million draft that might be presented at any moment. If presented, Morgan warned, "it will be all over by three o'clock."

Cleveland realized that Morgan was his only hope of avoiding a humil-
iating default. "What suggestions have you to make, Mr. Morgan?" he
asked.

Morgan made an astonishing offer. He and the Rothschilds, the two
most powerful forces in international banking, would purchase for the
government's account 3.5 million ounces of gold in exchange for thirty-
year gold bonds worth about $65 million. Further, he promised that the
gold, once in the hands of the government, would not flow out again, at
least for a while. In effect, Morgan was offering to act as the country's
central bank during the crisis, insulating the Treasury from market forces.
It was an awesome display of Morgan's faith in his own power.

The scheme worked, and, with confidence restored, the bonds were
sold at a handsome profit to the bankers. Cleveland, a sound-money man
to the core, never regretted taking Morgan up on the offer. But the silver
wing of the Democratic Party never forgave him for it.

The following year, the grip of the depression of the 1890s began to
lessen, and the political appeal of funny-money schemes therefore waned.
But William Jennings Bryan swept to his party's nomination by promising
to prevent the crucifixion of humankind upon a cross of gold. He was
soundly defeated, but for the next sixteen years, as the country matured
economically, the Democratic Party dragged a cross of silver through the
political wilderness.

R.I.P., ICC

In the Roman army, the soldiers' regular rations were principally in the form of large loaves of bread, each loaf enough for two soldiers for a day. This presented a big problem. As with every standing army before and since, life in the legions was largely a matter of hurry up and wait, and soldiers have a bad habit of fighting among themselves when they have nothing better to do. With the exception of women and gambling, nothing makes as convenient a *causus belli* among idle troops as food.

But the Romans, who had a genius not only for military matters but also for law, passed a nifty regulation to prevent fighting over the daily bread ration. When a pair of soldiers was issued a loaf of bread, the rule called for one soldier to divide it and the other soldier to take his choice of halves.

This is a perfect example of a self-enforcing law, a law so constructed as to make it in everyone's self-interest to act fairly. One would think that such laws would be used in every possible case, and doubtless they will be as soon as the Kingdom of Heaven on Earth arrives. But pending that event, they are likely to remain very rare. The reason is simple enough: Self-enforcing laws are in everyone's interest except for one group, the people who make and enforce the laws to start with. Those who work for government—legislators and bureaucrats alike—prefer to manage problems rather than solve them.

A classic example of what happens as a result of this predilection for management, not solution, is the Interstate Commerce Commission. On December 31, 1995, it finally closed its capacious doors after 108 years of managing a problem that could have been largely solved with a deft law. Indeed, through the immense inertia of politics, the ICC actually outlived the problem it was created to manage by several decades. That problem was the monopoly of overland transportation that railroads enjoyed in the nineteenth and early twentieth centuries and the economic power this monopoly gave them.

In fact, the modern world economy, which began to arise in the middle decades of the nineteenth century, came into being only because, for the first time in history, it became possible to move massive amounts of freight quickly and cheaply over long distances. But nineteenth-century railroads had very peculiar economics. They were very capital-intensive by the standards of the day and had virtually the same high maintenance costs regardless of whether business was brisk or slow. Railroads, therefore, were inherently a volume business, because they needed to spread their vast fixed costs over as much traffic as possible. That meant intense competition for market share.

The railroads tried forming cartels to allocate the traffic, but they often broke down, especially in bad times, and price wars resulted on routes where railroads competed with each other. But in turn, the price wars meant that the railroads often had to operate at a loss on the trunk lines that ran between major cities, such as Chicago and New York—the biggest trunk line of all—where the competition was at its most ferocious.

However, in those days, railroads not only operated trunk lines but also operated myriad branch lines running off the main ones to smaller cities and agricultural areas. On most of these branch lines, there was no competition, so the railroads, naturally, made the most of that fact to make up for losses they experienced on the trunk lines.

Just as naturally, this policy wasn't popular with the farmers and manufacturers living along these monopoly lines. As early as the 1860s, railroads had stirred up enormous resentment with their high-handed ways and their tendency to favor the powerful over the weaker with such devices as rebates. States, responding to political pressure, began to introduce regulation. Many states set up commissions to oversee the business, but these often proved ineffective, largely because the powerful railroad lobbyists saw to it that their powers were limited if not nonexistent.

Indeed, the commissions often became nothing more than covers for permitting railroads to behave as they pleased. One critic complained about the California Railroad Commission, which had been set up precisely to bring the Central Pacific Railroad to heel. "The curious fact remains," he wrote in 1895, "that a body created sixteen years ago for the sole purpose of curbing a single railroad corporation with a strong hand, was found to be uniformly, without a break, during all that period, its apologist and defender."

And as railroads amalgamated into networks spanning dozens of states, each state's power to regulate its own portion dwindled. In 1886 the Supreme Court, in *Wabash Railway v. Illinois,* ruled that the states had no power over railroads that were carrying goods coming from or going to another state. For all intents and purposes, that meant that states could not regulate railroads at all.

After *Wabash Railway v. Illinois,* therefore, the fight to change the behavior of railroads moved to Washington. But while the federal government, thanks to the commerce clause, had the undoubted power to regulate what had become a national transportation network, there was a good deal of question as to whether it had the ability. After all, Congress was faced with an aroused public on the one hand and the most powerful, not to mention richest, corporations in the country on the other. In those circumstances, politicians will always try to split the difference and make enough people happy to win the next election. The best solution will always rank far behind the most expedient.

What resulted, after a year of intense political sausage making, was, in the words of one historian, "a bargain in which no one interest predominated except perhaps the legislators' interest in finally getting the conflict . . . off their backs and shifting it to a commission and the courts."

A railroad commission, similar to those that had failed at the state level, was the only proposal seriously on the table. The rising political left instinctively looked to government, not markets, to protect its interests, and the railroads themselves were not averse to the idea, provided, of course, their own interests were carefully considered. Their economic and political power ensured that they would be.

As early as 1884, a vice president of the Pennsylvania Railroad, perhaps the most powerful railroad company in the country, had written that "a large majority of the railroads in the United States would be delighted if a railroad commission or any other power could make rates upon their traffic which would insure [*sic*] them six per cent dividends, and I have no doubt, with such a guarantee, they would be very glad to come under the direct supervision and operation of the National Government."

In other words, the railroads would have been perfectly happy to have a government-sponsored and -enforced cartel. The antirailroad forces, of course, wanted a commission that would set rates in the public interest, not the railroads' interest. The result, in the words of one congressman of the day, was "a bill that no one wants . . . and everyone will vote for."

The bill required that "all charges . . . shall be reasonable and just," but did not define what that might mean. And the commission that was set up had to use the courts to enforce any orders, a costly and time-consuming process. Even when the law was much strengthened in the Theodore Roosevelt administration and the ICC given the power to set rates, the railroads quickly learned how to manipulate it in their own interests, just as they had the old state commissions. American railroads began their long, slow decline.

The monopoly on long-distance freight hauling was broken in the 1930s by the nascent trucking industry, which, from its birth, was regulated by the ICC. In the 1970s—the nation's transportation industry by then a monument to inefficiency—the administration of Jimmy Carter removed most of the commission's power to set rates. In 1995 it finally expired, having had nothing to do for twenty years. Even the *New York Times,* hardly a passionate advocate of free markets, was not sorry to see it go. "As the decades wore on," a *Times* editorial that marked its passing noted, "it took as its interest the economic well-being of the industries under its purview. Its regulations jacked up prices and blocked entry by low-priced truckers and joint rail and truck services." In other words, the ICC had become precisely what the mighty Pennsylvania Railroad had wanted it to be in the 1880s, the leader of a cartel. That is no small part of the reason that both the ICC and the Pennsylvania Railroad are now on the ash heap of history together.

What might Congress, in a perfect world, have done instead? A self-enforcing solution would have been easy to craft. Congress could simply have required that each railroad publish a schedule of its freight rates for each commodity, on a per-mile basis, and require that those rates be uniform throughout the railroad's entire system and for each customer, providing severe penalties for under-the-table rebates.

Then the market forces that determined prices on the trunk lines would have been brought to bear on the branch lines, and the playing field would have been leveled by competition, not bureaucrats. And the inevitable co-opting of the regulators by the regulated would have been avoided for the simple reason that there would have been no regulators to co-opt.

ENGINE CHARLIE WILSON

IF YOU WANT TO know how much the world can change—and stay the same—in half a lifetime, consider the U.S. Defense Department, the General Motors Corporation, and the man who, forty years ago, epitomized them both, Charles E. Wilson.

In 1954 the Defense Department ran by far the most powerful military operation in the world. But that power came at a fearful cost to the American taxpayer. The Pentagon consumed 60 percent of the federal budget and one dollar out of every eight of GNP. Today, the Pentagon still commands unparalleled military power, but defense is only 21 percent of the budget and consumes one dollar of every twenty of GNP, a ratio that is increasing every year.

General Motors, meanwhile, was the world's largest industrial corporation. It dominated the American automobile business with a market share of over 50 percent and therefore dominated American business in general. More, it was the very model of how a giant economic enterprise should be run. Today, it remains the world's largest company, but its dominance of the automobile business is a fast-fading memory, with market share down to around 20 percent. And no one today would look to General Motors as a corporate exemplar. Indeed, for the last twenty years and more, it has been a pretty good example of how *not* to run a company.

Charles E. Wilson connects these two mighty organizations. From 1941 to 1953 he was president of General Motors and brought it to the peak of its economic power and reputation. From 1953 to 1957 he was secretary of defense and began the long, hard, bitterly fought campaign to get "more bang for the buck" out of the military.

Wilson was born in Minerva, Ohio, in 1890. According to him (the tale has the hallmarks of embroidered autobiography), his father had been a toolmaker, had organized a union local, and was a dedicated socialist. In college, Wilson followed his family's socialist traditions and supported Eugene V. Debs for president. He graduated from Carnegie Institute of Technology (now Carnegie-Mellon University) when he was only nineteen with a degree in electrical engineering, but, because of his youthful political adventures, had trouble getting a job as an engineer. For a while he worked as a patternmaker and became the business agent for the pattern-makers' local in Pittsburgh.

In later years he would keep his framed union card on his desk at General Motors. When he moved to the Pentagon, it was the only thing from his old office, other than family photographs, that he took with him.

He soon went to work for Westinghouse, however, and quickly attracted the attention of Benjamin G. Lamme, the company's chief engineer and one of the major figures in the early history of the commercial use of electricity. Wilson designed Westinghouse's first starter motor for automobiles and four years later was in charge of all the company's automotive electrical products. His talents as an executive were immediately clear.

After the First World War, Wilson moved to the Remy Electric Company, a subsidiary of General Motors located in Anderson, Indiana. He was soon general manager of that company and reorganized it, greatly increasing its profitability. In 1926 Remy merged with Delco, another GM subsidiary that produced electrical automotive equipment, and he became president. As always in mergers between companies in closely related fields, there was much overlap.

By restructuring the merged companies, Wilson was able to save $5 million, no small sum in the 1920s. But effecting the reorganization immediately would have cost 5,000 jobs in Dayton, where Delco was located. For an executive of his day, Wilson, perhaps thanks to his father, was always unusually sensitive to the needs and fears of the average worker. He postponed moving the jobs out of Dayton until new production could replace what was lost.

Such concern would characterize Wilson throughout his career at General Motors. It was Wilson who was in charge of the company's labor relations in the late 1930s and the one who accepted the United Auto Workers' organization of its workforce, ensuring that the entire industry would be organized. But he didn't stop there. It was Wilson who devised the cost-of-living raise to protect workers against inflation.

At this time the idea that "management" could be a formal discipline, one that could be taught and learned, rather than a seat-of-the-pants affair, was a very new one. In fact, the young Peter Drucker, today the grand old man of management science, began studying the structure of General Motors, a study that would result in his seminal book, *Concept of the Corporation,* in 1943.

By 1941, Wilson was president of General Motors (and soon was known as "Engine Charlie," to distinguish him from "Electric Charlie," the Charles E. Wilson who became president of General Electric at nearly the same time). When the war broke out, Engine Charlie threw his considerable energies into war production, making GM into one of the world's great military powers. During the war, the company produced one-quarter of the country's tanks, two-thirds of its heavy trucks, and three-quarters of its marine diesel engines. But the strain on Wilson, who never took a day off for two years, finally took its toll, and he collapsed with a stroke.

He was ordered to take six months off, agreed to take three, and spent the time thinking about the future of General Motors and its workforce. He came to some startling conclusions.

When he returned to work, he met with Drucker, who later remembered that of all GM's top executives, only Wilson took him and his study seriously. The rest were polite and helpful—the study had been initiated by the vice chairman of the board, Donaldson Brown, so they didn't have much choice—but they also clearly thought Drucker's study a waste of time. Wilson did not.

"I've been thinking about GM's future," he told Drucker. "To design the structure and develop the constitutional principles for the big business enterprise was the great achievement of the founding fathers of GM, the last generation. To develop citizenship and community is the task of the next generation. We are, so to speak, going to be the Jeffersonians to Mr. [Alfred P.] Sloan's Federalists."

This was exactly the conclusion that Drucker was heading toward, making the modern corporation a community of interests in a common cause, not a set of mutual antagonisms that was the legacy of the past.

Wilson and Drucker talked long about how to achieve that goal. And in the ensuing years Drucker and Wilson's staff worked out what has come to be called SUB, or Supplementary Unemployment Benefits. These would, in effect, guarantee workers against loss of income resulting from anything short of a major depression.

Drucker assumed that Wilson would implement such a scheme immediately. But Wilson was far wiser in the ways of unions and, especially, union leaders. He told Drucker: "*I* am never going to put it into effect. I grudgingly yield to a union demand for it when I have to."

"You mean your associates in GM management wouldn't go along with it unless they had to?" Drucker asked.

"No," Wilson answered, "my associates will accept my lead in labor relations; . . . But the union leaders won't go along unless it's a 'demand' we resist and they 'win.' "

It would be 1955 before the seed that Wilson planted with his contacts in the UAW turned into a full-fledged union demand for SUB. But when it did, the company "reluctantly" agreed to a plan that its own president, in fact, had developed.

Likewise, Wilson developed plans for a pension system to supplement Social Security. Drucker warned him that such a system, if the funds were invested in the stock market, would result in workers being the owners of American business in a few decades.

"Exactly what they should be," Wilson told him, unconcerned. Today, of course, pension funds are by far the largest owners of corporate stock in this country.

At the Pentagon, Wilson was fundamental in bringing the military fully into the atomic era and developing the doctrine of using "massive retaliation" to protect the country rather than the far more expensive conventional means. In his first year, backed by his boss, President Eisenhower, he slashed the budget by $5 billion and trimmed 40,000 from the Pentagon payroll.

If life were fair, liberals would hail Charles E. Wilson as a hero. And yet, in one of those ironies of history, Wilson is today remembered largely for a remark he never made, ugly words put into his mouth by antibusiness bigots.

On January 15, 1953, Wilson testified at his confirmation hearing before the Senate Armed Services Committee. The hearing was closed to the public and press, a much more common occurrence in those days than now, and Wilson was expecting no trouble. "I've got a feeling that I'm going to be pretty pleased and surprised at how easily those boys can be handled," he told reporters before entering the hearing room.

Well, welcome to Washington, Charlie.

Wilson was giving up a $600,000 salary to serve his country at $22,000 a year, and he probably felt that that was sacrifice enough. However, he also owned 40,000 shares of GM stock, and selling it would cost him a small fortune in capital gains taxes. But GM was the nation's largest defense contractor, so keeping it would be a clear conflict of interest. Even Republican senators gave him a hard time about it.

Senator Robert C. Hendrickson, Republican of New Jersey, asked Wilson if, faced with making a decision that would be in the interests of the country but extremely adverse to the interests of General Motors, he could make that decision.

"Yes, sir," Wilson replied briskly, "I could. I cannot conceive of one because for years I thought what was good for our country was good for General Motors, and vice versa. The difference did not exist. Our country is too big. It goes with the welfare of the country. Our contribution to the nation is considerable."

Wilson could hardly have imagined that this rather inelegant bit of Washington bomfog, uttered behind closed doors, would earn him a place in *Bartlett's Familiar Quotations*. But thanks to liberals horrified to find themselves out of power after twenty years and largely replaced with—ugh!— businessmen, it did exactly that.

They simply took what Wilson had said, shamelessly twisted it into "What is good for General Motors is good for the country," leaked it to the press, and repeated the lie endlessly, making Wilson sound like some latter-day corporate version of Marie Antoinette.

As his story clearly shows, he was anything but.

PART VIII

RETAILING AND REAL ESTATE

THE PERILS OF SUCCESS

In 1985 IBM HAD the greatest after-tax profit of any company in the history of the world: $6.58 billion. It bestrode the computer market like a colossus. But only seven years later, it had the greatest corporate loss in history up to that time: $5 billion. And the colossus of computing was a company owned by a supernerd Harvard dropout named Bill Gates, who hadn't even been born when IBM built its first computer.

How could so profound a reversal of fortune happen to so powerful a company in so short a time? Simple. In those seven years the computer world changed completely, but IBM didn't change at all.

IBM's greatness lay in mainframes, the powerful computers that are now indispensable to every big business and government agency. With the introduction of the revolutionary Series 360 system in the mid-1960s, IBM came to dominate the mainframe business worldwide. And once IBM mainframes were installed, companies were very reluctant to change to another brand, because the risk of a system crash and the consequent loss of data in the changeover was too high. IBM thus had a monopoly and could largely dictate to the market instead of the other way around.

But like all monopolies, IBM became fat, dumb, happy, and almost incredibly bureaucratic. One executive vice president, for instance, although among the top fifty people at IBM, still had no fewer than seven layers of management between him and the chairman. In many billion-dollar companies there aren't seven layers of management between the janitors and the chairman.

This, of course, stifled innovation and risk taking. Although IBM had been trying to develop a personal computer for years, it was only when the chairman cut through the bureaucracy and established a separate task force reporting directly to him, that the IBM-PC came into being in 1980.

It was one of the great commercial success stories of all time, and IBM quickly grabbed 80 percent of the exploding PC market.

But the PC, combined with the onrushing increase in the power of the microprocessors that are the heart of the beast, changed everything about the computer market. Only IBM didn't realize it. A mainframe company to the core, IBM thought PCs could be sold in the same way. But the two markets are utterly different.

The mainframe market consists of a few thousand executives who spend millions of dollars of company money on each machine, which is then run only by highly trained technicians. The PC market, however, consists of millions of individuals who spend a few thousand dollars, often of their own money, on each machine and then, as often as not, use it themselves.

Far worse for IBM, the mainframe generation cycle is about seven years. PCs have a new generation every year or year and a half. Hippopotamus IBM found itself in a race with a herd of gazelles named Microsoft, Intel, Gateway 2000, and Compaq, and simply could not change its ways to deal with the new reality until disaster forced it to begin the process in 1993.

A reluctance to change a winning formula that no longer applies has cost many a company its profitability and sometimes its very existence. Henry Ford's insistence that the Model T's 1908 technology was just what the people needed and wanted in the mid-1920s is perhaps the most famous example. But Sewell Avery's tenure at Montgomery Ward is also a cautionary tale worth the telling.

Born in 1874, Sewell Avery had ideas about how a company, or for that matter a society, should be run that were a bit old-fashioned even in the late nineteenth century. For most of his career, through the unstable boom of the 1920s and the utter gloom of the 1930s, these ideas stood him in good stead as a chief executive. Then the New Deal and World War II changed everything about the American economy except Sewell Avery.

Avery's family had become prosperous in the Michigan lumber trade and had investments in two gypsum companies. (Gypsum is the raw material from which plaster, and later wallboard, are made.) Young Sewell, fresh out of law school, went to work for one of these companies in 1893. In 1901 it merged with many other similar concerns to form the United

States Gypsum Company, known as the gypsum trust, or, inevitably, Big Gyp.

The new trust, as many of them did, took a long while to settle down internally, and in 1905 there was an explosion in company politics. Avery became president, explaining, "I came down last, and, lighting on top, I stuck." Avery proved to be exactly the right man for the job, running a very tight ship and turning the company from a regional to a dominant national building materials company. When the 1920s came along, the company was ready to take advantage of the building boom of that decade.

In 1919 U.S. Gypsum earned $1.1 million, more than twice its profits in any previous year. In 1926 its earnings peaked at over $10 million. But while Avery took advantage of the good times in the 1920s, he never fell for the idea that they would roll on forever. He had come of age in the depressed 1890s, and that fact, combined with a natural tendency to always see the glass as half empty, led Avery to be very wary about the future. He soon was known throughout the American business world as "Gloomy Sewell."

In 1929 Avery's predilection to expect the worst made him appear positively clairvoyant. In September of that year, the very month when, years later, economists would say the Great Depression began, Avery laid off 2,000 employees, almost half the firm's payroll. Further, he had squirreled away fully $35 million in retained earnings and had almost no long-term debt. As a result, not only was U.S. Gypsum able to survive the Great Depression, but it flourished, making a profit every year and extending its market share. It didn't even have to cut its handsome, 1920s-style dividend until 1933.

Montgomery Ward's story was the exact opposite. It had been perennially overoptimistic and had taken a bath in the short, sharp depression of 1920–21. In the prosperous days of the mid-1920s it began to transform itself from a catalog company into a major retail company as well. It had 10 stores in 1926, 248 two years later, and 554 in 1930. Even in that year of gathering depression, it opened 49 more stores. But it was no longer making a profit. In 1931 it lost $9 million, and its stock, which had peaked at 156⁷/₈ in 1929, could be bought for 6⁵/₈.

One of Montgomery Ward's principal stockholders at this time was J. P. Morgan and Company, and Morgan persuaded Avery to take over and be a new broom. Avery was certainly that. He wrote off unprofitable lines, closed stores, tightened central control, brought in new certified public accountants and told them to be ruthless, hired experienced store managers, and fired the catalog merchants who had been mismanaging the retail outlets.

It was an exhilarating time at Montgomery Ward. "I never saw such a mass movement forward in a business," one employee remembered. "Avery turned the place inside out, even to the fixtures and decorations. All the fellows were bustling and hustling to make the grade." Small wonder: In the first three years of the Avery regime, 22,000 out of a total of 35,000 employees left the company.

But Montgomery Ward was once again profitable, and its stock recovered sharply from its depression low. Sewell Avery, who had been granted large stock options as an inducement to take the job, became very rich.

As the economy slowly recovered after 1933, Avery could have borrowed money at very advantageous terms to begin a cautious expansion. Interests rates were very low, and corporate income taxes were very high, generously subsidizing interests costs. But Avery would have none of it. He regarded the New Deal and all it stood for as an abomination that would destroy the American economy in the long term. He especially hated labor unions. After one union won an election to represent 7,000 Montgomery Ward employees, only two direct orders from President Roosevelt himself got Avery to sign a union contract.

When a strike hit the company in 1943, Roosevelt seized Montgomery Ward under a wartime emergency measure after Avery refused to settle. Attorney General Francis Biddle flew to Chicago, hoping to effect a peaceful transfer of power from Avery to the government. Avery was not in a peaceful mood.

"To hell with the government," Avery yelled at him. "I want none of your damned advice." Prepared for this, Biddle had numerous MPs at his disposal and ordered two of them to lift the chairman out of his chair and haul him out of the building.

Avery had only words with which to respond, but he used the most contemptuous ones he could think of as he was carried away. "You . . . *New Dealer!*" he bellowed. The next day a photo of Avery in all his blue-suit-and-wingtip-shoes dignity being unceremoniously carted out of

Montgomery Ward was on the front page of nearly every newspaper in the country.

Avery was soon back in control and fully prepared to meet what he saw as the greatest challenge of the postwar economy: renewed depression. Avery, widely read, knew that one had followed every previous major war and was utterly sure that this one would be no different, especially with New Deal Democrats still in power. To be fair, Avery had lots of company in this opinion, for most of the nation's economists, their clouded crystal balls ever at the ready, also foresaw depression.

But the war had put large sums into the bank accounts of millions of citizens, while virtually no durable goods had been produced in the previous three and a half years, as war production had monopolized the nation's factories. So the pent-up demand was enormous, whereas the supply was, at least initially, very limited. The result, of course, was boom, not depression, and a lot of inflation to boot.

Most companies soon responded, including Montgomery Ward's archrival, Sears, Roebuck. But Avery, now in his seventies, had become a sort of reverse Herbert Hoover, insisting that depression was just around the corner. He kept his company's money in the bank. There would be no expansion at Montgomery Ward.

The results were disastrous. In 1946 it had been just about as big as Sears, with 628 stores and $974 million in sales, versus 603 stores and $1,045 million for Sears. By 1951, however, Sears's sales had reached $2.6 billion, while Montgomery Ward's were virtually unchanged at $1.1 billion.

In 1954 the stock market, after a quarter of a century, finally topped the highs it had reached in the early fall of 1929. Even Wall Street thought the Great Depression was over. A few months later Avery, who still did not, decided to resign.

Montgomery Ward stock jumped nearly 6 percent on the news, but the company would never again be in the top ranks of American retailing. In 2001, now just a subsidiary of General Electric, it was closed down.

NO RESPECT

If Rodney Dangerfield weren't a comedian, he'd probably be an executive. Executives don't get any respect either.

Alexander Graham Bell invented the telephone and has, naturally, a long entry in the *Encyclopaedia Britannica* and numerous cross-references. But his father-in-law, Gardiner Greene Hubbard, who merely invented AT&T, made Bell by far the richest inventor of the nineteenth century, and gave the country a phone system that has been the envy of the world ever since, goes entirely unmentioned.

Even the government gets in on the act. In 1993, the Clinton administration proposed that executives be the sole job category in the United States subject to government wage controls, by limiting the deductibility of executive salaries from corporate income taxes.

Now, certainly, some executives are overpaid, especially when the top management of a company controls the board of directors and the executives thus get to set their own salaries. But there are also overpaid movie stars and sports figures. Somewhere in the world there is probably an overpaid historian, although I've never met one.

But what's a good executive worth? Well, sometimes in American history he or she has been worth the whole company.

Henry Ford invented the mass-market automobile, and his engineering genius created both a great fortune and one of the world's largest corporations. But toward the end of his life, his slapdash, highly idiosyncratic, and increasingly paranoid approach to management went a long way toward wrecking both. Under Henry I, costs were estimated, to the extent they were estimated at all, by *weighing* piles of invoices. It was Henry Ford II—no genius, just a first-rate executive—who created the modern Ford

Motor Company (1999 sales: $162.5 billion) out of the nearly insolvent chaos left by his grandfather.

Or consider Sears, Roebuck. Having given their names to one of the most famous corporations in the world, both Richard Warren Sears and Alvah Curtis Roebuck are immortal. But it was the now-nearly-forgotten Julius Rosenwald who turned Sears, Roebuck from a shapeless, inefficient, rapidly expanding corporate mess into the retailing titan of much of the twentieth century. Indeed, there is probably nothing wrong with the modern-day Sears, Roebuck that a modern-day Julius Rosenwald couldn't fix, if only the company could find one.

Rosenwald was born in Springfield, Illinois, in a house only a block away from Lincoln's, in 1862. His father managed a clothing store, one of several in the Middle West that were owned by his wife's brothers and which he purchased from them a few years later. Leaving high school after two years, the young Rosenwald went to work for his uncles in New York, operated his own store there for a while, and then, moving to Chicago, opened a company that manufactured men's summer wear in 1885. The company flourished from the start, but ten years later, he sold out to purchase an interest in the even faster-growing Sears, Roebuck.

Richard Sears, trained as a railroad telegrapher, discovered he could sell in 1886, when he was twenty-three. A C.O.D. shipment of watches had been refused by a local jeweler in Redwood Falls, Minnesota, where Sears was agent for the Minneapolis and St. Louis Railroad. Sears made a deal with the shipper and sold the watches himself. Soon he was ordering more, and within six months, Sears had made $5,000—good money in 1886; it was enough to buy a comfortable house.

He quit the railroad and set up the R. W. Sears Watch Company. When watches started coming back for repairs, he hired Roebuck, a self-taught watchmaker. Before long they were partners and selling jewelry as well as watches. Sears began issuing a catalog and offering more merchandise.

It was soon obvious that Sears had a deep, intuitive feel for the commercial needs and aspirations of the people of rural America, and a genius for writing catalog and advertising copy that awakened those needs and aspirations. The 1892 catalog had 196 pages and offered everything from wagons to baby carriages, shotguns to saddles. Sales that year amounted to $276,980.

Over the next two years, in the teeth of the great depression of the early 1890s, the catalog expanded to 507 pages—nearly all of it written by Sears himself—and sales to $393,323. But profits did not expand commensurately. Swift corporate growth is often a messy affair, and many promising concerns do not survive the economic equivalent of adolescence. Sears, Roebuck's growth was messier than most, in no small part due to Richard Sears himself.

He was given to writing copy for merchandise he did not have in stock but which he thought might find a ready market. Being the genius he was, he was usually right. "Costs Nothing," he wrote in one catalog, "for $4.95 we will send C.O.D. subject to examination, etc. a fine black cheviot suit." When 25,000 orders avalanched into Sears headquarters in Chicago in response, he had desperately to cast about for a men's clothing company that could supply such an order, while his customers waited impatiently.

Sometimes Sears got a bit carried away with his catalog descriptions and strayed far beyond the literal truth. This, in turn, precipitated many returns of merchandise, always the greatest profit-gobbling threat to the mail-order business, for each one is a dead loss for the company, even if the merchandise can be resold. Sears learned his lesson—in later years he was fond of saying that "honesty is the best policy; I know because I've tried it both ways"—but hyperbole was always to be his stock-in-trade.

It was all too much for Roebuck, who possessed the very quintessence of the bean-counter mentality. In what may well be the worst investment decision in the history of American capitalism, he sold his interest in Sears, Roebuck to his partner in 1894 for $25,000. (Years later, at the beginning of the Great Depression, Roebuck, by then broke, applied for a job at the company that had once been half his. Asked if he was any relation to the founder, he admitted he *was* the founder and was immediately hired for promotional and ribbon-cutting purposes.)

But Sears, a salesman who "could sell a breath of air," was preoccupied with writing copy and dreaming up new items for the catalog. He still needed someone to count the beans and bring order to the sprawling, often chaotic company. Sears found a new partner when Aaron Nussbaum, who owned a firm that made pneumatic tubes, called on him hoping to sell a tube system. He sold the system and bought into the company with his brother-in-law, Julius Rosenwald. Sears, Roebuck's astonishing growth began immediately.

In 1895 Sears did a gross business of $800,000. By the turn of the twentieth century it was $11 million, surpassing Montgomery Ward, a company that was twenty years older. But Sears did not get along with Nussbaum. In 1901 he demanded that either Rosenwald and Nussbaum buy him out, or that he and Rosenwald buy Nussbaum out. Rosenwald had to choose between his brother-in-law and the man he knew was indispensable to the continued success of Sears, Roebuck. He chose Sears, and together they bought out Nussbaum's one-third interest for $1.25 million, fifty times what Roebuck had sold his half interest for only seven years earlier.

Yet Sears, Roebuck was now expanding so rapidly that they were able to pay Nussbaum off in only two years. No small part of this success was due to Rosenwald's executive abilities. He began to check Richard Sears's more extravagant flights of fancy in the catalog copy, greatly cutting down on returns from disappointed customers. In 1911 he set up one of the first corporate testing laboratories to ensure the quality of merchandise Sears bought from other firms.

Under Rosenwald's direction, new systems were instituted that made sure orders were processed promptly. Incoming orders were weighed (they averaged forty per pound) to indicate how many clerks would be needed. By 1906, when Sears, Roebuck moved into a vast new plant in Chicago, consolidating operations from dozens of locations, orders were averaging 20,000 a day, 100,000 a day during the Christmas season.

Each day of the week was assigned an order slip of its own color, so that delayed orders would stand out and get first attention. Conveyor belts and gravity chutes were installed to speed the flow of orders and merchandise, bringing everything together at an assembly point. Henry Ford inspected this system and was mightily impressed. The following year he adapted the assembly line principle to automobile manufacturing and changed the world. (One can only wonder if he noticed the weighing of incoming orders and misapplied it to invoices.)

Rosenwald was also way ahead of his time in employee relations. In 1916 he established the Savings and Profit Sharing Pension Fund of Sears, Roebuck. Employees could contribute up to 5 percent of their salaries, and the company contributed a portion of the profits according to a sliding scale—the more profits, the greater the percentage contributed to the fund, up to a limit of 10 percent. From the beginning, much of this fund was invested in Sears, Roebuck stock. So the Pension Fund not only greatly fostered employee loyalty—a hallmark of Sears for years—but also gave the employees a strong self-interest in the success of the company.

And succeed the company certainly did. By the mid–twentieth century, Sears, Roebuck was part of the very warp and woof of American civilization. The writer S. J. Perelman said that its catalog had the same effect on him as madeleines had on Marcel Proust. Senator Gene Talmadge thought that the Georgia farmer had only three friends in the whole world: Jesus Christ, Sears, Roebuck, and, of course, Gene Talmadge. Franklin Roosevelt joked that the way to convince the Soviet Union of the superiority of the American system would be to bomb it with Sears, Roebuck catalogs.

Unlike poor Roebuck, both Sears and Rosenwald died immensely rich, owing to Sears's genius as a salesman and Rosenwald's genius as an executive. The salesman left $25 million when he died in 1914, and the executive $17 million in 1932. Of course, by that time Rosenwald had given away to worthy causes fully $63 million.

Most of the article on Julius Rosenwald in the *Dictionary of American Biography*, the standard multivolume reference work on great Americans of the past, is devoted to detailing his endless charities. But guess how much of the article is devoted to his talents as an executive, talents that made his beneficence possible: exactly one sentence.

As I said, executives get no respect.

WHERE AND WHEN

IT IS A VERY old joke among real estate brokers that only three things determine the value of a parcel of land: location, location, and location. The reason the joke has been around so long, of course, is that it is mostly true. What's more, it is true not just on the microeconomic level of a city lot but on the macroeconomic level as well. New York City became the great American metropolis not because of its magnificent natural harbor but because of where on the globe that harbor was located.

What the joke does not take into account, however, is the dimension of time. For instance, around the turn of the nineteenth century my great-great-great grandfather, whose name I bear, exchanged thirty-five acres of undeveloped land in near-wilderness Tennessee for a horse and a saddle. It was, I suppose, a fair deal at the time. Today, alas for the family fortune, the horse is dead and the saddle worn out, but those acres are still there, now called downtown Nashville.

Time, to be sure, is the peculiar province of historians, not real estate brokers, and over the course of history, *when* has proved quite as important as *where*, for while a city cannot move, the tides of history most certainly can. When Venice was at the height of its glory, its location directly on the trade routes with the East made it a great power. Then the rise of the Ottoman Empire interrupted those routes, and the full-rigged ship opened the world's oceans to commerce. Venice's once incomparable location became a grave disadvantage, and it sank to the status of an exquisitely beautiful backwater.

Unless politically created like Washington, D.C., cities are not located where they are out of sheer whim. Although often lost in the mist of history, every city has an original raison d'être. Sometimes this is techno-logical: London is located at the first point from the sea where the Thames could be bridged using the techniques available to the Romans. Sometimes it is military: Paris began because the Île de la Cité at its heart was a natural fortress, moated by the Seine. Sometimes it is a natural resource, such as the freshwater springs that brought forth Los Angeles.

Most cities, however, come into being for economic reasons. Many arise at points where two streams of commerce join—such as St. Louis at the junction of the Missouri and Mississippi Rivers—or at a point where shippers have to "break bulk," that is, transfer freight from one means of transportation to another. The Dutch created New Amsterdam at the tip of Manhattan Island early in the seventeenth century because it was the obvious place to switch beaver pelts from Indian canoes to oceangoing sailing ships.

From the beginning New York's location had many natural advantages over other American ports. It was more centrally located than either Boston or Charleston and much closer to the open sea than either Philadelphia or Baltimore. Moreover, the Raritan River in New Jersey, the rivers of southern New England, Long Island Sound, and the mighty Hudson—great avenues of commerce in the preindustrial era—all led to New York harbor.

Still, New York was not the leading port during most of the colonial era. Philadelphia had a larger population, and Boston was surrounded by a more populous countryside. In 1770 New York ranked no better than fourth in tons of cargo arriving and clearing the port. Philadelphia led with 47,000 tons arriving, followed by Boston at 38,000 and Charleston at 27,000. New York had 25,000.

A few years later the American Revolution devastated New York. Under British occupation for seven years and swept by a disastrous fire that leveled more than 1,000 houses, its population declined steeply. Many of New York's merchants were either Tories by conviction or had hopelessly compromised themselves during the occupation. Many left the city when the British finally did on November 25, 1783. Still worse, the treaty of peace provided that all prewar debts owed to British merchants were due and payable with accumulated interest. Alexander Hamilton, among others, had a brisk law practice pursuing these debts.

But if the 1780s were a dismal time for the port of New York, the 1790s boomed. The start of the Wars of the French Revolution greatly increased demand for American products and American shipping. Although all American ports benefited, New York did best and by 1797 had pulled ahead of Philadelphia to become the busiest American port.

While New York was now in the lead, that lead was precarious. The city, however, had up its sleeve—or rather up the Hudson—one more locational advantage that was to make all the others seem insignificant: a gap in the chain of mountains that ran otherwise uninterrupted from Alabama to Maine and isolated the burgeoning Middle West from the East Coast.

Before the coming of the railroad, the cost of overland transportation simply prohibited moving bulky commodities such as agricultural products—which was all the Middle West had to sell—over the Appalachians to the eastern seaboard. The settlers had to consume them on the spot in a subsistence economy or ship them down the Ohio and Mississippi Rivers all the way to New Orleans and thence to the eastern seaboard and Europe.

It was Gouverneur Morris who first suggested capturing this trade by building a "Great Western Canal" from Lake Erie to the Hudson River near Albany, utilizing the fortuitous gap. But it was Governor DeWitt Clinton who made it nearly his life's work to push the canal scheme through to completion, despite often ferocious political opposition. Many of the senators and assemblymen from New York City, shortsighted even by the standards of politicians, opposed the idea, thinking it nothing more than an upstate boondoggle.

When the Erie Canal was finally completed in 1825, after eight years of digging done entirely by hand, a huge, statewide ceremony was held. A barrel of water from Lake Erie was transported by canal barge from Buffalo to Sandy Hook at the entrance to New York harbor. There Clinton poured it into the Atlantic, signifying the wedding of the waters that lay at opposite ends of the state. Along with the water from Lake Erie, water from the Rhine, the Ganges, the Nile, and twelve other great rivers of the world were also poured into the Atlantic. New York City, in its characteristically imaginative and unsubtle way, was boasting of its coming greatness as a center of world trade.

The boast was soon fulfilled. Before the canal, a ton of flour worth $40 could be shipped, overland, from Buffalo to New York in about three weeks at a cost of $120, quadrupling its price. On the canal the same ton could be transported in eight days at a cost of $6. With such changes in the economic equations, it is no wonder that New York soon became, in the words of Oliver Wendell Holmes, Sr., a "tongue that is licking up the cream of commerce and finance of a continent," and the greatest boom-town the world has ever known.

Between the opening of the canal in 1825 and the beginning of the Civil War thirty-six years later, New York grew so fast that it built on average some ten *miles* of newly developed street front per year. By 1860 New York handled fully two-thirds of the nation's imports and one-third of its exports. In other words, more than half of all American international commerce passed through the port of New York, largely thanks to its location 150 miles downriver from a gap in the mountains.

Now, it must be admitted that in history, if not real estate, location is not quite everything. From its earliest days New York was the most com-mercial-minded of American cities. The Puritans of Boston, the Quakers of Philadelphia, and the Catholics of Baltimore founded their cities first of all for religious reasons. But the Dutch founded New Amsterdam solely to make a buck. So busy were they buying beaver pelts that they didn't get around to building a church for fourteen years.

This commercial drive greatly contributed to New York's climb to the top and continues to characterize the city to this day. As Robert Green-halgh Albion points out in his magnificent *The Rise of New York Port, 1815–1860*, published in 1939, the aggressive and successful push by New York merchants to broker the trade between southern cotton growers and Euro-pean and New England textile manufacturers played a major part in the growth of the port, regardless of its location.

The southerners regarded themselves as gentlemen farmers and didn't want to grubby their fingers with anything so vulgar as money. The New Yorkers were only too glad to grubby theirs, in exchange, needless to say, for a piece of the action. By the time the southern states began to secede, the cotton trade had become so important to New York's economy that the mayor, Fernando Wood—"of whom no man need fear he holds too low an opinion"—went before the city council and proposed that the city follow the Confederacy out of the Union.

By the 1920s New York was the greatest port not only in the country but in the world as well, eclipsing London, and it maintained this hegem-ony for decades. But just as the tides of history and technology first brought Venice to greatness and then left it behind, so they continue to shift today. New York's near monopoly of transatlantic passenger travel, for instance, disappeared with the coming of the jet plane. Far more important have been the shifting patterns of world trade. Trade across the Pacific has been growing by leaps and bounds, whereas Atlantic trade has merely been steadily increasing. Today the West Coast's traffic with East Asian countries and Alaska far outstrips East Coast trade with Europe and Africa.

The result: In 1989 Los Angeles–Long Beach became the country's busiest port, and it shows every sign of continuing to increase its lead. There is a considerable irony here. You see, New York was founded on account of its great harbor, but Los Angeles was founded twenty miles inland and didn't have a harbor at all until an artificial breakwater was completed in 1914. Regardless, Los Angeles is located on the right ocean for the twenty-first century, and New York is not.

As they say, it's location, location, and location.

WOOLWORTH'S
CATHEDRAL

I met a traveller from an antique land
Who said: Two vast and trunkless legs of stone
Stand in the desert . . . Near them, on the sand,
Half sunk, a shattered visage lies, whose frown,
And wrinkled lip, and sneer of cold command,
Tell that its sculptor well those passions read
Which yet survive, stamped on these lifeless things,
The hand that mocked them, and the heart that fed:
And on the pedestal these words appear:
"My name is Ozymandias, king of kings:
Look on my works, ye Mighty, and despair!"
Nothing beside remains. Round the decay
of that colossal wreck, boundless and bare
The lone and level sands stretch far away.
                    —Percy Bysshe Shelley, "Ozymandias"

EVER SINCE TECHNOLOGY BEGAN to permit it, men of power have sought
immortality in stone. Knowing that their deeds, however important, were
ephemeral in the nature of things, they hoped that their tombs and statues
and palaces might remind the world of their greatness. Shelley, in his
famous and haunting sonnet, showed the essential barrenness of this idea,
but that hasn't stopped men in the least from erecting monuments to their
own memories.

Before the industrial revolution, politics and military conquest were
the main roads to power. With the advent of the steam engine, the instruments of choice by which men sought power began to change, as did the
means by which they displayed it. The opportunities for military conquest

shrank nearly to the vanishing point, but the opportunities to make a great fortune in business vastly expanded.

As early as 1868, James Gordon Bennett noted in the *New York Herald* how much things had changed and yet stayed the same. "Under our modern forms of government and in the advancing strength and intelligence of the people," he wrote in an editorial, "men no longer attempt to rule by the sword, but they find in money a weapon as sharp and more effective; and having lost none of the old lust for power, they seek to establish over their fellows the despotism of dollars."

If the wealth created by the industrial revolution never quite amounted to a "despotism of dollars," it certainly allowed the building of an unprecedented number of monuments to the glory of the creators of the new fortunes. The building of a suitable palace was usually the first step. The parade of mansions that slowly marched up New York's Fifth Avenue in the nineteenth century, each grander and more elaborate than the last, was a fantastic and—*pace* Shelley—now largely lost example.

Cornelius Vanderbilt was, in his day, the king of kings of American railroading and the richest self-made man in the world. He was quite comfortable living downtown in his relatively modest house on Washington Place and left Fifth Avenue to his children and grandchildren. But he couldn't entirely resist the temptation to immortalize himself. In 1869 he built a new freight warehouse in lower Manhattan for his New York and Hudson River Railroad, and he arranged for a grand monument to himself to be part of it. It amounted to nothing less than his autobiography, written in 100,000 pounds of bronze. The pediment of the building, 30 feet high and 150 feet long, was filled with depictions, in high relief, of Vanderbilt's career in ships and railroads. These flanked a central statue of the commodore himself, fully twelve feet high and weighing four tons.

Even before it was unveiled, the astonished *Herald* noted that "it is not so prodigious as the Pyramid of Cheops, nor so lofty as the Colossus of Rhodes, but it will do." (Vanderbilt's monument, alas, has also suffered the fate of Ozymandias's. Today only the central statue survives, placed high in front of Grand Central Terminal.)

Happily for ordinary mortals, Vanderbilt's expression of his egotism in bronze was an exception among nineteenth-century plutocrats. Instead of erecting statues to themselves, these men of fortune largely sought to attach their names to things that were both grand and useful, serving the public as well as the vanity of their creators. New York City alone is filled with these efforts: Carnegie Hall, the Cooper Union, Rockefeller University, Paley Park, and the Whitney and Guggenheim Museums are just a few examples.

But Frank Winfield Woolworth, the greatest merchant of his day, was, like Vanderbilt, an exception among the monument builders of the gilded age. And like Vanderbilt, he was not much given to charity. He had made a great fortune a nickel at a time, and he was accustomed to watching those nickels carefully. Worth $65 million, he was perfectly willing to keep his office staff late while he tracked down an unaccounted-for quarter, missing from his change purse.

For Woolworth, it wasn't enough that his monument be grand, like Vanderbilt's bronze; or grand and useful, like Carnegie's concert hall. It wasn't even enough that it be grand and useful and beautiful, like the New York Public Library.

Woolworth wanted his monument to be all that and *profitable* too. The man who invented the five-and-dime had every intention of building a moneymaking monument to carry his name down through the ages.

Woolworth's genius had been in seeing the possibilities in the low end of retailing. In 1879 he had set out on his own with a borrowed $410 and opened a store in Lancaster, Pennsylvania. He stocked it with "Yankee notions," the thread and needles and cheap tin cookware that peddlers had carried around rural America before the coming of the railroads. Nothing in Woolworth's store cost more than a nickel, and it was an immediate success. By the end of the year, he had 2 stores (and had raised his price limit to ten cents, hence the "five-and-dime"); by 1889, 12; by 1899, 54. In 1909 he owned 238 stores, and Woolworth was the best-known name in American retailing.

While Woolworth was by then an enormously rich man and lived in style in one of the mansions lining Fifth Avenue, he was dissatisfied. Although his name was associated with good value and utility, it was also, inevitably, associated with cheap, and Woolworth was sensitive on the subject. When the company had moved into new and luxurious offices in New York in 1905, Woolworth had exulted that "the five and ten cent business is no longer a Cheap John affair." But the offices were rented, not owned by the company. Woolworth wanted his own building, a building grand enough to proclaim to the world the glory of the name Woolworth.

Although he thought the Houses of Parliament in London to be the most beautiful building complex in the world and wanted his to be likewise in the Gothic style, Woolworth also wanted his building to be one of the new skyscrapers.

At the end of the nineteenth century two technologies, steel construction and the electric elevator, came together and made the skyscraper possible. Masonry buildings cannot be much more than ten stories high because the necessary thickness of their walls is a function of their height. But steel could soar to the sky. When the electric elevator was introduced in 1889 and made unlimited vertical transportation possible, buildings in New York, Chicago, and elsewhere began to do exactly that.

By the turn of the twentieth century a new world's-tallest-building was going up every few years, and the word *skyline* entered the English language in 1903. By 1909 the world's tallest was the Metropolitan Life Tower on New York's Madison Square, 700 feet high and modeled after the campanile in Venice's St. Mark's Square.

Woolworth began to buy land on Broadway, across from the southern tip of City Hall Park, and he hired the architect Cass Gilbert, whose Gothic-style design for a building at Sixty West Street he admired. At first Woolworth envisioned a building of moderate height, at least by skyscraper standards, perhaps twenty-five stories. Under Gilbert's prodding, however, Woolworth's ideas began to expand. The architect sent a surveyor out to find out exactly how tall the Metropolitan Life Tower was and then told his employer how high he had to go in order to have the world's tallest building bear the name Woolworth. Woolworth was aware of the advertising value and soon went along with the idea. Gilbert ended up designing a building 792 feet tall. Completed in 1913, it would hold the altitude record for fully seventeen years until it was finally surpassed by the Chrysler Building in 1930.

Woolworth, who knew a great deal about retailing but little if anything about building skyscrapers, supervised everything closely anyway, making a thorough pest of himself with Gilbert and Louis Horowitz, the contractor. At one point he wanted to know why somebody on the project, designated a "telephone boy," was being paid $2.50 a day. He even suggested that, since Gilbert and Horowitz were lucky to be connected with so prestigious a building, they should cut their fees. (Needless to say, they did no such thing.)

Woolworth was especially interested in cost control, perhaps, because he owned the building personally and intended to rent space in it to the Woolworth Company, the Irving National Bank, and others. And he paid for the entire project in cash, $13.5 million in all. The building—unique among New York skyscrapers—has never been mortgaged. But while Woolworth, as always, watched his nickels carefully, he was not afraid to spend as many as necessary to get top quality.

And top quality is exactly what Frank Woolworth got. No sooner was his building finished than he had the satisfaction of having it universally acclaimed a masterpiece. Gilbert had followed Louis Sullivan's dictum that a skyscraper should be "a proud and soaring thing," and Montgomery Schuyler, the leading architecture critic of his day, was dazzled. "How it cleaves the empyrean and makes the welkin ring as it glitters in the sunshine of high noon," he wrote. "How impressively it looms above its fellows in spectral vagueness, in the gray of the dawn or the haze of twilight."

No one has quibbled since. Today's leading architecture critic, Paul Goldberger, says that the Woolworth Building "has an almost Mozartian quality to it, a sense of light, graceful detail applied to a firm and self-assured structure." It is now a New York City landmark, and there can be few New Yorkers who do not hope that the curse of Ozymandias will long pass the Woolworth Building by.

Woolworth must also have been delighted that his building immediately became world famous and one of New York's foremost tourist attractions, depicted on countless postcards. Two hundred thousand people a year visited the building and paid to see the view from its observation level. (Now atop what is only New York's fourteenth-tallest building, the observation deck has been closed for many years.)

But I suspect that what made Woolworth happiest of all was that his "Cathedral of Commerce," grand and useful and beautiful as it was, immediately began to yield him a good, solid, 6 percent return on his investment as well.

UNINTENDED
CONSEQUENCES

THE LAW OF UNINTENDED consequences is nowhere more obvious than in the results of man-made laws. Prohibition, by eliminating demon rum, was supposed to alleviate poverty and disease. What we got was Al Capone. More recently, environmental laws have often served those who don't give a hoot about the environment but care very much about what is built in their own backyards.

Among the earliest environmental laws were zoning ordinances, and they have long been put to use by individuals pursuing their self-interests. In the 1970s, for instance, an exclusive private club in New York used the city's zoning laws, and not a little chutzpah, as nothing less than an instrument of alchemy, turning the thin air above its clubhouse into $5 million.

Zoning laws themselves came about because of the unintended consequences of steel construction and the electric elevator, which first appeared in the 1880s. Once limited to six or seven stories, buildings could now reach any height.

In 1915 the Equitable Building at 120 Broadway, just north of Wall Street, went up. The Equitable was built to maximize profit, plain and simple. The building fills an entire city block, rising straight up from the building line on all sides for forty stories. Naturally, there was an immediate outcry that New York's streets would be reduced to sunless canyons if many more such structures were built. The country's first zoning ordinance was the result, in 1916, and without a doubt made Manhattan a much more livable place than would otherwise be the case.

Over the years, New York zoning became more and more elaborate. Larger buildings could be negotiated with the city in exchange for public amenities, such as vest-pocket parks and subway entrances. Low-rise buildings next door could sell their "air rights," allowing taller buildings than would otherwise be possible. Building plans had to be approved by both citywide authorities and local community boards.

All this, of course, only complicated what has always been a very risky business. Real estate, especially in the dense commercial cores of great cities, is more subject to the vagaries of the business cycle, perhaps, than any other business there is, because the lead times between when large amounts of capital are risked and when income starts flowing in from tenants can be years long.

Major building sites must be assembled, often from dozens of bits and pieces. Old buildings must be demolished. Plans, permits, variances, waivers, and special legislation consume more time. Lawsuits, sometimes dozens of them, must be dealt with. The actual construction can take a year or more. At each stage more and more capital is committed. But no income is generated until the entire project is completed.

Thus, major-league urban real estate is not a game for amateurs or the faint at heart. And that's exactly who Fisher Brothers, a large New York real estate firm, thought it was dealing with when it decided to build a new office tower behind the Park Avenue clubhouse of the Racquet and Tennis Club in the early 1970s.

The Racquet Club traced its history back to 1875. From its inception, the club's membership had been made up of the more sports-minded male members of old New York society. Its clubhouse, an Italian Renaissance palazzo designed by McKim, Mead, and White, had been built in 1918 at Park Avenue and Fifty-second Street. Among its amenities are bedrooms, a dining room, a comfortable bar where very serious backgammon is played for very serious stakes, and courts for various indoor racquet games, including one of the country's half dozen or so court-tennis courts. (The game is a bit like squash, and the nice thing about it is that simply by taking it up, you are automatically one of the 100 best players in the country.)

When the club was built, Park Avenue north of Grand Central was lined with apartment houses designed for the very rich, exactly the sort of people who joined such clubs. By the 1960s, however, that part of Park Avenue had changed. The old apartment buildings had given way to towering office buildings.

Despite the affluence of the membership, by the 1970s the club's finances were in some peril, thanks largely to the soaring taxes on its prime real estate. It needed to raise cash if it was going to remain in its old location. The Racquet Club thought it saw opportunity in the Fisher Brothers project.

Fisher Brothers had paid $22 million for the land, about the last large site left in the east fifties. But the firm, too, had a problem. Although most of the projected building would have good views of Park Avenue over the low-rise Racquet Club, it did not have a Park Avenue address. This was thought essential to renting space at top prices, because side-street addresses in New York simply do not have the same cachet, or command the same rents, as avenue addresses. Fisher Brothers needed the Racquet Club's address and was prepared to rent it.

In most businesses, the needs of both parties would have quickly led to a deal. But this was New York, where hardball was, quite literally, invented. Meetings were held in 1973 and 1974, but no deal was struck because the club wanted an escalator clause to protect itself against inflation and Fisher Brothers wouldn't budge on that.

Then New York City's financial crisis hit, and the real estate market collapsed. For the next three years the Fisher Brothers lot—the meter on the $22 million it had borrowed to purchase the lot ticking away inexorably—lay empty. By 1977, however, things were looking up.

Fisher Brothers went back to the Racquet Club and offered a deal. If it could run an arcade through the club to its building, thus obtaining the precious Park Avenue address, it would pay the club $300,000 a year for the privilege. But the club said no. It insisted the club's architectural integrity had to be preserved and that its air rights had to be part of any deal.

So Fisher Brothers offered $600,000 for the entrance and the air rights, along with a modest escalator clause for inflation. The club thought the escalator should start at a cool $1.2 million a year. Fisher Brothers refused abruptly. The Racquet Club, however, remained confident it was in the catbird seat.

It was not. Fisher Brothers, after all, had not become the highly successful firm it was without having learned its way around the corridors of power in city government. First, it went to Manhattan Borough President Andrew Stein (to whose campaign coffers Fisher Brothers had been a frequent contributor) and asked him to give its lot a new address. In the time it takes to issue a proclamation, 42 East Fifty-second Street became One Park Avenue Plaza, and the market value of the Racquet Club's prestige address vanished.

Next, Fisher Brothers hired Skidmore, Owings, and Merrill, one of the city's premier architectural firms, to redesign the building. The architects were given instructions to design a first-class building with enough public amenities to justify floor-area bonuses equal to what Fisher Brothers could have acquired by buying the Racquet Club's air rights.

The architects came up with the idea of a public "galleria" running through from Fifty-second Street to Fifty-third Street and soaring fully sixty feet above street level. Sixty feet, by no coincidence, was exactly the height of the Racquet Club. It meant that all of the Fisher Brothers rentable floors would have views overlooking Park Avenue, thus commanding the highest rents. And the galleria, open to the public and even equipped with public rest rooms—a rarity in midtown Manhattan—would justify bonuses allowing a larger building.

Fisher Brothers quietly negotiated with the city to win approval of this scheme. Only when it had clinched the deal, in March 1978, did the Racquet Club learn that, far from having the Fisher Brothers against the wall, the club was about to be cut out of the action altogether.

It looked like game, set, and match for Fisher Brothers. But not quite. It turned out that some members of the Racquet Club were nearly as good at playing the game of New York real estate as other members were at high-stakes backgammon.

Only three weeks later a headline in the *New York Times* sent a chill down the collective spine of the Fisher Brothers: "Hotel Is Planned over Racquet and Tennis Club." The hotel, utilizing an alleyway behind the club as an entrance, would leave the club itself untouched. But it would rise 475 feet, right up to the Fisher Brothers's fortieth floor. Its tenants, then, instead of having a wonderful view toward the Seagram Building, St. Bartholomew's Church, and other splendors of New York's east side, would have a view of a brick wall a few feet away.

Fisher Brothers had already spent millions to buy the land and millions more to design and shepherd through the approval process a building that would cost $82 million to actually construct. The Racquet Club's hotel threatened ruination.

But could it be built? Legally, the answer was certainly yes. The proposed building's design was in strict conformity with the zoning law and thus could be built "as of right" without any negotiations with the city. And the Racquet Club was not a New York City landmark then (it is now).

But did the Racquet Club have the money and the expertise to build a hotel? Again, the answer was yes. Intercontinental Hotels, not only an owner and operator of large hotels but a builder of them as well, announced that it thought the scheme was feasible and worked with the club to refine the design. Brokers lined up lenders to finance construction. Structural engineers worked out ways of threading the hotel's support structure through the clubhouse without disturbing its major rooms.

Fisher Brothers was sure the plan was nothing but a holdup. However, it was now in a tough time bind. It received the last piece of paper needed to begin construction on June 9. Any delay in construction at this point cost thousands of dollars a day in extra interest payments, money that could only come from its potential profits.

Further, it had lined up a major tenant who agreed to take 300,000 square feet of space, provided it could move in by 1980. And provided also, of course, that Fisher Brothers guaranteed that it would not be looking out on a brick wall.

When Fisher Brothers failed to begin construction as soon as legally able, the Racquet Club suspected it had the firm on the run. The club was right. When the dust settled, Fisher Brothers paid $5 million for the empty air above the clubhouse.

PART IX

THE TELEGRAPH, TELEPHONE, AND TELEVISION

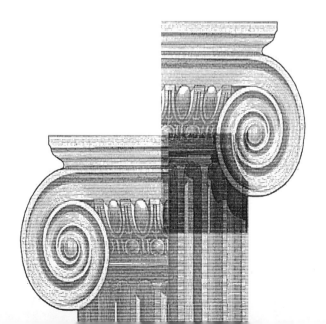

TECHNOLOGY OF THE FUTURE

IN MAY OF 1927, a secretary rushed into her boss's office shouting, "He did it! He did it! Lindbergh has landed in Paris!"

The boss was unimpressed.

"Don't you understand?" she asked. "Lindbergh has flown the Atlantic all by himself."

"A man can do anything by himself," the boss replied quietly. "Let me know when a committee flies the Atlantic."

The story, of course, is almost certainly apocryphal, but it demonstrates a fundamental aspect of the human condition: Genius, that strange and potent combination of insight, faith, determination, and—almost always—youth, inheres in *individuals*.

That's why, despite much recent talk, governments will never be any good at fostering new technologies; governments are nothing more than very large committees. Being endlessly pushed and pulled by conflicting, self-interested forces, governments are naturally inclined to split differences. Having to cater to the powerful, governments are wont to favor what *is* over what might be. Fearing accusations of wasting public money on crackpot schemes, governments must rely on senior experts, who all too often are already set in old ways of thinking.

The result is a rich literature of clouded-crystal-ball pronouncements, dead-end government research projects, and spectacularly missed opportunities. "Space travel is utter bilge," said Sir Richard Woolley, British astronomer royal, a mere thirteen years before the first moon landing. The Carter administration spent billions developing hopelessly uneconomic synthetic fuels. The Wright brothers had to go to a more war-minded Europe to find backing because the U.S. government saw no potential in airplanes.

But if it's any comfort to advocates of big government, even the geniuses who make the technological breakthroughs usually fail to foresee
how their creations will actually play out in the future. Like the rest of us,
they are too deeply embedded in the world they know. James Watt could
hardly have realized that his rotary steam engine would bring forth a
whole new civilization. Henry Ford sought only to free people from the
tyranny of the horse. He had no idea he was creating a profound instrument of social change.

Or consider Samuel F. B. Morse. Morse thought that his telegraph
would be limited to governments sending messages of extreme urgency.
That, after all, is what all earlier attempts to solve the problem of long-
distance communication had been used for. In fact, although he was over
fifty when he finally perfected his telegraph, he lived plenty long enough
to see the world remade by the product of his genius.

Born into a distinguished New England family in 1791, Morse was
trained as a painter, at which profession he scraped a most inadequate
living during much of his life. He had a genius for portraiture, but, like
so many failed artists, he denigrated what he was best at. Instead he aspired
to paint the sort of pictures he thought "important," large allegorical
canvases—then much in vogue—for which he had no more than a pedestrian talent. With much time on his hands, thanks to a lack of commissions, he dabbled in many ideas.

Returning from Europe in 1832, he talked on shipboard with Charles
Thomas Jackson, who had been doing research in electricity in Europe,
and then and there had his fundamental insight. "If the presence of electricity can be made visible in any part of the circuit," he said, "I see
no reason why intelligence may not be transmitted instantaneously by
electricity."

Morse seems to have thought that most of his conception was original
with him. In fact, hardly any of it was. And he would need fully twelve
years of determination and faith to perfect his system, getting much help
from others along the way.

The problem of transmitting information over long distances was as
old as empire. The Persians and the Incas developed elaborate messenger
systems over established roads to hold things together. Elizabeth I's government readied a series of bonfires across the south of England, so that
news of the arrival of the Armada in the Channel could be signaled in-

stantly to London. But it was only in the decade that Morse was born that a true long-distance communications network was devised, albeit so expensive only governments could afford it.

Beginning in 1794, Claude Chappe built a series of semaphore stations between Paris and important military posts such as the naval base at Brest. They were equipped with a mast and movable cross arms with flags. Spaced five to ten miles apart and worked by four or five people each, they were like a series of giant Boy Scouts wigwagging to each other across the French landscape. Using the semaphores, messages could be transmitted at a rate of several hundred miles a day, far faster than any other method of the time.

Of course, the system had numerous disadvantages besides expense. It was useless in bad weather or at night. And because each message had to be endlessly copied and repeated, the transmission error rate was extremely high. So the search continued for other means to move information quickly and began to center on one of the great scientific curiosities of the eighteenth century, electricity.

Electricity was first recognized as a separate phenomenon in the seventeenth century, but not until 1747 did Sir William Watson demonstrate that it was possible to transmit it down a metal wire and that this current could cause action at a distance. In the next decade Benjamin Franklin amused dinner guests by igniting spirits of alcohol from across the Schuylkill River, using an electric wire to convey the spark.

By the 1770s several people had had the idea that electricity flowing through wires might be used to convey information. The first system actually built, in Geneva in 1774, used one wire for each letter of the alphabet. The current would charge a pith ball with static electricity, which in turn would attract a bell, ringing it. This alphabetical carillon actually worked, after a fashion, but was hardly a practical system.

It was only after the invention of the electromagnet and much better batteries, in the first decades of the nineteenth century, that an electric telegraph really became possible. Instrumental in both these developments was Joseph Henry, a professor at Princeton and later the first director of the Smithsonian Institution. He generously shared his knowledge with Morse after Morse began coming to him for advice.

Henry also put Morse onto the final piece of the puzzle. Even the best-insulated wire loses electricity, limiting the distance a message can be carried. But Henry suggested using relays, electromagnetic devices that pick up the signal and generate it anew at full strength.

Morse put together a working model in one of the rooms of New York University. It consisted of batteries, 1,700 feet of wire coiled around the room, and, at each end of the wire, an electromagnet and a telegraph key for opening and closing the circuit. When the operator pushed down the key at one end, it closed the circuit, allowing a current to flow down the wire and activate the magnet at the other end, causing that key to click down in turn.

It was here that the only part of the Morse telegraph that was wholly Morse's came into play, his marvelously efficient code. Morse assigned patterns of dots and dashes to each letter, digit, and punctuation mark. Perhaps the most impressive aspect of the code is that Morse analyzed English letter frequencies and gave the shortest patterns to the most common letters. Morse had spent much time devising a means of recording the signals mechanically, his method for making the electricity "visible," but he soon learned that the code was so simple and easy to use that a trained operator could easily interpret it by ear and write it down directly.

Although Morse's model was extremely crude, it was enough to attract two partners: Leonard Gale, a professor at New York University, who filled in Morse's weak technical background, and Alfred Vail, a gifted mechanic whose father owned a prosperous ironworks in New Jersey. The Vails made a more sophisticated model to show Washington.

The government, handed the key to the future, was characteristically unimpressed, and no money was forthcoming for a real, long-distance demonstration. To get money from Congress, the partners took on a fourth partner, who was, conveniently enough, a congressman himself, F. O. J. Smith, known to his friends as Fog. Smith, chairman of the House Committee on Commerce, did not let a mere conflict of interest stand in the way of progress and pressed hard for an appropriation of $30,000 to build a test line from Baltimore to Washington. But for six long years he got nowhere with his fellow legislators (most of whom undoubtedly had conflicts of interest of their own to attend to).

Finally, in 1843, despite many rude jokes and disparaging remarks on the floor of Congress, Smith slipped his appropriation through in the frantic final minutes of a session. He promptly awarded himself the construction contract and botched it thoroughly, wasting fully $23,000 on shoddy wire and an attempt to lay the wires underground.

Starting the project over, they stretched the wires on poles, and on May 24, 1844, Morse, in the Capitol Building, signaled to Alfred Vail in Baltimore, "What hath God wrought!" and Vail repeated the message accurately.

The effect on the world of Morse's success was, well, electric. Within ten years of the first message, the United States was knitted together with 23,000 miles of wire, with thousands more being added every year. By the time of Morse's death in 1872, the telegraph reached from California to India. Because of it, railroads could operate safely at much higher speeds and much lower costs. Businesspeople could operate in a national market, with great economies of scale. The many regional stock exchanges could coalesce around the one in Wall Street, creating a market to rival London's. Newspaper readers could learn of distant news almost as soon as it happened. The world, thanks to Samuel Morse, shrank by several orders of magnitude.

All of this, of course, had been completely unforeseen by Morse. In fact, shortly after his success, Morse and his partners offered to sell the rights to the federal government for a mere $100,000. Fortunately for them, the government was even more myopic and turned them down flat.

It is a curious irony that, thirty years later, after Alexander Graham Bell successfully demonstrated his telephone, he, too, failed to grasp the immense potential. He, too, tried to sell his rights for the nice round sum of $100,000. But he didn't offer the rights to the government. He offered them to Western Union, which had come to dominate the telegraph business.

Western Union turned him down flat.

POSTALIZATION

IN STUDYING THE PAST, a historian often takes the appearance of a new word in the language as a signal that something was up at that moment and the public consciousness had changed. For instance, although scholars trace the birth of the modern world economy all the way back to the middle of the eighteenth century, when machinery and the factory system began to transform the British textile industry, it was only in 1848, as railroads, the telegraph, and—in Europe—political upheaval were sweeping through the daily lives of the people, that the term *industrial revolution* was coined.

Recently, however, I ran across a word that has *disappeared* from the English language, and its vanishment is eloquent, if silent, testimony to a fundamental change in the American political debate over economic policy. The word is *postalization*. Today, even without knowing exactly what it means, it probably sends an involuntary shudder down the spine of every believer in free markets. In the second decade of the twentieth century, however, to a lot of people it meant "progress."

In the 1990s, Congress voted sweeping changes in the federal law governing communications, designed to ensure maximum competition among local phone companies, long-distance carriers, cable television franchises, and others. The long-term trend in this direction has already borne much fruit. In 1980, 200 million overseas phone calls originated in the United States. Only seventeen years later, thirteen years after unbridled competition in long distance began and prices began to drop sharply, the number of overseas calls had soared to 4.2 billion.

But in the World War I era, the debate was not over how to foster competition in the communications industry, then dominated by a few giant companies, notably AT&T and Western Union. Rather, it was whether or not to bring all telecommunications under the control of the Post Office and thus extinguish what little competition there was. For one brief, inglorious year this actually came to pass.

Today, the telephone industry is in the process of reinventing itself. In the late nineteenth century, however, it had a much harder problem: to invent itself in the first place. One man, Theodore N. Vail, did such a good job of creating a continent-wide phone system that it lasted in the form he conceived for 100 years, avoiding postalization by the sheer quality of the service it offered.

The year after producing a working model in 1876, Alexander Graham Bell and several partners, notably Gardiner Greene Hubbard, who became Bell's father-in-law that year, formed the Bell Telephone Company, incorporated in Massachusetts. In 1878 he hired Vail as general manager. Vail had been born in Ohio in 1845 of Quaker parents. He went to work for the telegraph company and then went into the railway mail service, where he soon showed his talent for organization by radically improving its operations and routing system.

He was brought to Washington in 1873, when he was only twenty-eight, as assistant general superintendent of the railway mail service and three years later was named general superintendent. Gardiner Greene Hubbard then hired him to run the day-to-day operations of Bell Telephone.

From the beginning, telephony proved to be a very capital-intensive business, and in that year Bell and his partners sold a controlling interest in their enterprise to a group of Boston financiers in order to raise additional money. Because of the limited capital, Vail at first licensed numerous local exchanges, charging them twenty dollars a year per telephone, which allowed a rapid expansion of service at minimum cost to the company. As capital became available, however, the company also began taking an ownership interest and organizing these exchanges into larger, more efficient entities that were regional in scope.

In 1881 Hubbard purchased Western Electric to manufacture telephone equipment for the company and its subsidiaries. Finally, in 1885, he organized the American Telephone and Telegraph Company, as a subsidiary of Bell, to tie the various operating companies together with long-distance service. (In 1899, in an adroit move to escape the restrictive corporate law of Massachusetts, Bell Telephone became a subsidiary of AT&T, which was incorporated in New York.)

The first long-distance service, between Boston and New York, was initiated in 1884. The following year lines between New York and Philadelphia were installed. By 1892 AT&T long distance reached as far as Chicago. Significantly, the local operating companies that AT&T controlled were forbidden to connect with other operating companies directly. They had to use AT&T facilities.

By this time, the Bell system, with its control of the largest local operating companies and its now-spreading long-distance system, was dominant in the nascent American telephone industry. But while it was, increasingly, a monopoly, its ever-greater need for capital to expand the system (the number of telephones in operation in the United States nearly quintupled in the 1880s) forced it to be relatively efficient in order both to minimize the capital needed and to be able to sell stock and bonds in the market.

The Boston financiers who controlled the company, however, were primarily interested in immediate profit, not long-term growth. Vail, a true visionary, wanted to plow profits back into expanding and improving the system. In protest, he resigned as president in 1887.

By the turn of the twentieth century, AT&T had assets of $120 million, while all the independent phone companies together had assets of only $55 million. But the independents were expanding fast as the telephone began changing from a luxury to a necessity. To counter the new competition, AT&T was forced to slash rates and became much more customer-friendly. Still, it often acted like a monopoly in other ways. It refused to allow independent companies to connect with it, so these companies could not offer long-distance service. As a result, some cities had two different phone companies, one Bell, one independent. Increasingly, the Bell system used its monopoly of long distance as a lever to force the takeover of these independents.

But this rapid expansion stretched the company's finances, and it was forced to issue ever-increasing quantities of stock and bonds. J. P. Morgan became a major buyer of these securities, and by 1907 he had wrested control of the company from the Boston financiers. Morgan, a visionary like Vail, immediately asked Vail to return to the presidency of AT&T that he had resigned twenty years earlier.

AT&T had over 3 million phones in service by this time, but the company finances were in terrible shape, as was its public image—owing to often poor service and a still high-handed attitude. Staff morale was also very low. Vail set to work to correct these problems by creating a nationwide communication system that would be second to none.

He raised additional capital by offering securities at discount to stockholders, a tactic the company would use over and over again as the Bell system expanded by a factor of thirty in the ensuing decades. He greatly increased spending on research and development, pointing the way to the establishment of Bell Laboratories in 1925. He required all employees to be polite, something that Americans who have never had to deal with a government-owned phone company tend to take for granted.

He also set out, with Morgan's help, to control all telecommunications in this country, buying 30 percent of Western Union, as well as continuing to buy up independent phone companies. He often made use of Morgan's influence on Wall Street to squeeze their credit until they came to terms.

But antimonopoly pressure, especially after the Wilson administration came to office, forced Vail to retreat. In 1913, after Morgan's death, he sold Western Union and allowed, for the first time, the independent phone companies to connect with AT&T long-distance facilities.

Despite the changes Vail initiated at AT&T and its ongoing technological improvement, antimonopoly pressure continued. And in the peculiar tenor of the time, it was increasingly felt that the private quasi-monopoly enjoyed by AT&T should be converted into a complete public one, run by the Post Office. In the Wilson cabinet, the leading advocate of this idea, not surprisingly, was Albert Sidney Burleson, the postmaster general. He began to lobby Congress to authorize a takeover.

Several liberal congressmen took up the cry, notably David J. Lewis of Maryland, who formally called for the "postalization of the telephones and telegraphs." Naturally, this caused the prices of AT&T securities to tumble, but Vail, in his annual report for 1913, advised his stockholders to "rest quietly." Vail admitted that AT&T was, effectively, a monopoly, but he also pointed out, with a logic the left has never been able to grasp, that "all monopolies should be regulated. Government ownership would be an unregulated monopoly."

A government takeover was not a serious possibility until the country's entrance into World War I changed everything. The railroads were taken over temporarily in December that year, and congressional hearings were held in July 1918, to consider a similar takeover of telecommunications.

Postmaster General Burleson was heard at length; AT&T was not invited to testify. A joint resolution passed easily, and Wilson quickly took possession of "each and every telegraph and telephone system, and every part thereof, within the jurisdiction of the United States, including all equipment thereof and appurtenances thereto."

As a practical matter, the Post Office, in effect, hired AT&T to run its old business and only set rates. But whereas AT&T had had to ask to change rates, the Post Office could simply do so. It immediately did, and sharply upward, despite the fact that the primary benefit of government control was supposed to have been lower rates. And, in addition to higher rates, the government began charging a service connection fee, something AT&T had never done.

Public support for a permanent takeover evaporated with the increased rates and the end of the war. AT&T (and the other telecommunications companies) were returned to their owners only slightly more than a year after the takeover. The United States had dodged a socialist bullet and, as a consequence, continued to enjoy the finest, cheapest phone service in the world.

TECHNOLOGICAL
TURKEY

In 1979 RCA announced that it was developing what it called Selecta Vision, a process that, using Thomas Edison's basic technique for recording sound but now hooked up to a television set, produced pictures as well. Edison, no doubt, would have loved it. The public did not.

Selecta Vision came on the market in 1981, just when the VCR was catching on, and few people saw any reason to buy a machine that could play back but not record, when they could buy one that did both for the same price. In 1983 RCA sold only 250,000 Selecta Vision machines against 4 million VCRs sold by RCA and others. The following year it canceled the project, losing $575 million on what the company had once called its "Manhattan Project."

Certainly no one could argue that RCA hadn't produced a bomb.

Selecta Vision represented the end of a very long technological trail, for it had been 102 years earlier, in 1877, that the original, brilliant idea had suddenly flashed into the mind of Thomas Alva Edison. He had an assistant make a gadget consisting of a grooved metal cylinder that rotated and moved freely along a shaft when the shaft was cranked. To either side were diaphragms with a stylus in the middle of each that could come into contact with the groove on the cylinder. His assistant, a German immigrant named John Kreusi, asked what Edison intended to do with this gizmo. "I told him I was going to record talking," Edison remembered, "and then have the machine talk back. He thought it absurd."

Edison wrapped the cylinder in tinfoil, placed the stylus in the groove, and, turning the crank, shouted close to the diaphragm "Mary had a little lamb, its fleece as white as snow." Then he placed the other stylus at the beginning of the groove and cranked the cylinder a second time. Partially deaf since childhood, the inventor heard nothing and thought the experiment had failed. But the others had heard. Faintly but unmistakably, the machine had spoken in Edison's voice.

"Gott in Himmel," said Edison's assistant.

The idea that sound might be captured and preserved for posterity was considered as early as the 1830s, when light was first being captured and preserved by photography. But it was forty years before Edison discovered a practical method of doing so, a method both simple and profound.

The sound waves of Edison's voice caused the membrane of the diaphragm and thus its attached stylus to vibrate. As it moved along the groove on the cylinder, the vibrating stylus incised a pattern of hills and valleys in the tinfoil. When replayed, the pattern now made the stylus and the membrane vibrate, re-creating the original sound waves.

The inventor saw the commercial potential immediately, for he realized that "music can be crystallized as well." "I've made a good many machines," he told a New York newspaper reporter, "but this is my baby, and I expect it to grow up to be a big fellow, and support me in my old age." Edison was right. Vastly elaborated, his idea would be the basis of a great twentieth-century industry.

Edison's machine caused an immediate sensation. President Rutherford B. Hayes was so astonished by it at a late-night demonstration in the White House that he insisted that his wife get out of bed to see for herself. But although it was a sensation, it was still just a gimmick. It would be another decade before Edison's invention was a viable commercial product.

In 1885 C. A. Bell and Charles Sumner Tainter discovered that wax worked much better than tinfoil as a medium for recording sound waves. In the same decade Emile Berliner first used a flat disk with a spiral groove rather than a cylinder with a helical one. Around 1900, lateral recording, where the recording stylus vibrates back and forth rather than up and down as Edison's had done, came into use and much improved the fidelity. By the time of the First World War, the 78-rpm record had completely displaced the cylinder and could play four and a half minutes of music on a side.

At that time also Lee De Forest invented the electrical amplifier. By the early 1920s electronic methods began to replace acoustical recording and reproduction. In 1948 the long-playing record made it possible to play thirty minutes of uninterrupted music, and in 1958 stereo was introduced. By using both Edison's original up-and-down motion and the later lateral motion, stereo was able to record two channels in the same groove. For the first time, reproduced music began to sound much like live music.

But stereo was the last major elaboration of Edison's seminal idea to be commercially successful. Twenty years later, RCA pushed the technology one step farther still and stumbled into disaster. Today, digital technology has replaced Edison's analogue method of recording, and the DVD, with its many advantages over videotape, is taking over the market that Selecta Vision never found. The record is history, but thanks to Edison, the voices and music of a century will be with us forever.

Selecta Vision pushed a technology to its limits when another, better, technology was already beginning to supplant it. This is hardly the first time this has happened. In fact, clipper ships did exactly the same thing, with similar economic but quite different emotional results.

The full-rigged ship had come into being in the late fifteenth century. Over the next three centuries it was slowly refined and became the single greatest instrument in the spread of European civilization and power around the world. By the second decade of the nineteenth century, the standard commercial sailing ship was bluff-bowed and full-bottomed to maximize its cargo space, with a length-to-beam ratio of only about three-to-one. Such characteristics did not make for speed.

But some ships—privateers in the War of 1812 and the recently outlawed slavers among them—needed speed more than they needed cargo space. American naval architects, just beginning to convert their profession from an art to a science, began to produce them. The *Prince de Neufchatel*, a French-backed but American-built privateer, was so swift that when the British finally caught her, having mounted a major expedition to do so, they took her measurements and sent them off to the Admiralty for future reference.

Vessels called Baltimore clippers first appeared about this time and were famous for both their beauty and their speed. But Baltimore clippers were not clipper ships, being small and usually rigged as topsail schooners. And it was not the rigging but the hull—with its sharp, overhanging bow and deep draft at the stern—that made the Baltimore clipper so speedy. It was only a matter of time before someone adapted the Baltimore clipper's hull plan to a full-rigged, three-masted ship.

Exactly which ship was the first true clipper is much disputed among maritime historians. Carl C. Cutler, whose *Greyhounds of the Sea,* published in 1930, is still the definitive work on clippers, awards the title to the *Rainbow,* built in New York for the China trade in 1843.

Because of the great distance to the Orient and the need to coordinate sailing schedules with the monsoon, speed was important on this route. In addition, there was much competition every year among the New York and London merchants to deliver the first tea of the new crop. The early clippers were ideally suited to moving this high-value cargo.

Indeed clippers could not economically transport any freight that was not high value, for the price of their great speed was greatly restricted cargo space. As the race for speed among the clippers heightened, their hulls grew more and more extreme, their bows and sterns narrower. A true clipper had only about 55 percent of the cargo space available to an ordinary ship of the same length.

With their deep drafts, clippers were "stiff" and thus could carry much more canvas than other ships their size. The *Lightning*—appropriately named, for she was one of the fastest of them all—could carry fully 117,000 square feet of sail, more than two and two-thirds acres. All this sail area, of course, required a relatively large crew, and this further narrowed the possible profits.

The clippers, though, were only as fast as their captains were willing to drive them. And the clipper captains were as famous in their day as sports stars are now, competing just as fiercely to wring the last ounce of speed from the magnificent ships beneath their feet. Even in the laconic language of ships' logs one can sense the passion. On March 1, 1854, the master of the *Lightning* wrote "wind South, strong gales . . . 18 to 18½ knots per hour, lee rail under . . . distance run in 24 hours 436 miles." No sailing ship had ever traveled farther in a single day; it would be another thirty years before a steamship could make such sustained speeds.

Had the China trade remained the clippers' only purpose, they would be only a minor part of the history of sail. But the California gold rush changed everything. Suddenly thousands of people wanted to get to the gold fields as soon as possible and at any cost, while merchants were desperate to get merchandise to a market where eggs cost a dollar each and whiskey was forty dollars a quart.

Larger and still faster clippers were built to meet this sudden demand.

Flying Cloud made the New York–San Francisco run around the Horn in only eighty-nine days, a record never equaled under sail, except once by herself. The *Great Republic*, at 4,555 tons, was the largest wooden ship ever built, far larger than most steamships of her day.

It could not last. As the gold rush waned and steam technology improved relentlessly, the clippers made less and less economic sense. In 1853 120 clippers were launched in American yards. Two years later only 42 slid down the ways. In 1859 the last three ever built in this country were launched. Sailing ships designed for cargo, not speed, would continue to carry a majority of the world's ocean freight until after the turn of the twentieth century, but the brief days of the clippers were over.

When pushed to its limits, Edison's sound recording technology produced a soon forgotten commercial turkey called Selecta Vision. The full-rigged sailing ship, when pushed to *its* limits, produced a flotilla of uneconomic swans. Except in special circumstances the clippers couldn't make money and therefore lasted hardly longer in the marketplace than Selecta Vision. But they live on still in the American folk memory, for they were and remain the most beautiful and romantic creations of humankind ever to cleave the waves of the ocean sea.

THE DEATH OF A
MONOPOLY

MCI, the company that broke the monopoly that AT&T had on long-distance telephony in the United States and Canada, was sold in 1996 for $22 billion. That's not bad for a company that less than three decades earlier was having trouble borrowing $35,000. It is perhaps the greatest example of creative destruction in the modern history of capitalism.

Joseph Schumpeter, the great philosopher of capitalism, coined the term *creative destruction.* He was referring to the never-ending restructuring that takes place in a free-market economy as new technologies replace old ones and new companies outcompete their more established rivals. This is often a very painful process on the microeconomic level, as people lose their jobs and investors lose their capital. Indeed, the phenomenon of creative destruction played a major role in the rise of the left in the late nineteenth century as means were sought to avoid the pain without losing the benefits of a technologically progressive economy.

But after numerous experiments with noncapitalist and mixed economies in the twentieth century, creative destruction has turned out to be indispensable at the macroeconomic level. First, because the government owns the means of production in a socialist economy, political considerations, not economic ones, have always dominated decision making in such economies. And politicians will always try to preserve *what is* over fostering *what might be.* After all, *what is* votes and makes campaign contributions; *what might be* does not.

Second, all socialist economies have relied on monopolies to avoid "wasteful" competition and provide economies of scale. But without competition to keeps noses firmly applied to grindstones, all monopolies, whether owned by "the people" or owned by shareholders, tend to become fat, lazy, and uninnovative. Again *what is* becomes heavily favored over *what might be*. After all, creating *what might be* is a lot more work than maintaining *what is*. And if the customers have to come anyway for lack of choice, why work hard? Lions chase the slow gnus to get their supper, not the fast ones; so do we.

The inevitable result—from democratic, semicapitalist Britain in the years after World War II to the unspeakable tyrannies of Communist North Korea and Albania—has always been economic stagnation, lagging technology, and increasing relative poverty.

But even in the most capitalist countries, there have always been what economists call *natural monopolies*. These usually involve situations where such a heavy investment would be needed to provide competition, that it would raise the costs above any possible savings. Electrical utilities are a typical example.

The long-distance market in North America was, as late as the early 1980s, the greatest natural monopoly on earth. Today, however, it is a ferociously competitive industry, as the endless stream of television commercials demonstrates. What happened? Most important, the development of microwave transmission technology—one of the endless number of spinoffs from the invention of radar—made it possible for someone to compete with AT&T without duplicating Ma Bell's vast landline infrastructure. This broke the natural monopoly. All that was needed thereafter was to break the regulatory one. That was not easy, for the Federal Communications Commission was used to working closely with AT&T and had a natural tendency to favor it. Ironically, however, AT&T made, two decades apart, two trivial mistakes that each in no small way helped to end the monopoly.

First, an elephant named AT&T had once tried to squash a mouse called Hush-A-Phone. It is characteristic, indeed instinctive, of all monopolies to protect their turf and try to remove any potential competition or interference. Hush-A-Phone was so insignificant, however, that AT&T did not even notice its existence for nearly thirty years.

In 1921 a small company called Hush-A-Phone began to manufacture a device that could be fitted onto the mouthpiece of a phone. Because of its shape, it allowed the speaker to speak softly and be heard by the person at the other end, while people nearby in the room could not listen in. It was a purely mechanical device and in no way affected the operation of the individual phone to which it was attached or, still less, the network to which the phone was attached.

Then, in the late 1940s, an AT&T lawyer happened to be taking a lunchtime stroll in lower Manhattan when he noticed a Hush-A-Phone in a store window. Intrigued, he went in and bought one and took it back to AT&T headquarters. The company moved immediately to have the Federal Communications Commission forbid the use of Hush-A-Phone on all AT&T equipment. Because in those days customers rented their phones from AT&T rather than owned them, that meant, for all practical purposes, every phone in the United States. AT&T argued before the FCC that Hush-A-Phone might interfere with its equipment and might even cause a catastrophic failure of the system.

The FCC, all too used to saying "how high?" when AT&T said "jump," ruled against Hush-A-Phone. Hush-A-Phone, its very existence in mortal peril, appealed to the courts. The U.S. Court of Appeals for the District of Columbia, not surprisingly unable to see how a bit of plastic screwed onto the end of a phone could have any effect whatever on AT&T's continent-spanning network, ordered the FCC to reverse its decision.

The Hush-A-Phone case was important not in itself but in its use as precedent. From then on, AT&T would have to prove, not merely declare ex cathedra, that an attachment to its system would harm the system. With the contemporaneous onset of the electronic revolution (helped mightily by the invention of the transistor by—you guessed it—AT&T), this began to occur more and more often and AT&T's monopoly began to fray at the edges. It was MCI, however, that drove a stake through its heart.

Faced with a rising tide of complaints against AT&T's often high-handed ways, in 1959 the FCC had allowed companies to establish their own microwave communications networks that bypassed AT&T, but only for internal use. This meant, in effect, that only very large companies with far-flung operations, such as Boeing, could afford them. MCI wanted to set up a microwave communications system between St. Louis and Chicago that would function as a common carrier. In other words, anyone could use it by paying a fee to MCI. AT&T, needless to say, was aghast at the prospect.

MCI had started as a store selling two-way radios in Joliet, Illinois. Its owner, Jack Goeken, asked General Electric for the franchise in Springfield, Illinois, about 190 miles south of Joliet on the main route to St. Louis, and obtained it. Most of these radios were sold to truckers, but they had a range of only about fifteen miles. Worse, the dispatchers at either end of the St. Louis–Chicago corridor could not keep in touch with their truckers. Goeken figured if he could establish enough repeater stations along the route, he could sell a lot more radios. But to do this he needed the approval of the FCC. So in 1963 he and four partners each put up $600 and, with this war chest of $3,000, set off to get that approval.

The FCC, of course, was not supposed to be in the business of protecting AT&T's monopoly; its business was to see that the public interest was served. To prevent MCI from establishing a competitive system, therefore, AT&T had to show that MCI could not build its system at a cost that would allow it to charge competitive prices and hence the public would not be served by it and the license should be denied. And unfortunately for MCI, AT&T had virtually the only expertise in long-distance communications. The FCC had no real choice but to rely on it when making decisions. AT&T, needless to say, did not hesitate to use its monopoly on expertise in self-serving ways.

AT&T buttressed its argument that MCI couldn't operate at competitive prices with facts and figures that no one could effectively rebut. There is little doubt that the FCC would have gone along, but Jack Goeken had a stroke of luck and an AT&T employee made the other mistake. Goeken had heard at the FCC about a confidential report on microwave communications systems that AT&T had prepared for internal use only. He figured that the only hope of getting a copy was the direct approach, so he flew to New York, went to AT&T, and asked for a copy. Fortunately for him, it was a cold, snowy day in New York, and he had accidentally left his overcoat in the Hartford airport. The woman he talked to at AT&T simply assumed that, because he didn't have a coat, he must be an employee, and she told him the report was in the company library. He asked where—meaning where is the library—and, still operating under the assumption he was an employee, she apparently thought he meant where *in* the library. She wrote out an official interoffice request form with the document name and number. Goeken realized what was happening, had enough sense to shut up, and found the library on his own. The report was his, and with it AT&T would rebut itself, for the report contained much lower cost estimates.

It would take until August of 1969, six years after MCI filed its original application, before the FCC granted it a license to operate. But when it did, the camel's nose was under the tent of AT&T's vast and vastly profitable monopoly. Within a decade the greatest monopoly in history was history.

The result for AT&T has been an epic episode of creative destruction as it seeks to remake itself for a new competitive world. The process is by no means over. The results for the people at large, however, have been greatly improved service, swiftly falling rates, and a staggering rise in the use of long distance over the last two decades. The government stopped collecting statistics on toll calls in 1985 because the definition of a toll call had broken down in the face of competition. Overseas calls, however, show the rise clearly. In 1970 there were only 23.4 million of them. By 1980 the number had risen to 200 million, and in 1997 the number was 4.2 billion, 179 times as many as only twenty-seven years earlier. More, the cost has dropped dramatically. In 1970 the average overseas call cost $10.76. In 1994 it was $2.18. Add in the effects of inflation, and the cost of an overseas call is only about 5 percent of what it was two decades ago. Meanwhile, long-distance costs have dropped so dramatically that most businesses now happily pick up the tab for them with 800 numbers.

Many years ago the science writer Sir Arthur C. Clarke predicted that long distance would disappear by the end of the century, and a phone call would be a phone call whether it went next door or around the world. He's not far from being right, thanks to an ill-advised lawsuit and a lost overcoat.

DESI ARNAZ

Oscar Hammerstein I, the great theatrical impresario of the turn of the century, once famously said that "there is no limit to the number of people who can stay away from a bad play." Hammerstein, who had his share of flops, knew what he was talking about, and his dictum remains every bit as true today.

Of course, in Hammerstein's time the opposite—that there are strict limits on the number of people who can come to a *good* play—was equally true. Only about 1,800 people can fit into even the largest Broadway theater, so a sellout show has to run well over a year before 1 million people can get to see it.

Today, technology has changed that completely. A hit movie can be seen simultaneously in thousands of theaters. And because the actors don't get tired, there can be several "performances" a day. By the time *Titanic* had been out a year, something on the order of half the human race had seen it already.

Television is even more of a mass medium. When *Cinderella*, the only television musical written by Richard Rodgers and Oscar Hammerstein II (the grandson of the impresario), had its one performance, on March 31, 1957, it was seen by about 107 million people in this country. That's more people than had seen all the theatrical productions of Rodgers and Hammerstein's first musical, *Oklahoma!*, throughout the world, since the original had opened on Broadway fourteen years earlier to the day.

Television's unparalleled power to reach a mass audience is the reason that *Titanic* was not the biggest entertainment moneymaker of 1998. *Titanic's* worldwide box office was well over $1 billion, and that, to be sure, is a long way from hay. But it's chump change to the $1.7 billion that was paid for the syndication rights to *Seinfeld* in 1998, especially when you consider that a movie's take at the box office is gross and the sale of television syndication rights is pure, bottom-line profit.

Syndication is simply the sale of rights to broadcast old episodes of a television show. This is big business. Anyone with a couch and a clicker can, in the course of an evening, channel surf through the whole history of television sitcoms, from *The Honeymooners,* to *Bewitched,* to *M.A.S.H.,* to *The Mary Tyler Moore Show,* to *The Golden Girls,* to *Cheers,* to *Laverne and Shirley,* to *Cosby,* to *Seinfeld.*

One of the nicer aspects of syndication is that the major creative artists involved in the original production, not just the "suits" who finance it, are cut in on the action. Jerry Seinfield, who was a cocreator as well as the star of his eponymous sitcom, will bank an altogether tidy $225 million from the sale of its syndication rights.

The reason for this is not any excess gratitude on the part of the suits, I assure you. Rather, it is that the very idea of syndication was dreamed up by a very savvy businessman who happened to be the husband of—and straight man for—a very funny woman named Lucille Ball. Desi Arnaz's gifts as a performer helped mightily to make *I Love Lucy* the first great television sitcom. But it was his gifts as a businessman that made the Arnaz family seriously rich.

Desi Arnaz was born in 1917 in Santiago, on Cuba's southeastern coast. His family belonged to Cuba's small and privileged upper class; indeed his father was mayor of Santiago. When he was a teenager, however, a revolution against the utterly corrupt regime of President Gerardo Machado forced his family to flee to Miami, leaving their wealth behind. Desi got a job with a canary dealer, cleaning cages and delivering birds to stores, that paid fifteen dollars a week.

That was not bad money for a teenager in the middle of the depression. But when he was offered a job with a Latin dance band, at a seemingly princely thirty-nine dollars a week, he jumped at it. His family had wanted him to become a lawyer, and he had never even thought of a career in show business, but, like many a person before him, Desi Arnaz had stumbled upon his destiny.

Xavier Cugat, then the king of Latin music in this country, caught Desi's act one night and hired him, but for only twenty-five dollars a week. Desi took the job despite the salary cut and soon proved so popular that Cugat raised his salary to thirty-five dollars. Before long Desi decided he could do better on his own and told Cugat he intended to return to Miami and form his own band. Cugat, trying to keep him, told him he'd fail, but when Desi was adamant, offered to let him bill himself as "Desi Arnaz and his Xavier Cugat Orchestra."

Desi offered to pay a royalty for the use of his name, and Cugat asked how much. "The same as you paid me when I started, twenty-five dollars a week," Desi—already a businessman—told him. "And like you told me then, if we do good, we'll negotiate."

Desi's opening, with scratch musicians, two of whom were not even Latin, was a disaster. But the next night, desperate for a Latin beat his orchestra could play, he came up with the conga, then unknown in the United States. It was a sensation. Soon Desi was the lead at a New York nightclub called La Conga. It was there that he was spotted by Richard Rodgers and his then-partner Lorenz Hart and offered a part in their new musical, *Too Many Girls*. When *Too Many Girls* was made into a movie, he was offered the same part in the film. One of the other principals in the film was Lucille Ball.

They were soon married, and, if hardly Hollywood stars of the first rank, they made a very comfortable living in films, radio, and live theater. But after World War II ended, a new medium, television, began to make serious inroads on the audience for both films and theater. By 1948, the year Milton Berle first appeared on television, there were nearly 1 million sets in American homes. He was such a hit, however, that one year later there were 4 million and the number was climbing exponentially.

While still making pictures, Lucille Ball had been starring in a hit radio comedy called *My Favorite Husband*, and CBS wanted to transfer it to television. Lucy demanded that Desi be cast as her husband. The "suits" at CBS were appalled. "Who would believe her married to a wop?" asked one, not even getting his ethnic slurs straight.

"What do you mean nobody'll believe it?" asked Lucy. "We *are* married."

After much give-and-take, a pilot was shot of what was then called *The Lucille Ball–Desi Arnaz Show*. Because Desi was principally a singer and bandleader, not an actor, his part was, in effect, his real-life persona. And the original concept involved a good deal of his nightclub act.

In the early days of television, sponsors were usually involved in the actual production, rather than mere time-purchasers as they are today.

Cigarette manufacturers were major advertisers on television at that time, and Philip Morris was interested but wanted to judge reactions. So the kinescope (a film made off the television signal of the pilot—the only way then to preserve a live broadcast) was shown to a few people. One of these people was Oscar Hammerstein II, who, along with his many other talents, was known as a great "play doctor," someone who knew how to fix a show that didn't work.

His advice was succinct: "Keep the redhead, but ditch the Cuban." Told that was impossible, Hammerstein said, "Well, for God's sake, don't let him sing. No one will understand him. Make it a warm, human story built around a wholesome, lovable, dizzy couple."

I Love Lucy was born.

But if the basic creative decisions were made, the business ones were not. CBS wanted the series done live in New York. The East Coast was where the audience was, and if the show was done in Hollywood, the East Coast would have to see blurry kinescopes. Lucy and Desi wanted to stay in Hollywood, so Desi negotiated. He suggested using their production company, Desilu, to film the show ahead of time. This solved the quality problem but would considerably increase the production costs, originally budgeted at what now seems a minuscule $19,500 an episode. Desi, picking a figure out of thin air, guessed that the increase would amount to $5,000.

After much hemming and hawing, Philip Morris and CBS agreed to come up with an additional $2,000 each. But Lucy and Desi, who were to be paid $2,500 each and own half the show, would have to take a $1,000 salary cut between them on each of the thirty-nine episodes that were contracted for to make up the difference.

Desi made a counteroffer. He and Lucy would take the salary cut, provided CBS gave them sole ownership. Since in 1951 most television shows were done live and preserved only on kinescopes, yesterday's TV shows, CBS felt, were worth about the same as yesterday's newspapers. So CBS readily agreed. The suits figured they weren't giving up much.

But Desi knew that he and Lucy weren't giving up much either. "In our tax bracket," he explained, "we might have ended up with about $5000 of the $39,000 we were losing [in salary cuts]. So in effect, we were buying the other half of the series for $5000."

That, of course, turned out to be the bargain of the century. Because *I Love Lucy* was filmed, not performed live, for the first time in television there was something worth selling after the original broadcast was over. And because *I Love Lucy* turned into one of the biggest hits in the history of show business, there was no lack of offers to buy.

There still isn't. Today, nearly half a century after *I Love Lucy* premiered, the price of broadcasting a single episode is $100,000. That's not much compared to what *Seinfeld* will get in syndication, but it's twenty times what Desi Arnaz paid for half the rights to *all* the episodes.

PART X

AFTER HOURS

THE AMERICAN GAME

BASEBALL, we are told, is the American game, and much earnest nonsense has been written about how its attributes mystically reveal the American character. Baseball mirrors American life, it is said. It requires both teamwork and individual genius, involves squandered chances and answered prayers, measures the short term of the single game and the long haul of the entire season. It is all perfectly true, but I'm not sure how that differs from life anywhere else.

So what, then, makes baseball so red-white-and-blue American? Well, if Calvin Coolidge was right that "the business of America is business"—and the present writer is not about to argue with the notion—then baseball is most certainly the American game. Baseball, you see, was a business as well as a sport from its very earliest days.

Within twenty-five years of the game's appearance on the American scene in the 1840s, professional players had taken over baseball, and the displaced amateurs—unlike in football, track, and basketball—vanished from the game entirely beyond the purely local level. How a multibillion-dollar industry grew out of a child's game makes an interesting—and very American—story.

Like all great team sports (except basketball), baseball arose spontaneously from the human race's collective genius for play. Its ultimate origins lie in a game called rounders, played by village boys in England since time immemorial. Variations of rounders were known in both England and America by many other names, and one called baseball is even mentioned by Jane Austen in *Northanger Abbey*, written about 1798.

Exactly how rounders evolved into what we now know as baseball is unknown and quite probably always will be. But if baseball owes an undisputed debt to the English game, it was certainly in America where the crucial change was made, transforming a child's game of no great interest into a man's game that captured the imagination of the American nation.

In rounders, outs are made by throwing the ball at the runner and hitting him with it while he is off base. The use of a soft ball prevented fractured skulls, but a soft ball couldn't be hit very far. Once tagging the runner out with the ball was substituted for hitting him out with it, a hard ball could be substituted for the soft one, and baseball, that infinite interplay of just four human skills—hitting, running, catching, and throwing—could be born.

The game we call baseball emerged in New York City. Informal clubs, mostly made up of upper-middle-class men (that is to say, businessmen) would meet to play rounders. At first, winning was not nearly as important as the fun and the exercise. The camaraderie and informality were in all likelihood highly reminiscent of a modern backyard touch football game.

But as rounders evolved into baseball, matters became more serious. The clubs became formally organized and began playing each other occasionally. Rivalries developed between them, making winning more important. Spectators began showing up to watch these games and often to bet on the outcome. The gamblers, of course, wanted victory.

Until very recently, it was thought that the first reported game of baseball was a 23–1 shellacking of the Knickerbocker Club by the New York Club in 1846. But Edward L. Widmer, a Harvard graduate student, recently unearthed a newspaper box score for a game played in Hoboken, New Jersey, between the New York Club and a team from Brooklyn on October 21, 1845. The New York Club won the game 24–4 and even hit a grand slam.

Baseball's popularity slowly increased over the next ten years, and by 1855 there were a dozen ball clubs playing regularly in New York and Brooklyn. Then suddenly baseball exploded; by 1860 there were more than 125 clubs in the metropolitan area, and the game was spreading fast to other cities.

No small factor in this explosion was that the newspapers began reporting more and more baseball news and publishing statistics that allowed readers to compare teams and individual players. This, of course, greatly increased the club rivalries.

In 1857 representatives of fourteen clubs met and adopted the rules of the Knickerbocker Club as the official rules of baseball. In the next few years these rules would be adopted everywhere, extinguishing the other baseball-like games that had evolved from rounders and allowing clubs from different cities to play each other.

The following year the first umbrella organization was formed, the National Association of Base Ball Players. (Actually there was nothing national whatever about the teams represented, as they all came from the New York area, but that sort of P. T. Barnum–style exaggeration has always been typical of baseball. The first "World" Series was played in 1903, when no major league team was located west of St. Louis or south of Washington, D.C., let alone outside the United States.)

In 1860 the Excelsior Club of Brooklyn took the first road tour, a two-week jaunt through western New York State, playing local clubs and thrashing them all soundly. The Excelsior Club now took winning very seriously indeed. It chose its members not for their social attributes but for their skill at baseball. Before long, it recruited the game's first professional player, James Creighton. Creighton was a pitcher who delivered his pitches, at least according to one awed reporter, "within a few inches of the ground and they rose up about the batsman's hip, and when thus delivered, the result of hitting at the ball is either to miss it or send it high in the air."

Creighton couldn't afford to leave his job to tour with the club, but, because he possessed a pitch that would seem to have behaved in flat defiance of the laws of physics, the club was only too happy to compensate him for his lost wages.

By 1861 baseball had become so popular that two Brooklyn clubs even played a game in midwinter on ice skates. Although the results were more vaudeville than baseball, fully 10,000 people turned out to watch. These huge crowds did not go unnoticed by entrepreneurs.

The following year, William H. Cammeyer laid out the Union Grounds in eastern Brooklyn and allowed three clubs to use it for their home games, provided he was permitted to charge spectators ten cents each for admission. Other enclosed ball fields soon followed. The field owners, naturally, wanted the best possible teams in order to draw the largest crowds. They were a powerful force behind the increasing professionalization of baseball.

By the late 1860s there were three semiprofessional teams in New York and Brooklyn. In order to lure them to their fields, the owners began paying them a percentage of the gate. William H. Cammeyer paid the Brooklyn Atlantics 60 percent of their gate receipts, less expenses, to play at his field, the money being divided among the players. It was not a large leap from owning a ballpark and paying the players a percentage of the gate to owning the team and paying the players a salary. William Cammeyer took the team he formed, the ancestor of today's Los Angeles Dodgers, into the National League when it was formed in 1876.

The year 1869 saw the first completely professional team, the Cincinnati Red Legs. The team toured the country and did not lose a single game that year. Clearly if other teams were to compete with the Red Legs, they would have to become professional too. The amateurs still in the game protested, but it was too late. There was good money to be made in baseball, and market forces, as they usually do in the United States, took over. By 1874 serious amateur baseball was history.

Having become a business, baseball, like all other businesses, had to contend thereafter with two paramount considerations: how to attract paying customers, and how to divide the spoils between labor and capital.

To attract a larger and larger crowd, the rules of baseball slowly evolved. Hitters had been dominant in the early days, but with better balls, and better fields, the pitchers took over. In 1920, to increase the number of crowd-pleasing hits, such pitching tactics as spitballs were banned, and the livelier baseball was introduced. It worked. In 1919 Babe Ruth led the American League with twenty-nine home runs. In 1920 he led it with fifty-four, and the following year with fifty-nine, doubling his home-run output in two years.

When the pitchers again gained the upper hand in the 1950s and 1960s, thanks largely to the new specialty of relief pitching, the American League created (over the collective dead bodies of millions of baseball purists) the designated hitter in 1973. It has all worked. In 1876, the first year the National League operated, 343,750 people attended games, an average of only about 1,300 per game. In 1988 53.8 million went to major league games, far above the attendance at any other team sport. Countless millions also watched on television.

Negotiations between the owners and the players have not been as smooth. In 1869 the *New York Times* reported that players' salaries could be as high as $2,500 per year, an excellent wage for a young man in those days. As competition among the owners for baseball talent escalated, however, so did the salaries. The owners saw their profits being threatened and did exactly what you would expect nineteenth-century businessmen under the circumstances to do: They conspired to fix prices. In 1879 they added the so-called reserve clause to the standard player's contract, which in effect made it impossible for a player to move to another team without the consent of the owner of his present one. This clause not only prevented players from switching teams but worked wonders in keeping down player salaries.

Despite the Sherman Antitrust Act of 1890, this obvious combination in restraint of trade lasted almost a century, owing to some of the U.S. Supreme Court's most pixilated decisions. In 1923 Oliver Wendell Holmes simply declared baseball not to be a business, regardless of the 8.974 million people who paid good money to watch major league games that year. Not being a business meant the Sherman Antitrust Act didn't apply, and the semiserfdom of baseball players could continue.

When the reserve clause finally fell in 1975, salaries zoomed. In 1973 the highest-paid player in baseball pulled down $250,000 per year. In 1997 the *average* player earned $1,337,000. The owners, of course, are screaming poverty, but the operating profit of major league baseball continues to rise, although much more so for clubs in large media markets. Not bad for a game dreamed up on the streets of New York by some businessmen looking for exercise.

SAINT STRAUS

PEOPLE WHO OBTAIN THEIR view of the world only from movies and television know that businessmen come in three varieties. They can be crooks (*Wall Street*), incompetents (*Tucker*), or both (*The Solid Gold Cadillac*). Those of us who live in the real world know that businessmen come in the same infinite variety as any other group of human beings. A few are even saints. One of these was named Nathan Straus.

Born in Otterberg in Rhenish Bavaria in 1848, Nathan Straus was the second of the four children of Lazarus Straus. In 1852 his father immigrated to the United States and in 1854 sent for his wife and children. Unlike most Jewish immigrants, Straus did not settle in one of the major cities. Rather, he opened a small store in Talbotton, Georgia, where his children attended a log cabin schoolhouse. Being hundreds of miles from the nearest synagogue, the family went to the Baptist Church. The local circuit-riding preachers were awed, to put it mildly, by Lazarus Straus's ability to read the Old Testament in its original language. To them it was like hearing the word of God directly.

During the Civil War Lazarus Straus acquired a large stockpile of cotton, but in the disorders that followed the fall of the Confederacy, the cotton was burned and he was wiped out. Undaunted, he moved his family to Philadelphia and then to New York. There he opened L. Straus and Son, importers of fine china and glassware from Europe, in partnership with his eldest son, Isidor. (In 1912 Isidor would refuse to enter a lifeboat while women and children remained aboard the *Titanic*. He was lost along with his wife, who preferred death at her husband's side to life without him.)

Nathan joined the family business in 1881. The company had run the Macy's china and glassware departments under lease since 1874, and Nathan soon showed a flare for the sort of merchandising savvy that brings customers into a store and keeps them coming back. He dreamed up the idea of the depository account (an early version of the layaway plan). He provided rest rooms for customers and had emergency medical care on hand.

He was also extremely popular with the employees. Always a natty dresser, Nathan would wander around the store whistling the popular tunes of the day and having a good word for everyone. More practically, he provided the employees with a lunchroom and served food at cost.

In 1887 the Strauses acquired a half-interest in Macy's and a decade later became its sole owners. The store expanded steadily as they introduced more and more innovations. The Strauses invented bargain sales and exhibitions. They introduced odd pricing ($15.95 instead of $16.00) to give the customer the psychological sense of getting a bargain (and, not so incidentally, making it more difficult for the clerk to pocket the cash). By 1902, when Macy's moved to its present location in Herald Square, it was the largest store in New York. By then the family had also started the very successful Abraham and Straus store in Brooklyn and become very, very rich.

But moneymaking had never been their sole concern. Nathan dabbled in politics, serving as the city's parks commissioner from 1889 to 1893. The following year he was offered the Democratic nomination for mayor but turned it down. The brothers had also become considerable philanthropists. In the depression that racked the country in the 1890s, Nathan Straus did all he could to alleviate misery.

In the terrible winter of 1893–94, he provided meal tickets to fully 1.5 million people. The following year he supplied 2 million tickets for coal, food, and lodging at shelters he established. Deeply conscious of human dignity, he charged five cents for these tickets to those who could afford to pay, giving them away free only to those who could not. In this way, when coal was selling for twenty cents a pailful, he supplied it at five cents a pail to those who were merely poor, while giving away fully 2,000 tons to those who were desperate.

Great as was Straus's help to the poor and to other causes (such as his passionate support of Jewish settlement in what was then Palestine), it was in his tireless effort to secure a safe milk supply for the nation's children that he earned immortality.

Before the industrial revolution, the overwhelming majority of babies were fed at their mother's (or, if the family was rich enough, a wet nurse's) breast. But as women increasingly went to work in factories in the nineteenth century, they had to turn more and more to cow's milk to nourish their children. This posed no small menace.

Milk from both healthy cows and healthy humans is initially sterile, and is often referred to in industry ad campaigns as "nature's perfect food." Unfortunately, milk is quite as perfect a food for a myriad of microorganisms as it is for humans. As the cows were milked by unwashed hands, the milk poured into unsterilized containers and transported long distances from farms to cities, these microorganisms could enter and multiply quickly. Typhoid, diphtheria, various intestinal infections, and cholera can all be contracted from contaminated milk, although there may be no sign of spoilage. In one test, milk legally for sale at a grocery on Allen Street in New York City was found to contain bacteria at the rate of more than 125 *billion* per quart. There is no reason to think this was out of the ordinary.

As if the afflictions already mentioned were not bad enough, tuberculosis, the Victorian's "dreaded dark disease," can be carried by milk as well, and, worse, it is one of the few diseases that can get through nature's defenses and be transmitted directly through breast-feeding. Cows are quite as susceptible to TB as humans and often show few signs until they are near death.

For these reasons, milk, the staff of life to the young, was also the transmitter of death among urban children in nineteenth-century America. In the 1850s fewer than half the children born in New York City lived to see their fifth birthdays, and no one then knew why. Enter Louis Pasteur and Robert Koch.

Beginning in the 1850s and 1860s, Pasteur demonstrated that microorganisms were responsible for fermentation in wine and beer, for spoilage in milk, and for several diseases such as chicken cholera and anthrax. Koch found the organism that caused tuberculosis. The germ theory of disease was born.

In the early 1890s Nathan Straus kept a "high-bred cow" at his camp in the Adirondacks in order to supply the household with good, clean milk. Suddenly, the apparently healthy cow sickened and died. The autopsy revealed tuberculosis, and Straus was appalled.

It was not then certain that bovine TB was the same as the human variety; still, to Straus, who had no scientific training, "it was inconceivable . . . that the milk from tuberculous cows could be a safe food in its raw state." Straus also knew there was a solution at hand. Pasteur had shown that heating liquids to a point below boiling and holding them there for a period of time killed most disease-causing microorganisms, including Koch's deadly *Mycobacterium tuberculosis.*

Straus immediately saw to it that his own children drank pasteurized milk and characteristically set to work both to provide it to needy children and to have the process legally mandated for all milk sold. He set up milk stations in poor areas in New York City to give away pasteurized milk, and proof of the efficacy of the program was not long in coming. In 1871, 24 percent of babies born in New York City died before age one. But of the 20,111 children fed on pasteurized milk supplied by Nathan Straus over a four-year period, only six died.

In 1898 Straus served as the president of the city's Board of Health. He immediately donated pasteurization equipment to the city's orphans asylum. This grim institution received children abandoned by or removed from their families, so it is not surprising that they had a death rate four times that of children in general. In 1897, a typical year, 44 percent of the children housed there died. In 1898, with pasteurized milk the only change, the death rate at the asylum plunged to 20 percent.

With results like this, one would think that pasteurization would have swept the nation. Unfortunately, it faced fierce opposition from milk distributors, bureaucrats, and others. At one point Straus was even arrested for "adulterating" milk because he supplied mothers with infant formula. But he persevered until the evidence became overwhelming. In 1908, when the infant death rate had been cut in half by voluntary pasteurization, Chicago became the first city to require it, and New York finally followed suit in 1913.

In the course of his crusade, Straus established at his own expense 297 milk stations in thirty-six cities. Over the course of twenty-five years, 24 million glasses and bottles of safe milk were dispensed. The national death rate for children fell from 125.1 per 1,000 in 1891 to 15.8 per 1,000 in 1925, mostly thanks to pasteurization. Altogether it is estimated that the efforts of Nathan Straus directly saved the lives of 445,800 children.

Despite these prodigious outside activities, he remained active in the management of Macy's until 1914 and retired from business completely only in 1925, when he was seventy-seven. When he died in 1931, his estate amounted to $1 million, and he left not a penny of it to charity, explaining his reason in his will: "What you give for the cause of charity in health is gold, what you give in sickness is silver, and what you give in death is lead."

Today, New York City has a touching memorial to Isidor Straus and his wife—they who loved honor and each other above life itself—but there is none to Nathan. In a larger sense, however, there are thousands of memorials in every neighborhood of every city in the country. As Admiral George Dewey explained at the ground-breaking ceremony for one of the milk stations, "If all the little children whose lives . . . [Straus] saved could mass themselves around the building now to be erected, . . . [he] would have the most splendid memorial ever made to man."

So the next time you hear the laugh of a child or look into a little face shining with health, remember Nathan Straus, a saint who was, as it happens, a businessman.

THE PHILANTHROPIST

IT'S A STORY THAT has been told many times. The Hewlett-Packard Company was founded by two gifted tinkerers, David Packard and William Hewlett, in a garage in Palo Alto, California, in 1938, with $538 in capital. Its first product was an audio oscillator for testing sound equipment. Walt Disney quickly ordered eight of the devices to help in the production of *Fantasia,* and the company never looked back.

While Hewlett concentrated on the product side of the business, Packard headed the business side and ran a notably tight ship. (In 1961, when the company went public, several high executives, who were staying at a midtown hotel in New York, had to make their way to Wall Street for the ceremony via subway instead of a taxi, let alone a limousine. Unfortunately for them, the New York subway is distinctly stranger-unfriendly, and they got lost switching trains at Times Square and missed the ceremony.) But despite the occasional misplaced executive, Packard's methods were very successful. Today, Hewlett-Packard is a $31-billion-a-year company employing thousands and ensuring that the United States will maintain its lead in the dominant technology of the twenty-first century.

But if Packard was frugal about spending money, he was fabulously generous about giving it away. When he died in 1996 at the age of eighty-three, he left the bulk of his fortune to the foundation that he and his wife had established and already endowed with more than $1 billion. Thus the Packard Foundation enters the ranks of the great American eleemosynary institutions created in the twentieth century, along with the Carnegie Endowment and the Ford and Rockefeller Foundations.

But the men who founded these mighty institutions were hardly the first to use their wealth to help their fellow humans. Most of the great museums of New York, Boston, Philadelphia, Chicago, and elsewhere, after all, were built and filled with the donations of the very rich. One of the earliest of these national benefactors was a man now largely forgotten, except by New Yorkers, who see his name often around the great city. That name is Peter Cooper.

Like Packard, Cooper was a born tinkerer, very frugal about spending money, and notably generous about giving it away. And like Packard, he used these attributes to make and then largely distribute one of the great American fortunes.

Cooper was born in 1791 on Little Dock Street (now part of South Street) in New York City, the ninth child of the family. His family soon moved up the Hudson River to Fishkill, and his father, who had served as a lieutenant in the Continental army, had a series of businesses, working as a hatter, a brewer, a storekeeper, and a brick maker. He was not very successful in any of them, but his son helped him from a very young age and so grew up deeply familiar with small-scale industrial processes as well as the details of business keeping. In addition, he helped his mother around the house, including with the laundry. He soon invented a gizmo for pounding the dirty clothes, perhaps the world's first washing machine. He also designed a primitive mechanical lawn mower, although it was not built, at a time when the standard lawn mowers were called sheep.

Unfortunately, unlike David Packard, who received a world-class education in engineering at Stanford University, Cooper's family's relative poverty did not allow him to get more than about a year of formal schooling. But that was not uncommon at the turn of the nineteenth century, and engineering was a much simpler business then as well. When he was seventeen he was apprenticed to a carriage maker in New York City. During his apprenticeship, Cooper spent much time teaching himself by reading, and even by paying private tutors to teach him in the evening. It was this endeavor that gave him the idea of establishing evening classes to let working people gain a formal education. It was an idea that would blossom fifty years later into Cooper's greatest legacy and is now so common that it is hard to imagine that somebody had to think of it in the first place.

The apprenticeship agreement called for him to be paid twenty-five dollars a year plus room and board, but he was soon being so useful that his employer voluntarily doubled and then tripled his pay. At the end of his apprenticeship at age twenty-one, the carriage maker offered to lend Cooper the money he needed to set himself up in the carriage-making business, but Cooper declined. He didn't want to be in debt, for he had already learned to be very cautious about money. When he had first returned to New York City, he had taken his savings—ten dollars—and "invested" them in a lottery. He lost. Thereafter, he never again gambled, and he always paid his bills immediately. "I used to pay all my debts every Saturday night," he remembered as an old man, "and I knew that what I had left was my own!"

Cooper went to work in a woolen factory and again made himself indispensable. He invented a machine for shearing the nap off woolen cloth (it was based on his lawn-mower idea) and was soon being paid at the rate of $1.50 a day, then very good wages.

When he was twenty-two, Cooper married Sarah Bedell. It was to be a happy marriage, one that lasted fifty-six years and produced six children, although only two lived to adulthood. But Cooper felt himself to be drifting at this time. Late in life he said that he spent the first thirty years of his life getting a start, the next thirty making a fortune, and the last thirty doing good with that fortune. Thus he dates the start of his great success to the year he acquired a glue factory. Actually, he got the place at a discount, because he paid $2,000 in cash. So he had already acquired far more capital than the average man of his day.

Glue was not a very glamorous business, but Cooper suspected it would be a very profitable one. He was right. The factory was located at a place then deep in the countryside but which is now called Thirty-second Street and Park Avenue. Cooper immediately threw himself into both running the business (he did all the bookkeeping and office work himself for years) and improving his product line. At that time American-manufactured glue was of very poor quality, and most was imported from Europe at high prices.

Cooper quickly proved himself as adept a chemist as he was an engineer (although when one experiment went badly awry, it almost cost him the sight of one eye). The very first year he cleared $10,000 in the glue business—five times what he had paid for the entire concern. Soon he had a near-monopoly on glue in this country and was earning upward of $100,000 a year, a vast income for the 1820s. Cooper continued to live simply and to plow his profits into other investments, including, in 1828, a 3,000-acre parcel in Baltimore, where he and two partners built the Canton Iron Works.

It was hoped that the new Baltimore and Ohio Railroad, whose tracks ran nearby, would be a source of much business as well as a cheap means of transporting supplies and products. But the nascent B&O was near bankruptcy. Its few miles of tracks were so twisty that George Stephenson—who built the Liverpool and Manchester, the world's first commercially successful railroad, in 1828—declared that steam locomotives could not operate successfully on it. Cooper decided to prove the great engineer wrong. "I'll knock an engine together in six weeks," he declared, "that will pull carriages ten miles an hour."

This he proceeded to do. He found some old wheels that would serve, rigged them to a platform, sent to New York for a rotary steam engine he had had built for an earlier experiment, and bolted it to the platform and then added a boiler. So far so good, but now he had a problem: how to connect the boiler to the engine itself. What plumbing there was in 1830 was made of lead, which couldn't take the pressure or the temperatures of a steam engine. Iron piping simply did not exist yet in this country. So Cooper took a couple of old muskets, sawed off the barrels, and used them. Piece by improvised piece, he assembled the "Tom Thumb," the first locomotive built in the United States.

To everyone's surprise (except, I suspect, Peter Cooper's), the contraption worked, pulling a carriage loaded with forty people at a speed of up to eighteen miles an hour, then a breathtaking pace. Indeed, some of the passengers made a point of taking out paper and pencil and writing down coherent sentences while whizzing along to disprove the widely held belief that the human brain could not function when moving at such a speed.

Soon the Baltimore and Ohio Railroad was a going concern (quite literally in this case), and the value of Cooper's land in Baltimore soared. When he sold out a few years later, he took B&O stock in payment at a value of $45 a share, and a few years later sold it for $235 a share.

The Cooper industrial empire expanded rapidly after this, and within two decades he owned foundries, wire-making plants, blast furnaces, and rolling mills. By the 1850s 2,500 men worked for Peter Cooper, a large number when you consider that there would not be a single industrial enterprise listed on the New York Stock Exchange until the 1870s.

Even in the 1850s, when Cooper was in his sixties, he was looking for new technological worlds to conquer. In 1854 he helped to found—and served for more than twenty years as the president of—the New York, Newfoundland & London Telegraph Company. After many setbacks and constant infusions of new cash, much of it from Cooper, the company succeeded in laying the first successful Atlantic cable, a technological success that changed the world profoundly.

But by this time Cooper was also in the third phase of his life, the phase devoted to doing good works. He had always served on endless boards established to improve the quality of life in New York City. Now he resolved to do something more concrete. He established the Cooper Union in 1857 "for the advancement of science and art." The building itself was interesting, being the first "fireproof" building erected in the country (using cast-iron beams manufactured, of course, by Peter Cooper). In 1860 Abraham Lincoln gave his "House Divided" speech there.

But it is the Union, not the building, that is really interesting, for in addition to advancing art and science, it existed for the advancement of those who wished to advance themselves. It offered free courses (many given in the evening) and lectures on numerous subjects in science and the arts and maintained a reading room of which the general public was welcome to make use. This they did, often 2,000 a day. To this day, the Cooper Union remains the only private institution of higher learning in the country that does not charge tuition.

Toward the end of his life, Peter Cooper remarked that "I have always recognized that the object of business is to make money in an honorable manner. I have endeavored to remember that the object of life is to do good."

I do not know if David Packard knew those words, but he, too, lived by them.

BIBLIOGRAPHY

PART I. THE EARLY DAYS OF THE AMERICAN DREAM

Profits in the Wilderness

Bradford, William. *Of Plymouth Plantation, 1620–1647.* New York: Modern Library, 1967. (Edited by Samuel Eliot Morison.)

Innes, Stephen. *Creating the Commonwealth: The Economic Culture of Puritan New England.* New York: Norton, 1994.

Martin, John Frederick. *Profits in the Wilderness: Entrepreneurship and the Founding of New England Towns in the Seventeenth Century.* Chapel Hill, N.C.: "Published for the Institute of Early American History and Culture, Williamsburg, Virginia, by the University of North Carolina Press," 1991.

Morison, Samuel Eliot. *The Story of the "Old Colony" of New Plymouth.* New York: Knopf, 1960.

The Corners of Wall and Broad

Brooks, John. *Once in Golconda: A True Drama of Wall Street, 1920–1938.* New York: Harper and Row, 1969.

Gordon, John Steele. *The Scarlet Woman of Wall Street.* New York: Weidenfeld and Nicolson, 1988.

Greider, William. *Secrets of the Temple: How the Federal Reserve Runs the Country.* New York: Simon and Schuster, 1987.

Sobel, Robert. *The Big Board: A History of the New York Stock Exchange.* New York: Free Press, 1965.

Van der Zee, Henri, and Barbara Van der Zee. *A Sweet and Alien Land: The Story of Dutch New York.* New York: Viking, 1978.

Technology Transfer

Cameron, E. H. *Samuel Slater, Father of American Manufactures.* Bond Wheelwright Company, 1960.

Thompson, Mack. *Moses Brown, Reluctant Reformer.* Chapel Hill, N.C.: University of North Carolina Press, 1962.

Tucker, Barbara M. *Samuel Slater and the Origins of the American Textile Industry, 1790–1860.* Ithaca, N.Y.: Cornell University Press, 1984.

White, George S. *Memoir of Samuel Slater.* New York: August M. Kelley, 1967. Reprint of the 1836 edition.

King Cotton

Fogel, Robert William. *Without Consent or Contract: The Rise and Fall of American Slavery.* New York: Norton, 1989.

Hobhouse, Henry. *Seeds of Change: Five Plants That Transformed Mankind.* New York: Harper and Row, 1985.

PART II.   FARMING AND FOOD

The Tragedy of the Commons

Kurlansky, Mark. *Cod: A Biography of the Fish That Changed the World.* New York: Walker, 1997.

Sowing the American Dream

Dozynki, a Time of Joy. Middletown, N.Y. (?): Orange County Onion Harvest Festival Committee, 1983.

Everett, Dorothea D., and Fred Everett. "Black Acres, a Thrilling Sketch in the Vast Volume of Who's Who Among the Peoples That Make America." *National Geographic,* November 1941.

Headley, Russel, ed. *The History of Orange County.* Middletown, N.Y.: Van Deusen and Elms, 1908.

Jonas, Harold J. "A Preliminary History of Pine Island, N.Y." Address delivered at the Fortieth Annual Installation Dinner of Pulaski Fire Company, at the Polish Legion Hall, Pine Island, N.Y.: January 17, 1976.

Pine Island, the "Vegetable Garden of Orange County." Pine Island, N.Y.: Pine Island Chamber of Commerce, 1963.

"Something to Be Proud of: Story of the Gurda Family." In *Orange County Today: County Profiles.* N.p., n.d.

Yungman, Susan. "Faith of Our Fathers." N.p., n.d.

The Late, Great Liederkranz Cheese

Aszling, Richard. "The Story of Liederkranz." *Ohio Magazine,* May 1948.

Marquis, Vivienne, and Patricia Haskell. *The Cheese Book: The Definitive Guide to the Cheeses of the World.* Rev. ed. New York: Simon and Schuster, 1985.

Murphy, Mary E. (?) "Liederkranz Brand Soft Ripened Cheese." Columbus, Ohio: Borden Corporate Marketing Services, n.d. (but before 1982).

Stobart, Tom. *The Cook's Encyclopedia.* New York: Harper and Row, 1980.

Tannahill, Reay. *Food in History.* New York: Stein and Day, 1973.

Sawdust Pudding

Carson, Gerald. *Cornflake Crusade.* New York: Rinehart, 1957.

McLaughlin, Terence. *If You Like It, Don't Eat It: Dietary Fads and Fancies.* New York: Universe Books, 1979.

Nissenbaum, Stephen. *Sex, Diet, and Debility in Jacksonian America: Sylvester Graham and Health Reform.* Westport, Conn.: Greenwood Press, 1980.

Sokolow, Jayme A. *Eros and Modernization: Sylvester Graham, Health Reform, and the Origins of Victorian Sexuality in America.* Rutherford, N.J.: Fairleigh Dickinson University Press, 1983.

Tercentenary History Committee, eds. *The Northampton Book: Chapters from 300 Years in the Life of a New England Town, 1654–1954.* Northampton, Mass.: Tercentenary Committee, 1954.

PART III. MANUFACTURING AND MINING

Industrial Revolutionary

Bathe, Greville, and Dorothy Bathe. *Oliver Evans, A Chronicle of Early American Engineering.* Philadelphia: Historical Society of Pennsylvania, 1935.

Ferguson, Eugene S. *Oliver Evans, Inventive Genius of the American Industrial Revolution.* Greenville, Del.: Hagley Museum, 1980.

Norman, Bruce. *The Inventing of America.* New York: Taplinger, 1972.

Sewing and Reaping a Fortune

Brandon, Ruth. *A Capitalist Romance: Singer and the Sewing Machine.* Philadelphia: Lippincott, 1977.

The California Gold Rush

Andrist, Ralph K. "Gold!" *American Heritage,* December 1962.

Marks, Paula Mitchell. *Precious Dust: The American Gold Rush Era: 1848–1900.* New York: William Morrow, 1994.

Opportunities

Jones, Russell K. "He Went for the Gold." *Bulletin of the North Salem Historical Society* 9, no. 2 (June 1982).

Schart, J. Thomas. *History of Westchester County, New York.* Philadelphia: L. E. Preston, 1886. (See vol. 2, p. 510ff.)

The Revenge of the Trust

Connolly, C. P. "The Fight of the Copper Kings." *McClure's Magazine,* May, June, and July 1907.

Glasscock, C. B. *The War of the Copper Kings.* Indianapolis: Bobbs-Merrill, 1935.

McNelis, Sarah. "F. Augustus Heinze: An Early Chapter in the Life of a Copper King." *Montana Magazine of History* 2, no. 4 (October 1952).

Sales, Reno H. *Underground Warfare at Butte.* N.p., 1964.

Sanders, Helen Fitzgerald. *A History of Montana.* Chicago: Lewis Publishing, 1913.

PART IV. TRANSPORTATION

The Steamboat Monopoly

Haites, Erik F., James Mak, and Gary M. Walton. *Western River Transportation: The Era of Early Internal Development, 1810–1860.* Baltimore: Johns Hopkins University Press, 1975.

Hunter, Louis C. *Steamboats on the Western Rivers: An Economic and Technological Survey.* Cambridge, Mass.: Harvard University Press, 1949.

Sheehan, Paul. "What Went Right." *Atlantic,* August 1993.

To the Swiftest

Lane, Wheaton J. *Commodore Vanderbilt: An Epic of the Steam Age.* New York: Knopf, 1942.

The Atlantic Stakes

Brinnin, John Malcolm. *The Sway of the Grand Saloon: A Social History of the North Atlantic.* New York: Delacorte Press, 1971.

Hughes, Tom. *The Blue Riband of the Atlantic.* New York: Charles Scribner's Sons, 1973.

Maddocks, Melvin, and the editors of Time-Life Books. *The Atlantic Crossing.* Alexandria, Va.: Time-Life Books, 1981.

Maddocks, Melvin, and the editors of Time-Life Books. *The Great Liners.* Alexandria, Va.: Time-Life Books, 1978.

Post, Robert C. "The Thrall of the Blue Riband." *Invention and Technology,* winter 1996.

The Towering Boondoggle

Darton, Eric. *Divided We Stand: A Biography of New York's World Trade Center.* New York: Basic Books, 1999.

Gordon, John Steele. *The Scarlet Woman of Wall Street.* New York: Weidenfeld and Nicholson, 1988.

Smothers, Ronald. "Feud over How Port Authority Spends Money Creates an Impasse." *New York Times,* February 24, 2000.

"The Public Be Damned"

Croffut, William A. *The Vanderbilts and the Story of Their Fortune.* Chicago: Bedford, Clarke, 1886.

Nice Work If You Can Keep It

Collier, Peter, and David Horowitz. *The Fords: An American Epic.* New York: Summit Books, 1987.

Finch, Christopher. *Highways to Heaven: The AUTO Biography of America.* New York: HarperCollins, 1992.

Flink, James J. *The Automobile Age.* Cambridge, Mass.: MIT Press, 1988.

Howard, Frank. *Wilbur and Orville: A Biography of the Wright Brothers.* New York: Knopf, 1987.

Henry Ford's Horseless Horse

Collier, Peter, and David Horowitz. *The Fords, an American Epic.* New York: Summit Books, 1987.

Williams, Robert C. *Fordson, Farmall, and Poppin' Johnny, a History of the Farm Tractor and Its Impact on America.* Urbana, Illinois: University of Illinois Press, 1987.

The Man Who Saved the Cadillac

Collier, Peter, and David Horowitz. *The Fords: An American Epic.* New York: Summit Books, 1987.

Cray, Ed. *Chrome Colossus: General Motors and Its Times.* New York: McGraw-Hill, 1980.

Drucker, Peter F. *Adventures of a Bystander.* New York: Harper and Row, 1979.

Editors of *Automobile Quarterly. General Motors, the First Seventy-five Years.* New York: Crown, 1983.

Hendry, Maurice D. *Cadillac, Standard of the World: The Complete Seventy-five Year History.* New York: Automobile Quarterly Publications, 1973.

Keller, Maryann. *Rude Awakening: The Rise, Fall, and Struggle for Recovery of General Motors.* New York: Morrow: 1989.

Through Darkest America

Eisenhower, Dwight D. *At Ease: Stories I Tell My Friends.* Garden City, N.Y.: Doubleday, 1967.

Hulbert, Archer B. *The Path of Inland Commerce: A Chronicle of Trail, Road, and Waterway.* New Haven, Conn.: Yale University Press, 1920.

McCarthy, Joe. "The Lincoln Highway." *American Heritage,* June 1974.

Miller, Merle. *Ike the Soldier: As They Knew Him.* New York: Putnam, 1987.

Smartt, Vaughn. "1919: The Interstate Expedition." *Constructor,* August 1973.

PART V.   BANKING

We Banked on Them

Malone, Dumas. *Jefferson the President: First Term, 1801–1805.* Vol. 4 of *Jefferson and His Time.* Boston: Little Brown, 1970.

Ziegler, Philip. *The Sixth Great Power: A History of One of the Greatest of All Banking Families, the House of Barings, 1762–1929.* New York: Knopf, 1988.

The Freedman's Bank

Fogel, Robert William. *Without Consent or Contract: The Rise and Fall of American Slavery.* New York: Norton, 1989.

Osthaus, Carl R. *Freedmen, Philanthropy, and Fraud: A History of the Freedman's Savings Bank.* Urbana, Ill.: University of Illinois Press, 1976.

The People's Banker

Bonadio, Felice A. *A. P. Giannini: Banker of America.* Berkeley, Calif.: University of California Press, 1994.

Politicians Versus Bankers

Chernow, Ron, *The House of Morgan: An American Banking Dynasty and the Rise of Modern Finance.* New York: Atlantic Monthly Press, 1990.

PART VI. THE BUSINESS OF WAR

USS *Pork Barrel*

Bolander, Louis H. "The Ships of the Line of the Old Navy." *United States Naval Institute Proceedings,* October 1938.

Buckingham, John Silk. "The U.S. Navy in 1842." *United States Naval Institute Proceedings,* January 1967.

Chapelle, Howard I. *The History of the American Sailing Navy.* New York: Norton, 1949.

Cowburn, Philip. *The Warship in History.* New York: Macmillan, 1965.

Gruppe, Henry E. *The Frigates.* Alexandria, Va.: Time-Life Books, 1979.

Lavers, Brian. *The Ship of the Line.* London: Conway Maritime Press, 1983.

Whipple, A. B. C. *Fighting Sail.* Alexandria, Va.: Time-Life Books, 1978.

Paying for the War

McPherson, James M. *Battle Cry of Freedom.* New York: Oxford University Press, 1988.

Oberholtzer, Ellis Paxson. *Jay Cooke: Financier of the Civil War.* Philadelphia: George W. Jacobs, 1907.

Unger, Irwin. *The Greenback Era.* Princeton, N.J.: Princeton University Press, 1964.

The Armor-Plate Scandal

Hessen, Robert. *Steel Titan: The Life of Charles M. Schwab.* New York: Oxford University Press, 1975.

Serrin, William. *Homestead: The Glory and Tragedy of an American Steel Town.* New York: Times Books, 1992.

The American Superweapon

Hoopes, Roy. *Americans Remember the Home Front.* New York: Hawthorn Books, 1977.

Kennedy, David M. *Freedom from Fear: The American People in Depression and War, 1929–1945.* New York: Oxford University Press, 1999.

Nelson, Donald M. *Arsenal of Democracy: The Story of American War Production.* New York: Harcourt, Brace, 1946.

Phillips, Cabell. *The 1940s: Decade of Triumph and Trouble.* New York: Macmillan, 1975.

PART VII. BUSINESS AND GOVERNMENT

The Great Crash (of 1792)

Brandt, Clare. *An American Aristocracy: The Livingstons.* Garden City, N.Y.: Doubleday, 1986.

Gordon, John Steele. *The Great Game: The Emergence of Wall Street as a World Power, 1653–2000.* New York: Scribner, 1999.

Miller, John C. *Alexander Hamilton: Portrait in Paradox.* New York: Harper and Row, 1959.

Sobel, Robert. *Panic on Wall Street: A History of America's Financial Disasters.* New York: Macmillan, 1968.

The Other Great Depression

Bailyn, Bernard, et al. *The Great Republic.* Boston: Little, Brown, 1977.

Chernow, Ron. *The House of Morgan.* New York: Atlantic Monthly Press, 1990.

Smith, Page. *The Rise of Industrial America.* New York: McGraw-Hill, 1984.

Strouse, Jean. *Morgan: American Financier.* New York: Knopf, 1998.

R.I.P., ICC

Friedman, Lawrence M. *A History of American Law,* 2d ed. New York: Simon and Schuster, 1985.

Hadley, Arthur T. *Railroad Transportation—Its History and Its Laws.* New York: G. P. Putnam's Sons, 1886.

Engine Charlie Wilson

Ambrose, Stephen E. *Eisenhower: The President.* New York: Simon and Schuster, 1984.

Brendon, Piers. *Ike: His Life and Times.* New York: Harper and Row, 1986.

Drucker, Peter F. *Adventures of a Bystander.* New York: HarperCollins, 1991.

New York Times, obituary of Charles E. Wilson, September 27, 1961.

PART VIII.   RETAILING AND REAL ESTATE

The Perils of Success

Carroll, Paul. *Big Blues: The Unmaking of IBM.* New York: Crown, 1993.

Grant, James. *Money of the Mind: Borrowing and Lending in America from the Civil War to Michael Milken.* New York: Farrar Straus Giroux, 1992.

No Respect

Collier, Peter, and David Horowitz. *The Fords: An American Epic.* New York: Summit Books, 1987.

Harris, Leon. *Merchant Princes: An Intimate History of Jewish Families Who Built Great Department Stores.* New York: Harper and Row, 1979.

Mahoney, Tom, and Leonard Sloane. *The Great Merchants: America's Foremost Retail Institutions and the People Who Made Them Great.* New York: Harper and Row, 1966.

Where and When

Albion, Robert Greenhalgh (with the collaboration of Jennie Barnes Pope). *The Rise of New York Port, 1815–1860.* New York: Charles Scribner's Sons, 1939.

Burnham, Alan. *New York Landmarks*. Middletown, Conn.: Wesleyan University Press, 1963.

Miller, Nathan. *The Enterprise of a Free People: Aspects of Economic Development in New York State During the Canal Period, 1792–1838*. Ithaca, N.Y.: Cornell University Press, 1962.

Shaw, Ronald E. *Erie Water West: A History of the Erie Canal, 1792–1854*. Lexington, Ky.: University of Kentucky Press.

Woolworth's Cathedral

"F. W. Woolworth Co. 100th Anniversary." New York: F. W. Woolworth, 1979.

Goldberger, Paul. *The Skyscraper*. New York: Knopf, 1985. (Paperback edition)

Spencer, Klaw. "The World's Tallest Building." *American Heritage*, February 1977.

Winkler, John K. *Five and Ten: The Fabulous Life of F. W. Woolworth*. New York: Robert M. McBride, 1940.

Unintended Consequences

Goldberger, Paul. *The City Observed: New York*. New York: Vintage Books, 1979.

Horsley, Carter B. "Hotel Is Planned over Racquet and Tennis Club." *New York Times*, March 31, 1978.

Smith, C. Ray. "Squaring Off on Park Avenue: A Gentlemen's Club K.O.'s the Real-Estate Kings." *New York*, November 27, 1978.

PART IX.   THE TELEGRAPH, TELEPHONE, AND TELEVISION

Technology of the Future

Davidson, Marshall B. "What Samuel Wrought." *American Heritage*, April 1961.

Oliver, John W. *History of American Technology*. New York: Ronald Press, 1956.

Postalization

Brooks, John. *Telephone: The First Hundred Years*. New York: Harper and Row, 1976.

Coll, Steve. *The Deal of the Century: The Breakup of AT&T*. New York: Atheneum, 1986.

Technological Turkey

Clark, Ronald W. *Edison: The Man Who Made the Future*. New York: G. P. Putnam's Sons, 1977.

Cutler, Carl C. *Greyhounds of the Sea: The Story of the American Clipper Ship*, 3rd ed. Annapolis, Md.: Naval Institute Press, 1984.

Laing, Alexander. *The American Heritage History of Seafaring America*. New York: American Heritage Publishing, 1974.

Tunis, Edwin. *Oars, Sails, and Steam: A Picture Book of Ships*. New York: Thomas Y. Crowell, 1952.

Wachhorst, Wyn. *Thomas Alva Edison: An American Myth*. Cambridge, Mass.: MIT Press, 1981.

The Death of a Monopoly

Kahaner, Larry. *On the Line: The Men of MCI—Who Took on AT&T, Risked Everything, and Won!* New York: Warner Books, 1986.

Kraus, Constantine Raymond, and Alfred W. Duerig. *The Rape of Ma Bell: The Criminal Wrecking of the Best Telephone System in the World.* Secaucus, N.J.: Lyle Stewart, 1988.

Stone, Alan. *Wrong Number: The Breakup of AT&T.* New York: Basic Books, 1989.

Desi Arnaz

Arnaz, Desi. *A Book.* New York: William Morrow, 1976.

Brochu, Jim. *Lucy in the Afternoon: An Intimate Memoir of Lucille Ball.* New York: William Morrow, 1990.

Harris, Warren G. *Lucy and Desi: The Legendary Love Story of Television's Most Famous Couple.* New York: Simon and Schuster, 1991.

Rodgers, Richard. *Musical Stages: An Autobiography.* New York: Da Capo Press, 1995. (Reprint of the 1975 edition)

Sanders, Coyne Steven, and Tom Gilbert. *Desilu: The Story of Lucille Ball and Desi Arnaz.* New York: William Morrow, 1993.

PART X.   AFTER HOURS

The American Game

Adelman, Melvin L. *A Sporting Time, New York City and the Rise of Modern Athletics.* Urbana, Ill.: University of Chicago Press, 1986.

Dickey, Glenn. *The History of the National League.* New York: Stein and Day, 1979.

Durso, Joseph. *Baseball and the American Dream.* St. Louis: Sporting News, 1986.

Ritter, Lawrence S. *The Glory of Their Times.* New York: Macmillan, 1966.

————. *The Story of Baseball.* New York: William Morrow, 1983.

Saint Straus

Dillon, John J. *Seven Decades of Milk, a History of New York's Dairy Industry.* New York: Orange Judd, 1941.

Mahoney, Tom, and Leonard Sloane. *The Great Merchants.* New York: Harper and Row, 1966.

Pamphlet, no author, no title, no date [1913]. In New York Public Library under call number (Straus) AN n.c. 10, no. 10.

Spargo, John. *The Common Sense of the Milk Question.* New York: Macmillan, 1910.

Straus, Lina Gutherz. *Disease in Milk, the Remedy Pasteurization.* New York: Dutton, 1913.

The Philanthropist

Lyon, Peter. "The Honest Man." *American Heritage,* February 1959.

Nevins, Allan. *Abram S. Hewitt with Some Account of Peter Cooper.* New York: Octagon Books, 1967.

Raymond, Rossiter W. *Peter Cooper.* Boston: Houghton Mifflin, 1901.

Scott, Reverend W. *Peter Cooper, the Good Citizen.* New York: Church and Home Publishing, 1888.

INDEX

A

Abraham and Straus, 253
Adams, Charles Francis, 94
Adventurers, 4, 5
Age of sail, end of, 149
Agricultural depression, 133
Agriculture, 34
    machinery in, 33, 105–7
"Air rights," 211–12, 213, 214, 215
Airline industry, cartels in, 75–76
Airplanes, 85, 100, 205, 219
Alabama, 21
Albion, Robert Greenhalgh, 204
Alexander, Catherine, 170
Alexander, William, 170
Allen, Paul, 62
Almy, Brown, and Slater (co.), 16
Aluminum, 165
Alvord, John W., 129, 132
Amalgamated Copper Company, 68–71
America (ship), 148
American dream, 30, 34
American League, 250
American Revolution, 170, 174, 202
American River, 57
American Telephone and Telegraph
    Company (AT&T), 196, 224,
    225–28
    monopoly, 234, 235–38
Ancillary fortunes, 63–66
Ancillary opportunities, 62–63
Annenberg, Walter, 62–63
Apex law, 69–70
Apple I computer, 62
Archimedes' screw, 49
Arkwright, Sir Richard, 14
Armor-plate scandal, 158–61
Army Air Force, 165

Arnaz, Desi, xiii, 240–43
Arthur, Chester, 158
Articles of Confederation, 170
Ashton-Tate, 111
Assembly line, 101, 199
Association of Licensed Automobile
    Manufacturers (ALAM), 102–3,
    104
Atlantic cod, 26–29
Audiences, mass, 239–40
Automobile, xii, 85, 101–4, 133, 196
    evolution of, 111
    luxury, 112, 114
Automobile industry, 80, 102–3, 111,
    114, 183
    assembly line in, 199
    unionization, 184–85
Avery, Sewell, 192–95

B

Babbage, Charles, 101
Bacon, Roger, 101
Ball, Lucille, 240, 241, 242
Baltimore, 202, 204
Baltimore and Ohio Railroad, 47, 260
Baltimore clippers, 231–33
Bank failures, 140, 175
Bank of America, 134, 137–38
Bank of California, 66
Bank of D. O. Mills, 65–66
Bank of England, 60
Bank of Italy, 136–37
Bank of New York, 171
Bank of the United States, 171
Banking Act of 1999, 139
Banking crisis (1933), 138
Banking industry, 133–34, 137
Banking law, 139–40

Banking system, 128, 141
Banks/banking, 124–25, 126–27,
    139–43
  branches, 129, 130, 134, 137
  Freedman's Savings and Trust Com-
      pany, 128–32
  regulation of, 134
Barbary pirates, 124–25
Baring, Alexander, 124, 126
Baring, Sir Francis, 124, 125, 126–27
Baring Bank, 123
Baring Brothers, 123–27
Barton, Samuel, 98, 99
Baseball, 247–51
Basques, 27–28
Battery Park City, 95
Bell, Alexander Graham, 196, 223, 225
Bell, C. A., 230
Bell Laboratories, 227
Bell Telephone Company, 225, 226, 227
Bennett, James Gordon, xi–xii, 207
Berliner, Emile, 230
Bethlehem Iron Company, 158–59
Biddle, Francis, 194
Bingham, William, 124, 170
Bismarck Schlosskaese, 37, 38
Black Ball Line, 87
Black-dirt country, 30–34
Blacks
  and Cadillac, 113
  freed, 128–29, 132
Bland-Allison Act, 176
Blue Riband, 85, 90
Board of Naval Commissioners, 150
Bond drive, 155–56
Bonds, selling, 124, 125
Boone, Daniel, 5
Borden Company, 39
Boston, Massachusetts, 26, 43, 202, 204,
    258
Boston and Montana (co.), 68
Branch banking, 129, 130, 134, 137
Brayton, George B., 101
Brick (cheese), 35
Brooklyn Atlantics, 250
Brown, Donaldson, 185
Brown, Moses, 15–16
Bryan, William Jennings, 141, 176, 178
Bryant, William Cullen, 129, 130
Bull wheel, 108–9

Bureau of Internal Revenue, 154
Burleson, Albert Sidney, 227, 228
Business, 98
  baseball as, 247–51
  in modern era, xi–xii
  opportunities in, 207
Business history, xii–xiii
Butte, Montana, 67–71
Butte Hill, 69, 70

C

Caboto, Giovanni (John Cabot), 27
Cadillac, 111–14
California
  banking law, 137
  travel to, 58–59, 64–65
California gold strike/rush, 57, 58–61,
    232–33
  D. O. Mills in, 63–66
California Railroad Commission,
    180–81
Cambrian explosion, 110
Cameron, Simon, 131
Cammeyer, William H., 249, 250
Canada, 29
Canadian Ministry of Agriculture, 28–29
Canadian Pacific, 68
Canal ring, 93
Candler, Asa, 91
Canton Iron Works, 260
Capitalism, 56, 91, 123, 127, 234
  near misses in, 105
Carburetor, 101, 102
Carnegie, Andrew, xii, xiii, 158–59, 160,
    208
Carnegie Endowment, 257
Carnegie Hall, 208
Carnegie Steel Company, 159–60
Cartels, 75
  ALAM, 102–3
  government in, 75–76
  railroad, 180, 182
  steamboating, 80–81
Carter, Jimmy, 182
Carter administration, 219
Cartier, Jacques, 27–28
Catalog sales, 197–98
Catholics, 204

CBS, 242
Central bank, 9–10
Central Pacific Railroad, 180–81
Chappe, Claude, 221
Charles I, 4
Charleston, 202
Chase, Salmon P., 129, 154–55
Chase Manhattan Bank, 92, 134
Chase National Bank, 140–41
Cheese, xiii, 35–39
Chemical, 134
Chicago, 209, 255, 258
Chimelowski, Walter, 33
China trade, 232
Cholera epidemic, 42
Chopping cotton, 21
Chrysler Building, 209
Cincinnati Red Legs, 250
Cities
    location, 201–2
    real estate in, 212
Civil War, 61, 128, 129, 150, 176, 204,
    252
    paying for, 152–56
Clancy, William F., 69–71
Clark, Enoch W., 154
Clark, William A., 67, 69
Clarke, Sir Arthur C., 238
Clermont (steamboat), 78, 80
Cleveland, Grover, 159, 177–78
Clinton, De Witt, 93, 203
Clinton, William, 139
Clinton administration, 196
Clive, Robert, 170
Cloth, 13–14, 52
Cloth industry, 19, 20
Cloth making, 53
Clothes, ready-made, 56
Clothes manufacture, 52–53
Coca-Cola, 35, 91
Cod (Kurlansky), 28
Cod fishing, 26–29
Collins, Edward Knight, 87–90
Columbus, Christopher, 3, 27
Columbus Savings and Loan Society, 136
Combinations in restraint of trade, 75
Commerce clause, 181
Communication, long-distance, 220–23,
    237, 238
Communications industry, 224–28

Compaq, 192
Competition, 234–35
Computer, 62, 101, 110–11, 134
Computer market, 191–92
Concept of the Corporation (Drucker), 185
Confederacy, 153, 156, 204, 252
Congress, 129, 166, 177, 222, 224, 227
    banking law, 141–42
    and Freedman's Bank, 129, 130, 131
    and ICC, 181, 182
    monetary policy, 176
    ships-of-the-line program, 149, 150
Connecticut River Valley, 6
Continental Congress, 170
Cooke, Henry, 154
Cooke, Jay, 154–56
Coolidge, Calvin, 247
Cooper, Peter, 129, 258–61
Cooper, Sarah Bedell, 259
Cooper Union, 208, 261
Copper, 67–71
Copper trust, 68–69, 70
Copper Trust (co.), 70
Cornelius Vanderbilt (steamboat), 81–85
Corner (the), 8–12
Corporation(s), 4, 185–86
Costs, socialized, 26
Cotton, 18–22
Cotton gin, 20–21
Cotton trade, 16, 20, 21, 22, 204
Coudert, Frederic, 103
Coward, Noel, xi, 18
Crash of 1792, 169–73
Crash of 1893, 177
Crash of 1987, 173
Creative destruction, 234–35, 238
Creighton, James, 249
Croffut, William A., 98
Cugat, Xavier, 240–41
Cumberland Road, 116
Cunard, Samuel, 87, 88–89, 90
Cutler, Carl C., 232

D

Daly, Marcus, 67
Daniels, Josephine, 161
De Forest, Lee, 230–31
de Gaulle, Charles, 35

Debs, Eugene V., 184
Deere, John, 106
Delco, 184
Democracy, 139
Democratic Party/Democrats, 147, 178
Deposit insurance, 142–43
Depression(s), 169, 174–78, 193, 195
    of 1890, 175, 178, 198
    see also Great Depression
Desilu (co.), 242
Dewey, George, 256
Dickens, Charles, xii, 87
Dietary advice, 40–44
Dinkins, David, 126
Disease, milk and, 254
Disney, Walt, 257
Distribution costs, 76
Douglass, Frederick, 132
Dresser, Clarence P., 97, 98, 99
Dreystadt, Nicholas, 111, 112–14
Drucker, Peter, 185–86
Duer, William, 169–72
Durant, William, 103

E

East India Company, 4
Eastern Airlines, 75
Economic decisions, 91, 92–93
Economic growth, 60–61
Economic history, xi, 30
Economic mistakes, 91, 93
Economics, 8, 110
Economies
    centrally planned, 163
    creative destruction, 234–35
Economies of scale, 33, 223, 234
Economy
    American, 76, 133, 143, 174–75
    effect of monopolies on, 157
    modern world, 173, 180, 224
    of the North, 156
    in the South, 154
    wartime, 163, 164, 165–66
Edison, Thomas Alva, 52, 100
    sound recording, 229–30, 231, 233
Eisenhower, Dwight, 119, 186
Electric Boat, 158

Electric elevator, 209, 211
Electric starter, 111
Electric Vehicle Company, 102
Electricity, 67, 220, 221–22
Electronic revolution, 236
Elizabeth I, 220
Emerson, Ralph Waldo, 43
Empire State Building, 92
Engine(s), 111
    four-cycle, 101
    see also Internal combustion
    engine; Steam engine
England
    and Barbary pirates, 125
    cloth industry, 19, 20
    joint-stock company, in, 3, 4
    secrets of textile industry stolen from,
        xiii, 14–16
Entrepreneurs, 7, 62
Equitable Building, 211
Erie Canal, 92–93, 94, 203–4
Erie Railway, 92–95
Evans, Oliver, 47–51
Excelsior Club, 249
Executives, worth of, 196–97, 200

F

Factory system, 224
FDIC, 142
Federal Communications Commission
    (FCC), 235, 236, 237, 238
Federal Reserve System, 12, 141
Federalists, 126
Fiat money, 153
Financial panics, government action in,
    173
Firestone, Harvey, 118
First Transcontinental Motor Convoy,
    117–19
Fisher, Joshua, 6
Fisher Brothers, 212, 213–15
Fisk, Jim, 10
Fitch, James, 6
Fitch, John, 77
Flatboats, 77
Flour mills, 47, 48–50, 51
"Flying shuttle," 14

Food, industrialized, 35–36
Ford, Henry, xiii, 47, 101, 102–4, 111–12, 192, 196, 199, 220
   Fordson tractor, 105, 108, 109
Ford, Henry, II, 196–97
Ford Foundation, 257
Ford Motor Company, 102, 104, 196–97
   Edsel, 91
Fordson tractor, 105, 108, 109
France, 35, 39, 125, 148
   and Louisiana Purchase, 126–27
Franklin, Benjamin, 21, 115, 221
Free market, 8, 12, 224
   rules of, 110
   signals sent by, 25–26
Freedmen, Philanthropy, and Fraud (Osthaus), 128
Freedman's Savings and Trust Company, 128–32
Freight, transporting, 76, 77, 78
Frey, Emile, 38
Frick, Henry Clay, xii, xiii, 159, 160
Friedman, Milton, 76
Frigates, 148–49
Froelich, John, 107
Frontier, 4–5
Full-rigged ship(s), 3, 201, 231–33
Fulton, Robert, 78
Fur trade, 6, 9

G

Galbraith, John Kenneth, 133
Gale, Leonard, 222
Gates, Bill, 62, 191
Gateway 2000, 192
General Court, 6
General Electric, 195, 237
General Foods, 39
General Motors Company, 111, 112, 113–14, 183, 184–86, 187
Germ theory of disease, 254
Getty, J. Paul, 30, 34
Giannini, Amadeo Peter, 134–38
Gibbons v. Ogden, 79
Gilbert, Cass, 209–10
Gilbert, Parker, 141

Ginning, 20
Glass, Carter, 141–42
Glass-Steagall Act, 139–40, 142
Glue business, 259
Goeken, Jack, 237–38
Gold, 10–11, 57–58, 61, 137, 177, 178
   density of, 58
   in world financial system, 60
Gold corner, 11
Gold standard, 60, 153, 156, 175–76, 177
Goldberger, Paul, 210
Gould, Jay, 10
Gould, Stephen Jay, 110
Government
   and cartels, 75–76
   and depression(s), 175–78
   in/and economic crisis, 169–73
   and monopolies, 77, 79
   monopsonies, 158, 161
   and passenger ship business, 87, 88, 89
   raising money, 153
   and technologies, 219–20, 222–23
Government regulation
   of economy, 133
   of railroads, 180–82
Graham, Sylvester, 41–44
Grahamites, 43–44
Grant, Ulysses S., 166
Great Britain, 148, 149, 235
   see also England
Great Depression, xiii, 137, 169, 174, 195, 198
   automobile market, 111, 112–13
   and banking industry, 133–34, 139, 140
   U.S. Gypsum in, 193
Great Man theory, 3
Great North Road, 76
"Great Western Canal," 203–4
Greeley, Horace, 43, 59
Greenback Party, 156
Greenbacks, 153, 156
Greenspan, Alan, 169
Gresham's law, 10, 153, 176
Greyhounds of the Sea (Cutler), 232
Guggenheim Museum, 208
Gypsum trust, 193

H

H. J. Heinz and Company, 35–36
Hamilton, Alexander, 16, 124, 170, 171,
    172–73, 202
Hammerstein, Oscar, I, 239
Hammerstein, Oscar, II, 239, 242
Harper's Magazine, 44
Harper's Weekly, 96
Harrison, Benjamin, 159
Hart, Lorenz, 241
Hayes, Rutherford B., 230
Hedley, William, 100–101
Heinze, F. Augustus, 67–71
Hendrickson, Robert C., 187
Henry, Joseph, 221–22
Henry Ford Company, 111
Henry Hope and company, 127
Henry J, 111
Hewlett, William, 257
Hewlett-Packard Company, 257
Hillman, Sidney, 163
History, 3
History of Montana, A (Sanders), 69
HMS *Victory*, 148, 150
Holland, 3, 4, 9
Holmes, Oliver Wendell, 251
Holmes, Oliver Wendell, Sr., 204
Homestead strike, xii, 159
Homestead Works, 159, 160
Hooker, Thomas, 5
Hoover, Herbert, 195
Horowitz, Louis, 209–10
Howe, Elias, 55, 56
Hubbard, Gardiner Greene, 196, 225
Hudson Railroad stock, 10
Hudson River, 77, 78, 95, 202, 203
Hudson River Association, 80
Hughes, Howard, 105
Humphreys, David, 125
Hundred Days, 140
Hunt, Nelson Bunker, 10–11, 12
Hunt, William Herbert, 10–11, 12
Hush-A-Phone, 235–36

I

I Love Lucy (TV program), xiii, 240,
    242–43

IBM, 191–92
Immigrants, 30–31, 37, 136
Indians, 5, 6, 9, 202
Indigo, 19, 20
Industrial process
    integrated, automatic, 49
Industrial revolution, 14, 19, 123, 149,
    224
    agricultural machinery in, 106
    in America, 16, 80
    founding father of American, 47
    sewing machine in, 53
    wealth created by, 207
Industrialization, 52, 53
Industry (American)
    war production, 162–66
Inflation, 10, 153, 175–76, 195
Infrastructure, 115–16
Insurance companies, 139
Intel, 133, 192
Internal combustion engine, 101, 107,
    117
Internal Revenue Act, 154
International Harvester (co.), 107, 108,
    109
International Hotels, 215
Interstate Commerce Commission (ICC),
    179–80, 182
Interstate Highway System, 116, 118,
    119
Inventions, 100–101
    P. Cooper, 258, 259
    O. Evans, 47
    I. Singer, 54
Investment banking, 124, 143
Invisible hand, 53
Isthmus of Panama, 58–59, 60, 64
Italian-American Bank, 136

J

J. P. Morgan and Company, 140, 143,
    193–94
Jackson, Andrew, 16–17, 129
Jackson, Charles Thomas, 220
Japan, 162
Jay Cooke and Company, 154
Jefferson, Thomas, 49, 106, 125, 126,
    134, 139, 172

Jobs, Steven, 62, 101
John Deere Company, 106, 107
Joint-stock company, 3–4, 5
Joy, Henry B., 116

K

Kay, John, 14
Keelboats, 77
Kellogg brothers, 44
Ketchup, 35–36
Kinescope, 242
King, Rufus, 125
Knickerbocker Club, 248–49
Knudsen, William S., 163
Koch, Robert, 254, 255
Kraft General Foods, 39
Kreusi, John, 229, 230
Krupp (co.), 160
Kurlansky, Mark, 28

L

L. Straus and Son, 252–53
Labor costs, 19, 20, 53, 106
Lamme, Benjamin G., 184
Law, George, 81, 82–85
Law of unintended consequences, 211
Lee, Henry, 170
Leffingwell, Russell, 141, 143
Leland, Henry M., 111
Lewis, David J., 227
Liederkranz (cheese), 35, 38–39
Liederkranz Society, 38
Lincoln, Abraham, 77, 115, 153, 261
Lincoln Highway, 116, 117
Liverpool and Manchester Railway, 93,
    101, 260
Livingston, Edward, 78
Livingston, Robert R., 77–79, 126
Livingston, Walter, 169–70, 171, 172
Loans
    in Civil War, 154–55
Locomotives, 100–101, 115, 260
London, 124, 201–2, 204
Los Angeles, 202, 205
Los Angeles Dodgers, 250

Louisiana Purchase, 77, 124, 125–27
Lucille Ball–Desi Arnaz Show, The, 241

M

McClure, Charles W., 117
McCormick, Cyrus H., 108
McDonald's, 36
Machado, Gerardo, 240
Machinery, 224
    automatic, 49
    laborsaving, 106
McKim, Mead, and White, 212
Macomb, Alexander, 170–71, 172
Macy's, 252–53, 256
Mail-order business, 198
Mainframes, 191–92
Management, 185
Manhattan, 92, 95, 211
Manufactures, American, 13
Market, laws ruling, 8
Market forces, 182
Market share, competition for, 180
Marketplace, xi, xii
Marshall, George C., 162
Marshall, James, 57, 59
Marshall, John, 79
Martin, John Frederick, 4
Mass media, 239–40
Mass production
    luxury cars, 113–14
Massachusetts Bay Colony, 4, 28
Massive retaliation doctrine, 186
Maybach, Wilhelm, 101, 102
MCI, 234, 236–38
Mercedes-Benz, 113–14
Merchant banking, 124
Merchants' Bank of Erie County, 63
Mergers, 133, 184
    banks, 134, 139
Merrimac, 150, 158
Metropolitan Life Tower, 209
Mexican War, 57
Microprocessor, 110
Microsoft, 133, 192
Microwave transmission technology,
    235, 236–38
Middle West, 203
Military monopsonies, 158–61

Milk, 37
Milk supply, safe, 253–55
Mills, Darius Ogden, 63–66
Mills, Edgar, 63, 65
Mills, James, 63, 65
Mississippi Delta, 21
Mississippi River, 51, 77, 125–26, 202, 203
Mississippi River Valley, 77, 78
Missouri River, 202
Model T, 103, 105, 108, 109, 192
Monetary policy, 176, 177
Money supply, 9, 172, 176
Monitor, 149–50, 158
Monopoly(ies), 75, 133, 234–35
    AT&T, 234, 235–38
    causing economic dislocations, 157, 158
    government-granted, 76–79
    IBM, 191
    overland transportation, 180–82
    steam navigation, 77–79
    telephone industry, 226, 227
    see also Natural monopolies
Monopsony, 157–61
Monroe, James, 126
Monroe Cheese Company, 37–38, 39
Monterey Jack (cheese), 35
Montgomery Ward, 192, 193–95, 199
Monuments, 206, 207–10
Moral hazard, 142
Morgan, J. P., 68, 175, 177–78, 226, 227
Morgan Stanley, 143
Morris, Gouverneur, 203
Morris, Robert, 124
Morse, Samuel F. B., 53, 220–23
Moscow Company, 4
Muck soil, 31, 32, 33, 34
Mule train, 33
Murray, James, 68

N

Nabisco, 36
Napoleon Bonaparte, 124, 126, 127
Nashville, Tennessee, 201
Nation-state, 4

National Association of Base Ball Players, 249
National banks, 134
National Cordage Company, 175
National debt, 155, 156
National League, 250
Nationsbank, 134
Natural monopolies, 235
Naval power, 148, 158, 160
NDAC (National Defense Advisory Commission), 163
Nelson, Donald, 163–66
New Amsterdam, 202, 204
New Deal, 140, 141, 147, 163
    Avery and, 192, 194
New Deal Democrats, 195
New England, 16, 28
    settlement of, 4–7
New Orleans, 77, 78, 126, 203
New South, 21
New World, 18, 19, 37, 42
New York, Newfoundland & London Telegraph Company, 261
New York and Hudson River Railroad, 207
New York Bay, 91–92
New York City, 33, 34, 92, 115, 209, 210, 261
    baseball in, 248–50
    buildings created by plutocrats, 208
    center of world trade, 201–5
    Fifth Avenue, 207, 208
    immigrant population, 53
    Kleindeutschland, 37
    memorial to I. Straus, 256
    museums, 258
    pasteurized milk, 255
    port, 88
    taxi cartel, 75
    zoning laws, 211–15
New York Club, 248
New York harbor, 83, 86, 93, 201, 205
New York Herald, 56, 81, 82, 83, 89, 96, 207
New York Public Library, 208
New York State, 77, 93–94
    slavery in, 21
New York State Assembly, 99
New York Stock Exchange, 10, 75, 173, 260

New York Subtreasury, 177
New York Times, 81, 97, 182, 214, 250
Newspaper(s), xii
Newton, Sir Isaac, 60
Nielsen, A. C., 63
"Nifty fifty," 133
Norfolk Naval Yard, 150
North (the)
    Civil War, 61
    Civil War financing, 152, 153–54,
        156
    industry in, 21–22
North American fishing banks, 28–29
North Atlantic, 89, 90
North Korea, 25, 235
Northwest Passage, 27
Nussbaum, Aaron, 198, 199
Nutrition, 40–41, 43

O

Oceans
    common ownership of, 26–29
Ohio River, 203
Oil industry, xii
Old economy, 52
Old South, 21
Oliver, James, 106
Oklahoma! (musical), 239
Onion farming, 32–34
OPM (Office of Production Manage-
    ment), 163
Opportunities, 30, 31, 62–63, 67
Orange County, 31, 34
Oregon (steamboat), 81–85
Organization, 3–4, 5
Orukter Amphibolos, 50–51
Osthaus, Carl R., 128
Other Great Depression, 174–78
Otto, Nikolaus, 101
Overland transportation
    Erie Canal in, 203–4
    railroads' monopoly of, 180–82
Ownership
    socialized, 26–29

P

Packard, David, 257, 258, 261
Packard Foundation, 257

Paley, William S., 62
Paley Park, 208
Pan American, 75
Panama City, 59
Panic of 1907, 71, 137
Paris, 202
Parsons, Joseph, 6
Partnership(s), 3
Passenger ship business, 86–90
Pasteur, Louis, 254, 255
Pasteurization, 255
Patent Board, 49
Patent pool, 56
Patents
    automobile, 101–2, 103–4
    cotton gin, 20
    flour-mill process, 49
    sewing machine, 55, 56
Pearl Harbor, 151, 163
Pecora, Ferdinand, 140–41
Pennsylvania Railroad, 180, 182
Pennsylvania Society for Discouraging
    the Use of Ardent Spirits, 42
Pension system(s), 186
Pentagon, 183, 184, 186
People's history, 3
Pepsi-Cola, 34
Pepsico, 36
Perelman, S. J., 200
Persians, 220
Personal computer, 110, 191–92
Personal computer industry, 62
Philadelphia, 202, 203, 204, 258
Philadelphia and Reading Railroad, 175
Philanthropy, xii, 253, 257–61
Philip Morris, 39, 242
Philipse, Frederick, 9–10, 11, 12
Pilgrims, 28
Planters, 4, 5
Plow, 106
Plunkett, George Washington, 30
Plymouth Colony, 4
Politicians, 91, 93, 94
Politics, 139
    and banking law, 140, 142
    Jeffersonian, 173
Polk, James K., 59
Poor Richard's Almanack (Franklin), 115
Pork-barrel projects, 147–48, 149–51
Port Authority of New York and New
    Jersey, 91–92

Post Office, 225, 227, 228
Postalization, 224–25, 227–28
Potter, Stephen, 82
Power, acquisition and display of, 206–7
Power takeoff (PTO), 109
Privateers, 231
Productivity, 76, 106
Profits in the Wilderness (Martin), 4
Public (the)
    Vanderbilt's comment regarding, 96, 99
"Puffing Billy," 100–101
Puritans, 5, 6, 28, 204
Pyramids, 147
Pythagoras, 40

Q

Quakers, 204

R

R. W. Sears Watch Company, 197
Racing, 80, 85
    automobile, 103
    steamboats, 81–85
Racquet and Tennis Club, 212–15
Railroad commissions, 180–82
Railroads, 47, 51, 53, 59–60, 85, 93–
    94, 100–101, 116, 223, 224
    infrastructure, 115
    miles of track, 60
    monopoly of overland transportation,
        180–82
    overexpansion, 175
    Vanderbilt and, 97–98, 99
RCA
    Selecta Vision, 105, 229, 231
Real estate, 201, 212, 213
Recession, 174
Reconstruction, 156
Relays, 222
Remy Electric Company, 184
Retailing, 208
Rice, 19
Rise of New York Port, 1815–1860, The (Al-
    bion), 204

Ritz Crackers, 36
Rivers, commerce on, 76, 77, 202
Roads, 76, 116–19
Robber barons, xii
"Rocket," 101
Rockefeller, David, 92
Rockefeller, John D., xii
Rockefeller, Nelson, 92
Rockefeller, William, 68–69
Rockefeller Foundation, 257
Rockefeller University, 208
Rodgers, Richard, 239, 241
Roebuck, Alvah Curtis, 197, 198, 200
Rogers, Henry H., 68–69
Roosevelt, Franklin D., 140, 141, 142,
    194, 200
    and World War II, 162, 163, 164
Roosevelt, Theodore, 38, 182
Rope trust, 175
Rosenwald, Julius, 197, 198–99, 200
Rothschilds, 178
Rounders, 247–48
Royal Mail Ship (RMS), 87
Royal Navy, 148–49, 170
Rubber, 164–65
Rumsey, James, 77
Russell Sage Foundation, xii
Ruth, Babe, 250
Ryan, Thomas Fortune, 102

S

Sacramento, 65
Sage, Russell, xii
Sailing ships, 76, 88, 231, 233
    passenger service, 87
St. Lawrence River, 27
St. Louis, 202
San Francisco, 58, 64–65, 66, 118
    earthquake, 136–37
San Ildefonso, treaty of, 126
Sanders, Helen Fitzgerald, 69
Santayana, George, 132
Sarnoff, David, 62
Savings and loan industry, 128, 142
Savings and Profit Sharing Pension Fund
    of Sears, Roebuck, 199–200
Schumpeter, Joseph, 234

Schurz, Carl, 38
Schuyler, Montgomery, 210
Schuylkill River, 50, 51
Schwab, Charles, 160
Sears, Richard Warren, 197–200
Sears, Roebuck, 163, 164, 195, 197–200
Second Bank of the United States, 129
Securities Act of 1933, 143
Seinfeld (TV program), 239–40, 243
Seinfeld, Jerry, 240
Selden, George B., 101–2, 103, 104
Selecta Vision, 105, 229, 231, 233
Self-enforcing law(s), 179, 182
Senate Armed Services Committee, 186–87
Sewing, 53
Sewing machine, 53, 55
Shelley, Percy Bysshe, 206, 207
Sherman, John, 155
Sherman, William T., 155
Sherman Antitrust Act, 157, 251
Sherman Silver Act, 176, 177
Ship-of-the-line program, 148–51
Ships
    see Full-rigged ship(s); Sailing ships; Steamships
Short sellers, 8, 11
Shreve, Henry, 78
Silver, 176–77, 178
Silver market, corner on, 10–12
Silver standard, 10
"Silver Thursday," 12
Singer, Isaac Merrit, 53–56
Skidmore, Owings, and Merrill, 214
Skyscrapers, 92, 209–10
Slater, Samuel, xiii, 15–17
Slave labor, 19, 21–22
Sloan, Alfred P., 185
Smith, Adam, 28, 53, 99, 157, 176
Smith, F. O. J. (Fog), 222–23
Smith, John, 28
Socialist economies, 234–35
Soft drinks, 35
Soule, John L. B., 59
Sound recording, 229–31, 233
South (the), 22
    Civil War, 61, 128
    Civil War financing, 152, 153–54, 156

cotton in, 18–19
slavery in, 21
Southern Tier, 92–93
Soviet Union, 163, 200
SPAB (Supplies, Priorities, and Allocations Board), 163
Spain, 3, 18, 22, 126
Speculation, 170–72
Speed, lust for, 81
Sperry, Anson, 131–32
Spice Islands, 27
Spinning jenny, 14
Spinning wheel, 13
Spruce Goose (airplane), 105
Standard Oil, xii, 69, 71, 157
Stanley Steamer, 111
State commissions overseeing railroads, 180–81
Steagall, Henry B., 142
Steam engine, 47, 48, 49, 50–51, 100–101, 123, 206, 220, 260
    in agriculture, 106–7
Steam navigation
    monopolies, 77–79
Steamboats, 51, 76, 77–79, 80–81
    racing, 81–85
Steamships
    passenger service, 87, 88–89
Steel construction, 209, 211
Steel manufacturers, xii, 158–61
Stein, Andrew, 213
Steinbeck, John, 169
Stephenson, George, 53, 101, 260
Stock market, 52
Stock-market crashes, 169
Stone, Melville E., 97, 98
Stone, Oliver, xii
Straus, Isidor, 252, 256
Straus, Nathan, 252–56
Strutts, Jedidiah, 15
Stuyvesant, Peter, 9
SUB (Supplementary Unemployment Benefits), 186
Sugar, 18–19
Sullivan, Louis, 210
Sumerians, 36–37
Sumner, Charles, 129, 131
Supreme Court, 181

Sutter, John, 57
Syndication rights, xiii, 239–40

T

Taft, William Howard, 103
Tainter, Charles Sumner, 230
Talmadge, Gene, 200
Taxation, 154
Technological overreach, 105
Technology, 3
    conceptualizing new, 105
    fishing, 29
    flour mills, 48–50
    governments and, 219–20
    mass media, 239–40
    new, 110
    and skyscrapers, 209
    steamboat, 77
    supplanted by new, 231–33, 234
    textile production, 13–15
    transportation, 85
Telecommunications, 225, 227–28
Telegraph, 53, 60–61, 220–23, 224, 261
Telephone, 223
Telephone industry, 225–28
Telephone system, 196, 228
Telephony, 225, 234
Television, 239–40, 241–43
Television industry, 62–63
Textile industry, 13–17, 52, 204, 224
Textile machinery
    plans for, carried from England, xiii, 14–16
Textile weaving, 13–14
Tiffany's, 11
Titanic, 91, 115, 252
Titanic (film), 239
Tobacco, 19
Tode, Adolph, xiii, 37–38
"Tom Thumb," 260
Town founding, 5, 6–7
Townsend, E. J., 63
Tractor, 105, 107–9
Tragedy of the commons, 26–29
Trail, British Columbia, 68
Transatlantic passenger travel, 205

Transatlantic trade, 86–87
Transportation, overland, 76–77
Transportation industry, 182
Transportation market, 76–79
Transportation technology, 85
Treasury Board, 170
Treasury notes, 153, 154
    see also U.S. Treasury
Treaty of Guadalupe Hidalgo, 57
Trevithick, Richard, 47, 100
Truck farming, 33
Trucking industry, 182
    cartels in, 75, 76
Trusts, 68–69, 193
Tuberculosis, 254–55
TV Guide, 63

U

Union Pacific Railroad, 60
United Auto Workers (UAW), 184–85, 186
United Copper Company, 71
United States
    and Baring Brothers, 124–27
    economic growth, 60–61
    foodstuffs, 35
    infrastructure, 115–16
United States Gypsum Company, 192–93
Upland cotton, 21
U.S Army, 117–19
U.S. Court of Appeals for the District of Columbia, 236
U.S. Defense Department, 183
U.S. Department of Agriculture, 36
U.S. Navy, 148–51, 158, 160, 161
    and World War II, 162
U.S. Steel, 160
U.S. Supreme Court, 79, 251
U.S. Treasury, 10, 11, 125, 129, 170–71, 172–73, 176, 177, 178
    gold reserve, 177
USS Alabama, 149–50
USS New York, 150, 159
USS Pennsylvania, 150–51
USS Vermont, 150
USS Virginia, 149

V

Vail, Alfred, 222, 223
Vail, Theodore, N., 225, 226, 227
Vandenberg, Arthur, 142
Vanderbilt, Cornelius, 10, 80–81, 82–85, 99, 207–8
Vanderbilt, William Henry, 96–99
VCR, 105, 229
Venice, 201, 204
Vesta (ship), 89
Vinci, Leonardo da, 47
Visicalc, 110–11

W

Wabash Railway v. Illinois, 181
Waldo, Cornelius, 5
Wall Street, 9, 10, 75, 94, 115, 142, 153, 169, 173, 177, 195, 223, 227
  banks, 140
  corners, 10, 11, 12
  crash, 174, 175
  Heinze and, 71
Wallace, Henry, 164
Wampum market, 9, 10, 11
Wang Laboratories, 110
War Department, 152–53, 156
War of 1812, 148–49, 231
"War of the Copper Kings," 69
War production, 162–63, 185, 195
War Production Board, 164–65, 166
Wars, paying for, 152
Wars of the French Revolution, 202–3
Washington, D.C., 129, 201
Washington, George, 13, 14, 15, 49, 116
Watson, Sir William, 221
Watt, James, 48, 49, 50, 51, 123, 220
Wealth, 18, 67, 207
Wealth of Nations (Smith), 28
Webster, Daniel, 79
West (the), 176
West Indies, 9, 18–19, 28, 37
Western Electric, 225
Western Union, 223, 224, 227

Westinghouse, 184
Westminster, Duke of 96
Whitney, Eli, 20
Whitney, William C., 102
Whitney Museum, 208
Widmer, Edward L., 248
Wiggin, Albert, 140–41
Wilson, Charles E. ("Electric Charlie"), 185
Wilson, Charles E. ("Engine Charlie"), 183–87
Wilson, Woodrow, 137, 141, 161, 228
Wilson administration, 227
Wing-warping, 100
Winton, Alexander, 102
Winton Motor Carriage Company, 102
Wirt, William, 79
Wood, Fernando, 204
Wood, Jethro, 106
Woolley, Sir Richard, 219
Woolworth, Frank Winfield, 208–10
Woolworth Building, 208–10
Woolworth Company, 210
WordPerfect, 111
Wordsworth, William, xiii
World trade, 205
World Trade Center, 91, 92, 94–95
World War I, 107–8, 116–17, 156, 161, 224–25
  and postalization, 227–28
World War II, 185, 192, 195
  war production, 162–66
Wozniak, Stephen, 62, 101
Wright, Isaac, 86–87
Wright, Orville, 100, 219
Wright, Wilbur, 100, 219

Y

Young Millwright and Miller's Guide, The (Evans), 50

Z

Zieber, George B., 54–55
Zoning laws, xiii, 211–15